THE DEVELOPMENT OF Samuel Beckett's FICTION

THE

DEVELOPMENT

OF

Samuel Beckett's

FICTION

Rubin Rabinovitz

UNIVERSITY OF ILLINOIS PRESS

Urbana and Chicago

Publication of this work was supported in part by a grant from the Eugene M. Kayden Fund.

Earlier versions of portions of this book appeared in *Modern Fiction Studies* (Autumn, 1974), *Modern Irish Literature*, ed. R. Porter and J. Brophy (Iona College Press, 1972), *Samuel Beckett*, ed. E. Morot-Sir, H. Harper, and D. McMillan (University of North Carolina Press, 1976), *Yeats, Joyce, and Beckett*, ed. K. McGrory and J. Unterecker (Bucknell University Press, 1976), and *Samuel Beckett*, ed. M. Beja, S. E. Gontarski, and P. Astier (University of Ohio Press, 1983), and permission to reprint this material is hereby gratefully acknowledged.

Library of Congress Cataloging in Publication Data

Rabinovitz, Rubin.
  The development of Samuel Beckett's fiction.

  Includes index.
  1. Beckett, Samuel, 1906–   —Fictional works.
I. Title.
PR6003.E282Z7887 1984   823'.912   83-4850
ISBN 0-252-01095-7

To Margit

Contents

Preface

One of my concerns in this book has been to discuss the new techniques that Samuel Beckett developed early in his career as a novelist, in the period before he began to write in French. I have attempted to show how Beckett's innovations resulted in a type of writing which—even when it initially seems impenetrable or meaningless—is very rich in significance. Such an approach, I hope, will make his works more accessible.

For this reason it may be appropriate to begin by thanking those who have made Beckett's writing more accessible to me. The late William York Tindall kindled my interest in Beckett; his intelligence and conviviality, like his scholarship, will long be remembered. I am indebted to Ruby Cohn, who contributed many astute insights and suggestions as my book was nearing completion. Raymond Federman was very generous with advice, encouragement, and help. Deirdre Bair, who read the book in manuscript form, also made many valuable comments.

Beckett's writing has attracted many other outstanding scholars. I learned a great deal from the books and essays of John Fletcher, Melvin J. Friedman, Lawrence Harvey, Edith Kern, Hugh Kenner, Vivian Mercier, and Eugene Webb. For their fine criticism as well as their stimulating conversation, many thanks to Porter Abbott, Linda Ben-Zvi, Enoch Brater, Susan Brienza, Mary Doll, Judith Dearlove, Stan Gontarski, Lawrence Graver, David Hayman, David Hesla, James Knowlson, Jeri Kroll, Dougald McMillan, Angela Moorjani, Edouard Morot-Sir, Kristin Morrison, J. D. O'Hara, John Pilling, Dina Sherzer, and Jennie Skerl.

My colleague Michael Preston deserves special thanks for his work in preparing computer-generated concordances for some of Beckett's writings. I benefited from the expertise of two other colleagues, Reg Saner and Richard Schoeck, who clarified a number of scholarly questions. Alan Mandelbaum kindly took the time to read the chapters where Dante's works are discussed. Paul Levitt and James Kincaid, when each was chairman of my department, helped provide me with released time to do my research. Mark Wishingrad, my research assistant, earned his salary many times over. My former students—there are too many to list by name—contributed to my understanding of Beckett's works with their comments and questions.

I am happy to acknowledge the support generously provided by the Columbia University Council on Research in the Humanities, the National Endowment for the Humanities, the University of Colorado Council on Research and Creative Work, the University of Colorado Kayden Faculty Manuscript Prize Committee, and the University of Colorado Committee on Scholarly Publications. My book could not have been completed without this assistance.

Finally, I am grateful to Samuel Beckett for having taken the time to answer my queries, for having given me permission to consult his unpublished works, and, most of all, for having written his books.

THE DEVELOPMENT OF Samuel Beckett's FICTION

1

Beckett's Beginnings

Samuel Beckett's early fiction has received relatively little critical attention. *Molloy* (according to some authorities), or *Watt* (according to others), or *Murphy* (a few concede) is the book that marks the boundary between juvenilia and genius. The works that precede these are usually given a kindly dismissal, as if they would wither under the harsh glare of critical illumination. The most damning evidence is delivered by Beckett himself: when asked about his early stories and novels, he freely confesses that all of them are failures.

But Beckett also claims that *Murphy* is "derivative, trivial and without major import."[1] *Watt* he dismisses as "an unsatisfactory book," written "with a view to not losing my reason."[2] He says that *Molloy* was conceived on "the day I became aware of my own folly."[3] "The End" he calls "rubbish"; *Mercier and Camier* is a work for which he feels "loathing."[4] The *Texts for Nothing* are "abortive" and "failures."[5] *How It Is* he considers "very bad writing."[6] *Waiting for Godot* is a "bad play" written in a "facile attempt to make quick money."[7] *Endgame* is a "three-legged giraffe," and *Happy Days*, "another misery."[8] His poetry he considers "the work of a very young man with nothing to say and the itch to make."[9] His essays on art and aesthetics are "best forgotten."[10]

Stepping back to look at his works retrospectively, Beckett has concluded that there is "something wrong with all of them."[11] Such comments are based in part on modesty and in part on discomfort. It is difficult for artists to discuss their own works, even more for perfectionists to praise them. Taking Beckett's self-evaluations at face value is clearly a risky business.[12]

If Beckett's early works seem inferior to those that came later—and they often are—such a comparison finally means little. Beckett's best works are extraordinarily good; how bad the rest of them are is an issue to be judged on its own merits. Stories about mediocre artists suddenly blossoming into genius gain wide currency, perhaps because of the hope they generate in aspiring geniuses. But Beckett, lacking the requisite mediocrity, never underwent this kind of transformation.

Beckett's career did develop in an unusual way, and this helps explain why his early works received so little notice. After World War II he began to write plays and for the most part abandoned poetry and criticism. Around the same time he decided to compose his works in French instead of English. With the success of *Waiting for Godot* he quickly became famous. Many people, hearing of Beckett for the first time, assumed that he was a new French playwright. Understandably, his earlier works were neglected.

Beckett's early fiction, however, is important for a number of reasons. His development as a writer is best observed in his fiction, the only genre he worked in consistently throughout his career. Many of the innovative devices that would reappear in his later works were introduced in his first stories and novels. The narrators in these works often comment on the style they are using and on relevant aesthetic ideas. Such explanations are rarely given in the later works, although many of the same methods and principles are still operative. If the explanatory passages sometimes seem overly self-conscious, they are nevertheless useful for understanding Beckett's innovations. In some of the early works Beckett, mocking conventional fictional techniques, purposely introduces stylistic lapses and then—in case no one had noticed—points them out. This makes it easy to underestimate these works: if their apparent shortcomings are readily discerned, their strengths are not.

Original writing, when it first appears, often seems flawed or unintelligible. Beckett makes this point in his first published work, an essay in which he defends *Finnegans Wake* from the charge that it is unnecessarily obscure. If Joyce's novel seems puzzling, says Beckett, the fault is not the author's. Readers' problems come as a result of their "rapid skimming and absorption of the scant cream of sense. . . ."[13] The effort made to understand an innovative work is the price one pays for its originality. Beckett's comments about Joyce's writing also hold for his own; both their styles are very demanding. Like Joyce, Beckett is not concerned that his imperious attitude may reduce the size of his audience; the door is always open for dissatisfied customers to patronize another shop.

In 1928 Beckett met Joyce, and they became friends. Beckett undoubtedly learned a good deal from Joyce, but the degree to which he was influenced by Joyce is often overestimated. In his essay on *Finnegans Wake* Beckett makes it clear that he shares Joyce's views on the importance of originality in art. But Beckett—even carried away by youthful hero-worship—never persuaded himself that imitating Joyce's style was a way of making his own more original.

There is nevertheless a widely held belief that Beckett's early works are little more than pastiches of Joyce's. Beckett sometimes did use Joycean devices, but it is important to note how he used them. In his first novel, *Dream of Fair to Middling Women*, there is an interior monologue that resembles Joyce's. But the novel also contains a passage in which Beckett's narrator complains about "the fuss that went on about the monologue and dialogue and polylogue and catalogue, all exclusively intérieur."[14] This is a hint that the novel's Joycean passage is a parody, and not an imitation.

On one of the infrequent occasions when Beckett discussed his own writing without disparaging it, he denied that he was influenced by Joyce.[15] Though Beckett parodied Joyce and other authors he admired, he also worked to develop his own style. He rejected many traditional novelistic devices and introduced others of his own invention, and these often are initially puzzling. Some critics, mystified by Beckett's more difficult passages, decided they were meaningless; others labeled them indecipherable statements about the impenetrability of existence—which amounts to the same thing. But Beckett's lack of meanings is less often a problem than his readers' inability to discover them.

In Beckett's writing, the elements that seem chaotic or devoid of significance are usually those that are most innovative. The same is true in other types of twentieth-century art. To be sure, a few modern artists have striven for total emptiness and meaninglessness. But not Beckett: his writing may be difficult, but it is not incomprehensible. Careful readers are rewarded with insights that clarify his ideas; indifferent readers are rewarded accordingly.

Notes

1. Deirdre Bair, *Samuel Beckett: A Biography* (New York: Harcourt Brace Jovanovich, 1978), p. 479.

2. "Unsatisfactory," Bair, p. 364; "not losing my reason," letter to the author from Samuel Beckett, Dec. 3, 1972. Beckett made a similar comment to Richard Seaver: he said *Watt* was "only a game, a means of staying sane, a way to keep my hand in"; Richard Seaver, "Introduction," *I Can't Go On, I'll Go On: A Selection from Samuel Beckett's Work* (New York: Grove Press, 1976), p. xxxi.

3. Gabriel d'Aubarède, "Waiting for Beckett," trans. Christopher Waters, *Trace*, no. 42 (Summer, 1961), p. 158.

4. On "The End," Seaver, p. xxv; on *Mercier and Camier*, Bair, p. 634.

5. Seaver, p. xxxix.

6. Bair, pp. 512, 515.

7. *Ibid.*, pp. 383, 479.

8. On *Endgame*, Alan Schneider, "Beckett's Letters on Endgame," in *The Village Voice Reader*, ed. Daniel Wolf and Edwin Fancher (Garden City, N.Y.: Doubleday, 1962), p. 183; on *Happy Days*, Bair, p. 557.

9. Lawrence Harvey, *Samuel Beckett, Poet and Critic* (Princeton, N.J.: Princeton University Press, 1970), p. 273.

10. John Fletcher, *Samuel Beckett's Art* (London: Chatto and Windus, 1967), p. 20.

11. Ruby Cohn, "The Beginning of *Endgame*," *Modern Drama*, 9 (Dec., 1966):323.

12. When asked by an interviewer to evaluate a book on his own works, Beckett gave an opinion but then qualified it by saying, "You can't really judge your own work"; see David Gullette, "Mon jour chez Sam: A Visit with Beckett," *Ploughshares*, 1 (June, 1972):68. Beckett wrote to Alan Schneider, "the less I speak of my work the better"; see Schneider, p. 185. And he told John Gruen, "It is impossible for me to talk about my writing. . . . I can only estimate my work from within"; see John Gruen, "Samuel Beckett Talks about Beckett," *Vogue*, 154 (Dec., 1969):210.

13. "Dante... Bruno. Vico.. Joyce," in *Our Exagmination Round his Factification for Incamination of Work in Progress* (1929; rpt., London: Faber and Faber, 1972), p. 13.

14. *Dream of Fair to Middling Women* (TS), p. 39. The typescript is in the Dartmouth College Library, Hanover, N.H.; I am grateful to the officers of the Dartmouth College Library for permitting me to consult this source. The Joycean interior monologue is on p. 74.

15. Gruen, p. 210. John Pilling has described the "pervasive and misleading tendency in early Beckett criticism that attempted to derive Beckett from Joyce . . ."; see "Beckett's 'Proust,'" *Journal of Beckett Studies*, no. 1 (Winter, 1976), p. 25.

2

Innovation and Obscurity in Beckett's Early Fiction

The innovative passages in Beckett's fiction raise many problems of interpretation. Often difficulties arise when Beckett dispenses with conventional novelistic techniques and introduces formal experiments. In his essay on *Finnegans Wake* Beckett accuses modern readers of being so conditioned by traditional fiction that they consider the form of the writing as a peripheral adjunct of the content. "You are not satisfied," he says, "unless form is so strictly divorced from content that you can comprehend the one almost without bothering to read the other."[1] One reason for the hostility to *Finnegans Wake,* Beckett feels, is that Joyce's audience does not know what to make of a work where form and content are united: "Here form *is* content, content *is* form. You complain that this stuff is not written in English. It is not written at all. It is not to be read—or rather it is not only to be read. It is to be looked at and listened to. [Joyce's] writing is not *about* something; *it is that something itself.*"[2]

Two years after this essay was published, Beckett made a similar point about Proust's fiction: "For Proust, as for the painter, style is more a question of vision than of technique. Proust does not share the superstition that form is nothing and content everything, nor that the ideal literary masterpiece could only be communicated in a series of absolute and monosyllabic propositions. For Proust the quality of language is more important than any system of ethics or aesthetics. Indeed he makes no attempt to dissociate form from content. The one is a concentration of the other, the revelation of a world."[3] If Proust's fiction is like painting in its union of form and content, Beckett's—like abstract art—sometimes permits form to gain the upper hand.[4]

In *Watt* the narrator's reference to incidents "of great formal brilliance and indeterminable purport" hints at such a dominance of form.[5] The long boring passages in the novel, listing the arrangements of Mr. Knott's furniture or the glances exchanged by members of a committee, may seem pointless at first. But as eventually becomes apparent, the prolix style is used to demonstrate that reality contains oceans of tedium, tedium which conventional literature bridges with an *et cetera*. Traditional novelists describe boredom; Beckett's method is to offer demonstrations. He stresses a similar idea in a description of Joyce's style: "When the sense is sleep, the words go to sleep. . . . When the sense is dancing, the words dance."[6]

The boring lists in *Watt* tempt the reader to consider skipping over them; yet they might contain something noteworthy, so one plods on.[7] This results in uncertainty and frustration—feelings very much like Watt's when he submits to the irrational rules at Mr. Knott's house. In using techniques like these, Beckett indicates that he is willing to abandon the principle that art must always be interesting or pleasing. Many things in nature are unpleasant and (according to another time-honored aesthetic principle) art is supposed to follow nature. In his first published essay Beckett indicates that he cares little about appeasing those whose casual reading results in "dribbling comprehension"; in "Assumption," his first published story, he announces that he will not gratify readers who are looking for mere prettiness.[8]

An important element in Beckett's writing is its unbending honesty. In *Murphy* a character named Neary says, "Let our conversation now be without precedent in fact or literature, each one speaking to the best of his ability the truth to the best of his knowledge."[9] The irony in Neary's comment is double-edged: Beckett is serious about trying to express the truth. Reality is often misrepresented, in life as well as in literature, and his revolutionary idea is to depict it as accurately as possible. As Beckett moves toward this goal, he re-examines a number of aesthetic ideas that have usually been taken for granted. The traditional devices used to promote verisimilitude ostensibly give truthful representations of reality but actually often do the opposite. They force writers to pretend that fictional events actually occurred when every reader knows they are imaginary. Most works of fiction conform faithfully to the reality of the outer world, as if their authors were convinced that an untethered imagination would drift off irretrievably when its connections with the world were severed. But in fact, verisimilitude can restrain the imagination. It directs attention toward an area that is perceived indirectly (the space-time world, which is filtered through the senses) and away from the locus of direct experiences, the mind.

One aspect of the problem Beckett is addressing was raised by Plato. In the last book of *The Republic* Plato concludes that because art represents material entities, it is subservient to material reality. No matter how faithful the artistic representation, it never can duplicate the object that exists in the outer world.[10] When (as in Plato's case) the determining aesthetic criterion is an artist's ability to replicate material objects, the resultant art does contain a tacit admission of its inferiority to a higher reality. Plato's argument is sometimes dismissed as simplistic, but if his assumptions are granted, his conclusions make sense. Moreover, there exists a widespread belief that artistic reality is in some essential way inferior to material reality. A connotation of mendacity clings to words like fiction, romance, acting, fable, and device. The idea that art presents a distorted form of reality is pervasive, even if only on a popular level.

As Raymond Federman points out, Beckett "unmasks the counterfeit aspects of fictional realism. . . ."[11] By emphasizing the distinctions between imaginative and historical reality, Beckett satisfies even the most literal-minded demands for truthfulness. One way he does this is to admit that the action in his fiction is not a description of events which occurred in the external world. He is never apologetic about such admissions. What he describes did occur, in his imagination; this in no way suggests an inferior level of reality. Beckett sees the reality of art as an alternative to the deceptive impressions one has of the material world. Such impressions may be vivid, but they are based on sensory information that is often unreliable.

A critical view of material reality is an important theme in Beckett's writing. According to Lawrence Harvey, Beckett once remarked that two philosophical ideas are useful for understanding his works. The first is from the works of Arnold Geulincx, the seventeenth-century Belgian philosopher: "Ubi nihil vales ibi nihil velis" ("Want nothing where you are worth nothing"). The second passage is from Democritus: "Nothing is more real than nothing." To these Harvey adds another of Beckett's favorite quotations, Berkeley's "essere est percipi" ("existence is to be perceived").[12] Geulincx describes the futility of volition in the material world, Democritus indicates that an understanding of the material world founders on paradox, and Berkeley denies the real existence of the material world. These arguments against materialism on volitional, rational, and phenomenological grounds run parallel to Beckett's aesthetic critique of materialism. Here he follows Schopenhauer, both in rejecting materialism and in holding that art can provide a path to a higher plane of reality. In his essay on Proust, Beckett pays homage to Schopenhauer's aesthetic theories and argues that art can cut through the illusory reality based on sensory responses to the phenomena of the material world.[13]

Beckett makes it clear that he is as interested in the laws of the mind as he is in physical laws.[14] In *More Pricks than Kicks* the narrator toys with his obligation to follow time-space rules: "Let us call it Winter," he says, "that dusk may fall now and a moon rise."[15] In *Murphy* the narrator calls attention to a violation of the laws of physics: "Miss Carridge's method of entering a private apartment was to knock timidly on the door on the outside some time after she had closed it behind her on the inside. Not even a nice hot cup of tea in her hand could make her subject to the usual conditions of time and space in this matter."[16] If Miss Carridge's actions had conformed to the usual conditions of physical reality, the passage would have been less interesting—which is a reason Beckett violates them.

In *Watt* there is a description of fish that "are forced to rise and fall, now to the surface of the waves and now to the ocean bed." Anticipating the reaction of literal-minded readers, the narrator asks: "But do such fish exist?" He then answers his own question: "Yes, such fish exist, now."[17] The zoology of the outside world is irrelevant; the fish exist in the world of the novel. Similarly, when Kate Lynch is described as a bleeder, the narrator of *Watt* includes this footnote: "Haemophilia is, like enlargement of the prostate, an exclusively male disorder. But not in this work."[18]

An aesthetic theory that frees art from the obligation to represent material events has broad implications for literature. If one dispenses with verisimilitude, the rules for characterization, appropriate dialogue, motivation, chronological sequence, and realistic setting become less important. Some of these devices, like characterization and motivation, promote the illusion that it is possible for a writer to understand the workings of another person's mind. But Beckett believes that third-person descriptions of mental processes are usually trivial or misleading. The intrinsic self of another person is unknowable; we see other people as objects in space and time, phenomena in the macrocosm. In *Proust* Beckett agrees with Schopenhauer that the outer reality is a projection of a person's own will.[19] Realistic writers who believe they are modeling their characters on people in the outer world may in fact be presenting images that originate in their own minds. The intrinsic reality of a person (in Schopenhauer's terminology, a person's aspect as thing-in-itself) always remains hidden from others.

Beckett uses a number of techniques to dispel the illusion that his characters can be equated with people in the outer world. He reminds readers that they have before them, not life, but a book by Samuel Beckett. In *More Pricks than Kicks* Beckett includes an acknowledgment to himself as the author of a well-turned phrase.[20] The narrator of *Dream of Fair to Middling Women* reveals that his name is "Mr Beckett," and there is a narrator called Sam in *Watt*.[21] At the same time, the peripheral figures in these novels are denied the rounding effect of conventional characterizations and begin to resemble puppets.

Dylan Thomas noticed this occurring in *Murphy* and assumed that it was an inadvertent flaw. According to Thomas, Neary is a failure as a character: he is "a slap-stick, a stuffed guy, when he moves; his mind is Mr. Beckett's mind. . . ."[22] But this is an effect of Beckett's refusal to provide conventional characterizations. Nor was he unaware of the apparent flaw: at one point his narrator indicates that most of the characters in *Murphy* are puppets.[23]

One learns nothing about the backgrounds or outward appearances of the characters in "Assumption." The narrator of *Dream of Fair to Middling Women* bluntly refuses to give characterizations.[24] In *More Pricks than Kicks* the narrator says of one character, "There was nothing at all noteworthy about his appearance"; of another one he says, "it would be waste of time to itemise her."[25] The reasons for Beckett's elimination of traditional forms of characterization begin to emerge in *Murphy*. Near the beginning of the novel Mr. Kelly asks Celia to tell him about Murphy. This device for leading into characterizations must have been shopworn when, in the *Iliad,* Priam asked Helen to describe the Greek heroes. Like a well-trained student writer, Mr. Kelly refers to all of the prescribed questions: he inquires about "the who, what, where, by what means, why, in what way and when." The narrator compares Mr. Kelly to Quintilian—an indication that Beckett is familiar with the rhetorical rules he is about to abandon.[26] After hearing Mr. Kelly out, Celia tells him that Murphy is Murphy. A tautology is the best response when the interrogator is persistent and the question unanswerable.

Watt figures in a similar episode. Mr. Hackett, curious about Watt, asks Mr. Nixon to supply a few biographical details. "Nationality, family, birthplace, confession, occupation, means of existence, distinctive signs," says Mr. Hackett, "you cannot be in ignorance of all this." Mr. Nixon can be: he is. He insists he knows nothing about Watt, that nothing is known.[27] Hackett's quest for the *haec* of Watt founders on Nixon's *nichts.*[28] Mr. Kelly similarly searched in vain for the *quel* of amorphous Murphy.

Soon after the Hackett-Nixon conversation a newsagent named Evans is introduced. Unlike Watt, Evans is given an ample characterization. The narrator describes his hair, his moustache, his typical expression, his height, his way of walking. One learns that Evans never removes his cap, that he is a cyclist, that he plays chess. Caps, bicycles, chess—readers familiar with Beckett's earlier novels will expect this character to play an important role in the forthcoming action. Mr. Evans, however, never appears again.[29]

Beckett indicates that this is no oversight when he repeats the joke with another of the novel's minor figures: "The postman, a charming man, called Severn, a great dancer and lover of greyhounds, seldom called. But he did sometimes, always in the evening, with his light eager step and his dog by his side, to deliver a bill, or a begging letter." This curtain raiser is also Mr. Severn's final appearance in the novel.[30]

Many of Beckett's novels contain refusals to speculate about the characters' actions. Pretending to be concerned about maintaining verisimilitude, the narrator of *More Pricks than Kicks* explains why he will not go into the reasons for the hero's impending suicide attempt: "we feel confident that even the most captious reader must acknowledge . . . the verisimilitude of what we hope to relate in the not too distant future. For we assume the irresponsibility of Belacqua, his faculty for acting with insufficient motivation, to have been so far evinced in previous misadventures as to be no longer a matter for surprise."[31] A tap of the wand, and the inability to explain Belacqua's behavior is transformed into a shining example of consistent characterization. For conventional narrators, the hero's suicide attempt might be an occasion for extensive psychological probing—but not for Beckett's narrator. He only shrugs: "How he had formed this resolution to destroy himself we are quite unable to discover. The simplest course, when the motives of any deed are found subliminal to the point of defying expression, is to call that deed *ex nihilo* and have done. Which we beg leave to follow in the present instance."[32] The narrator's tone is playful, but his assertion that the intrinsic self of another person cannot be known is meant to be taken seriously.

This idea is related to a pattern in many of Beckett's early novels: though the protagonist's mind is described, his external characteristics are not, and the reverse is often true for the other characters. One learns little about Murphy's appearance, but an entire chapter is devoted to a description of his mind. Conversely, the narrator has a good deal to say about Celia's physical attributes—he provides readers with a list of her body measurements—but he discloses little about her thoughts. Such characterizations are less whimsical than they appear to be. The narrator usually knows the protagonist's thoughts because both of them are aspects of the author's mind (in some works the narrator even hints that the protagonist is his alter ego).[33] But the narrator lacks direct access to the thoughts of the other characters, and must content himself with summaries of their actions and external qualities. Describing one of Proust's characters, an impressionist painter, Beckett says he is concerned with "what he sees and not what he knows he ought to see. . . ."[34] The same can be said for Beckett himself.

Beckett's innovative ideas about characterization lead to another effect: when his characters become less vivid, readers are more easily involved in the action. It may seem that the very opposite should be true. One way of justifying conventional characterization is to assume that it increases the emotional intensity of a work by making characters so lifelike that readers readily identify with them. But this type of characterization induces readers to believe in intermediary figures who dilute the intensity of an author's expression. The quality of any reader's emotional response is limited by his or her ability to identify with a particular character. Beckett's method is to confront readers with difficulties in the work that replicate the ordeals his characters undergo. In this way he introduces an immediacy that surpasses the vicarious experience of being told about another person's actions.[35]

Moreover, Beckett also reverses this process. His characters often express emotions similar to those his readers may at the moment be feeling. Hackett and Kelly, when they demand characterizations, are also articulating Beckett's readers' needs. Watt's desire to learn more about Mr. Knott is described in such a way that it runs parallel to the reader's curiosity. Beckett uses a similar device in his drama. In *Waiting for Godot* Vladimir and Estragon speak about their boredom at the very point when members of the audience, responding to the lack of action in the play, are likely to be growing restless. When Godot does not appear, Vladimir asks the boy about him; his questions have probably also occurred to members of the audience. This is why Beckett refuses to say who Knott is or what Godot represents. If narrow meanings are assigned to these characters too quickly, an important dimension of Beckett's art is lost.

In their search for knowledge about the nature of reality, Beckett's characters come away with few answers. These characters are not unintelligent; they often learn a good deal about reality and see the world with unusual clarity. But they also discover that ultimate answers are hard to come by. Beckett's method is based on a union of form and content: the structures of his works create situations resembling those that are being described. In Beckett's fiction, readers, characters, and author are all challenged by the same elusive reality; and all experience the same sense of despair when, after attempting to plumb its depths, they fail.

Notes

1. "Dante... Bruno. Vico.. Joyce," in *Our Exagmination Round his Factification for Incamination of Work in Progress* (1929; rpt., London: Faber and Faber, 1972), p. 13.

2. "Dante... Bruno," p. 14. The italics are Beckett's.

3. *Proust* (1929; rpt., New York: Grove Press, 1957), p. 67.

4. Useful discussions of the form-content question can be found in Lawrence Harvey, *Samuel Beckett, Poet and Critic* (Princeton, N.J.: Princeton University Press, 1970), p. 435; John Fletcher, *Samuel Beckett's Art* (London: Chatto and Windus, 1967), p. 12; Tom Driver, "Beckett by the Madeleine," *Columbia University Forum*, 4 (Summer, 1961):23.

5. *Watt* (1953; rpt., New York: Grove Press, 1959), p. 74.

6. "Dante... Bruno," p. 14.

7. Many of the lists are in fact important in another way: they seem complete but often contain errors or omissions. See John Mood, "'The Personal System'—Samuel Beckett's *Watt*," *PMLA*, 86 (Mar., 1971): 255–65. The significance of such errors and omissions will be discussed in the chapters on *Murphy*.

8. "Assumption," *Transition*, 16–17 (June, 1929):268–71. Reprinted in *Transition Workshop*, ed. Eugene Jolas (New York: Vanguard Press, 1949), pp. 41–44. The quoted passage is from *Transition Workshop*, p. 42; "dribbling comprehension" is from "Dante... Bruno," p. 13.

9. *Murphy* (1938; rpt., New York: Grove Press, 1957), p. 214.

10. Plato makes this argument in the tenth book of *The Republic*. He concludes that "the imitator or maker of images knows nothing of true existence; he knows appearances only"; see *The Republic*, trans. B. Jowett (New York: Modern Library, n.d.), p. 369 (X, 601).

11. Raymond Federman, *Journey to Chaos: Samuel Beckett's Early Fiction* (Berkeley: University of California Press, 1965), p. 7.

12. Harvey, pp. 267–68. The translations are my own. There are allusions to all three passages in *Murphy*. Geulincx, p. 178; Democritus, p. 246; Berkeley, p. 246. "Esse est percipi" is the motto of Beckett's *Film*. The significance of these quotations will be discussed subsequently.

13. *Proust*, pp. 8, 66–69. For material on Schopenhauer's influence, see Harvey, pp. 73–78; David Hesla, *The Shape of Chaos* (Minneapolis: University of Minnesota Press, 1971), Ch. II; F. N. Lees, *Memoirs and*

Proceedings of the Manchester Literary and Historical Society, 1961–62, p. 39; John Pilling, *Samuel Beckett* (London: Routledge and Kegan Paul, 1976), pp. 126–27; and subsequent chapters of this book, especially those on *Murphy* and *Watt*.

14. For example, when Molloy refers to the laws of his mind, he is parodying Archimedes' principle that a body immersed in water will displace an amount of water equal to its own volume. Molloy speaks of knowing "the laws of the mind perhaps, of my mind, that for example water rises in proportion as it drowns you . . ."; *Molloy* (New York: Grove Press, 1955), p. 16.

15. *More Pricks than Kicks* (1934; rpt., New York: Grove Press, 1970), p. 20.

16. *Murphy*, p. 68.

17. *Watt*, p. 120.

18. *Ibid.*, p. 102.

19. *Proust*, p. 8.

20. *More Pricks*, p. 176.

21. *Dream of Fair to Middling Women* (TS, Dartmouth College Library, Hanover, N.H.), p. 166; *Watt*, pp. 153 *et passim*.

22. Dylan Thomas, "Documents: Recent Novels," *James Joyce Quarterly*, 8 (Summer, 1971):291; the review originally appeared in the *New English Weekly*, Mar. 17, 1938.

23. *Murphy*, p. 122.

24. *Dream*, p. 10.

25. *More Pricks*, pp. 27, 105.

26. *Murphy*, p. 17. As Quintilian mentions, his questions are based on Aristotle's categories; see Quintilian, *Instituto Oratoria*, III, vi, 23ff., and Aristotle, *Categoriae*, Ch. 4.

27. *Watt*, p. 21.

28. Sidney Warhaft connects Hackett with *haecceitas*, Watt with *quidditas*; see "Threne and Theme in *Watt*," *Wisconsin Studies in Contemporary Literature*, 4 (Autumn, 1963):267. Beckett uses the word "haecceity" in *More Pricks than Kicks* (p. 147).

29. Evans is introduced on p. 25 of *Watt*, described on pp. 25–26, and never again mentioned thereafter.

30. *Watt*, p. 69. Earlier, Arsene mentioned a consumptive postman (p. 47); this may (or may not) be Severn. There are no other references to Severn in the novel.

31. *More Pricks*, p. 89.

32. *Ibid.*

33. In *More Pricks than Kicks*, for example, the narrator refers to the protagonist as "my little internus homo" (p. 38).

34. *Proust*, p. 66.

35. A good discussion of how Beckett uses form to accomplish this can be found in H. Porter Abbott's *The Fiction of Samuel Beckett: Form and Effect* (Berkeley: University of California Press, 1973), pp. 61 *et passim*.

3

"Assumption" and the Aesthetics of Silence

Beckett's first published work of fiction is the short story "Assumption," which appeared in 1929.[1] "Assumption" is in many ways innovative: Beckett avoids using traditional devices like plot, characterization, dialogue, and motivation, and instead relies on metaphor and paradox to suggest shadowy meanings. An example occurs in the opening sentences of the story: "He could have shouted and could not. The buffoon in the loft swung steadily on his stick and the organist sat dreaming with his hands in his pockets."[2] The story begins with a contradictory statement ("could have . . . could not"), a precise linguistic configuration that demonstrates the inadequacy of language. The next sentence seems ambiguous until one realizes that the setting is neither a religious service nor a concert—unexpectedly there has been a shift from literal to figurative description. The conductor and organist are metaphorical representations of psychological impulses: one demands an utterance; the other, capable of producing it, does not. This type of metaphor, in which characters are used to represent psychological entities, is very common in Beckett's later fiction. In *How It Is*, for example, one similarly encounters a conflict between figures who represent expression and silence.

A pivotal idea in "Assumption" emerges in these first two sentences. The image of the conductor and organist is part of a sustained metaphor that runs through the story and links themes related to verbal, emotional, sexual, and artistic expression. The metaphor also introduces a problem that is important both in the form and in the content of the story: how best to express the idea of withheld expression.

"Assumption" is about an artist who strives to create a work that, without itself interrupting silence, will suggest silence to others. One of the artist's experiments involves using gestures to draw attention to himself and then uttering an explosive whisper that leaves everyone speechless. He knows this approach will not produce the ideal oxymoron, expressive inexpressiveness. Nevertheless, he refuses to give up; here, as in the *Unnamable*, the hero persists in his quest even when he believes it is futile to go on.

Beckett's protagonist is encumbered by emotional needs that run counter to those imposed by his art. His suppressed feelings demand expression: he feels a scream welling inside him, a "wild rebellious surge that aspired violently towards realization in sound" (p. 42). But he is afraid to release his pent-up emotions, and uses all his self-control to remain silent. As he struggles to keep the scream from escaping, he meets a woman who tempts him to express himself in another way—sexually. Her "clear, steady speech" gnaws away at his silences, and he is resentful (p. 43). Eventually, however, weakened by the effort of containing the scream, he yields to her. Though their love-making is ecstatic, he feels remorse afterward. They make love again, and again he is filled with regret. The hero's recurring euphoria and depression transform him into a figure who, like Adonis, is caught up in a cycle of death and resurrection: "Thus each night he died and was God, each night revived and was torn, torn and battered with increasing grievousness, so that he hungered to be irretrievably engulfed in the light of eternity . . ." (p. 44).

These overpowering emotions consume what remains of the hero's self-restraint, and the suppressed scream bursts forth: "While the woman was contemplating the face that she had overlaid with death, she was swept aside by a great storm of sound, shaking the very house with its prolonged, triumphant vehemence, climbing in a dizzy, bubbling scale, until, dispersed, it fused into the breath of the forest and the throbbing cry of the sea" (p. 44). The story ends as the woman caresses the "wild dead hair" of her lover.

As the title of the story suggests, the godlike hero has achieved assumption. The apotheosis has Christian as well as classical associations: the Feast of the Assumption commemorates the Virgin Mary's being received into heaven.[3] This provides a connection between the hero's desire to maintain his virginity and his role as creator. Other definitions of assumption—arrogance and taking into union—refer to the woman's "enormous impertinence" when she intrudes on the hero's silence and then seduces him (p. 43). The hero's belief that he will be able to maintain silence after becoming involved with her is an invalid assumption and introduces another meaning of the word. Beckett ingeniously uses the different ideas associated with assumption to link various elements in the story with the central theme of expression versus reticence.

This theme is also related to the innovative style in "Assumption." At one point, when the narrator discusses art, it becomes evident that his comments are relevant to the story itself: "To avoid the expansion of the commonplace is not enough; the highest art reduces significance in order to obtain that inexplicable bombshell, perfection. Before no supreme manifestation of Beauty do we proceed comfortably up a staircase of sensation, and sit down mildly on the topmost stair to digest our gratification: such is the pleasure of Prettiness. We are taken up bodily and pitched breathless on the peak of a sheer crag: which is the pain of Beauty" (p. 42). The struggle for perfection; the reduction of significance; the refusal to pamper readers with sensational effects, or with what is merely pretty; the conviction that beauty cannot be achieved easily: these principles govern the style of "Assumption" as well as many of Beckett's later works.

The narrator's comment about the reduction of significance indicates why the idea of expressive silence is central in "Assumption." Just as his protagonist cannot scream silently, Beckett cannot write a story without using words. But the elements in the story that are suppressed, omitted, or enigmatic contribute to the attempt to use silence creatively. Intensified by the whisper that precedes it, threatened by the scream that finally emerges, the silence finally becomes powerfully expressive. Instead of inundating readers with kinetic effects, Beckett creates a looming reservoir of potential meanings.

A similar image is used in the story: the pent-up scream is compared to water behind a weakening dam. But if the hero's dam breaks down, Beckett's reservoir of suppressed meanings is maintained. One learns that the hero is afraid to scream, but not why, or what the scream represents. A similar situation occurs in *Molloy:* the protagonist says that his "long silent screams" are dangerous but never explains why.[4] Here, as in "Assumption," ambiguity makes the scream portentous and—by permitting readers to project their own feelings into the situation—enhances the story's universality. The suppressed meanings give readers an uneasy sense of the obscure emotional forces that finally overwhelm the protagonist.[5] Ominous reticence, with its intimations and unstated possibilities, can be as threatening as more direct forms of communication. In "Assumption" Beckett transforms this psychological insight into an aesthetic principle.

Notes

1. *Transition,* 16–17 (June, 1929):268–71. Reprinted in *Transition Workshop,* ed. Eugene Jolas (New York: Vanguard Press, 1949), pp. 41–44.

2. *Transition Workshop,* p. 41. Subsequent page references in this chapter are to this work.

3. Assumption is celebrated on August 15. In the Eastern Church this feast (which is celebrated on the same day) is called "Falling Asleep." There may be a connection between Mary's sleeplike death and the deathlike state of the hero after he sleeps with the woman (p. 44).

4. *Molloy* (1951; rpt., New York: Grove Press, 1970), p. 109.

5. There is a similar idea in *Murphy.* At one point Murphy says to Ticklepenny, " 'Have a fire in this garret before night or—.' " The narrator then adds, "It was an aposiopesis of the purest kind. Ticklepenny supplied the missing consequences in various versions, each one more painful than any that Murphy could have specified, terrifying taken all together"; *Murphy* (1938; rpt., New York: Grove Press, 1957), p. 164.

4

Dream of Fair to Middling Women and the Life of the Inner Man

In 1932 Beckett completed his still-unpublished first novel, *Dream of Fair to Middling Women.*[1] The title contains joking references to Tennyson's "A Dream of Fair Women" as well as to Chaucer's *Legend of Good Women*—even in his debut as a novelist Beckett was not overly burdened by diffidence toward other writers.[2] At times his narrator holds forth on the weaknesses of novelists whose style he feels is superannuated: "To read Balzac is to receive the impression of a chloroformed world. He is absolute master of his material, he can do what he likes with it, he can foresee and calculate its least vicissitude, he can write the end of the book before he has finished the first paragraph, because he has turned all his creatures into clockwork cabbages and can rely on their staying put whenever needed or staying going at whatever speed in whatever direction he chooses" (pp. 106–7). The narrator of *Dream* refuses to indulge in such artifices of plot manipulation: he claims he is "neither Deus enough nor ex machina enough . . ." (p. 104). A cohesive plot makes him uncomfortable: "The only unity in this story," he says, "is, please God, an involuntary unity" (p. 118). After listing a few possibilities for a character's final scene he says, "that ought to dénouer that"—as if he really had provided a denouement (p. 132). When the narrator finally does revert to old-fashioned methods, he cannot help grumbling. It is with very bad will indeed, he says, that he approaches "the gehenna of narratio recta" (p. 150).

After this prospectus it should be clear why the plot is difficult to follow, let alone summarize. The story, set in Dublin, deals with the activities of a young man, Belacqua (he is named for a character in Dante's *Purgatorio*). Belacqua is blessed with a multitude of acquaintances—the novel has over a hundred characters—but he is not very sociable. Sought out by friends, pursued by women (most of them extraordinarily beautiful), Belacqua mainly enjoys communing with himself. About halfway through the novel Belacqua goes to Germany to be with his fiancée, the Smeraldina-Rima. Not unexpectedly, the visit is a fiasco and he returns to Dublin. This central event gives the story a beginning, middle, and end, and some of the book's episodes hint at the vestiges of a plot. But such lapses into conventionality serve only to heighten the parody: when traditional techniques are not immediately banished from the novel, it is so they can be pilloried later on.

The characterizations, like the plot, are quite unconventional. The narrator freely confesses that his characters are no more realistic than Balzac's "clockwork cabbages"; revelers at a party, for example, are dismissed as "masks," and Belacqua's friend Chas is called a "machine" and a "clockwork fiend" (pp. 185, 180–81). The protagonist is admittedly an imaginary figure: "There is no real Belacqua, it is to be hoped not indeed, there is no such person" (p. 108). When the Smeraldina-Rima is brought on stage for her first important scene (she will rape the hero), the narrator says, "The Smeraldina-Rima is not demonstrable" (p. 11). Rejecting conventional modes of characterization, he lists the things he will not reveal about her: "Milieux, race, family, structure, temperament, past and present and consequent and antecedent back to the first combination and the papas and mammas and paramours and cicisbei and the morals of Nanny and the nursery wallpapers and the third and fourth generation snuffles . . ." (p. 10).

As an alternative to traditional novelistic methods, Beckett relies on an "aesthetic of inaudibilities" something like the one he introduced in "Assumption" (p. 126). Details of the aesthetic are revealed when Belacqua describes a book he hopes to write—its similarity to *Dream of Fair to Middling Women* is hardly coincidental. Belacqua's book will be one "where the phrase is self-consciously smart and slick." But its meaning will emerge, not in clusters of words, but from the interstices that separate them. "The experience of my reader," says Belacqua, "shall be between the phrases, in the silence, communicated by the intervals, not the terms, of the statement . . ." (p. 123). According to Belacqua, there is a precedent for his method in the music of Beethoven:

> I think of his earlier compositions where into the body of the musical statement he incorporates a punctuation of dehiscence, flottements, the coherence gone to pieces, the continuity bitched to hell because the units of continuity have abdicated their unity, they have gone multiple, they fall apart, the notes fly about, a blizzard of electrons; and then the vespertine compositions eaten away with terrible silences . . . and pitted with dire stroms of silence, in which has been engulfed the hysteria that he used to let speak up, pipe up, for itself. (P. 124)

Here, as in "Assumption," the silence is suggestive; much of the expression that might have been overt is implied. Belacqua describes a similar effect in a Rembrandt painting, where he discovers "the implication lurking behind the pictorial pretext threatening to invade pigment and oscuro . . ." (p. 123).

In a letter written to his friend Axel Kaun in 1937, Beckett discusses a similar idea and Beethoven is again used as an example: "Shall literature alone be left behind on that stale old path long ago abandoned by music and painting? Is there something paralyzingly sacred involved in the abnormality of the word which doesn't belong to the principle of the other arts? Is there any reason why that terribly arbitrary materiality of the word's surface should not be permitted to dissolve, like, for example, the tone's surface devoured by those great black pauses in the Seventh Symphony of Beethoven . . . ?"[3] Belacqua's goal resembles the one Beckett defines here: to provide a literary counterpart to the silence and emptiness in the works of Beethoven and Rembrandt.

Silence is an integral part of this aesthetic, but Beckett is not—as some critics hold—striving for the literary equivalent of empty canvases or music without notes. Positive elements are always present in his works to define the emptiness. Beckett's spaces depict an arid vastness that overwhelms the reader; they do not suggest. as empty canvases do, a poverty of talent moving toward its logical destination. Total silence poses few difficulties in conception or execution, but using silence creatively is another matter entirely. As Belacqua says when he discusses Beethoven's silent pauses, it took "as bloody a labour . . . as any known to man" to produce them (p. 124). Similarly, in *Murphy*, Beckett refers to the "silence not of vacuum but of plenum."[4]

Though Beckett uses self-canceling statements in *Dream of Fair to Middling Women*, the work as a whole never collapses into a void of negated meaning. At times the narrator, seemingly incapable of mastering even the most rudimentary fictional techniques, confesses that one of his descriptions is inaccurate or worthless. But the juxtaposed elements—the weak passages and the self-criticism—remain in a state of balanced antithesis without eliminating one another. The result is a form of litotes that leads to new levels of meaning. The self-criticism can be seen as Socratic irony—the key issue is not the author's incompetence but the overwhelming difficulty of his task. Every artist encounters insuperable problems when it comes to depicting the essential aspects of human reality: the inner self defies being represented. "The reality of the individual," Belacqua observes, "is an incoherent reality and must be expressed incoherently" (p. 91). It is not that Beckett lacks the skill to use conventional methods of characterization; rather, he is unwilling to use them. He intentionally weakens fictional devices which suggest that human reality can be transcribed and sometimes uses self-canceling statements for this purpose. As the narrator says, "little by little Belacqua may be described but not circumscribed; his terms stated but not summed. And of course God's will be done should one description happen to cancel the next . . ." (p. 111). The distorted surface reality in *Dream* is a reaction to the kind of fiction where thoughts are attributed, and motives imputed, too readily. One really knows little about the motives for the simplest decision or the mechanisms involved in making it. Beckett is concerned with "the inner man, its hunger, darkness and silence"—one cannot even use the pronoun "his" in referring to it (p. 35).

Beckett's rejection of conventional characterizations calls attention to the aspects of human reality that are ignored because they are imperfectly understood. For Beckett, the terra incognita of human geography is more interesting than the areas that have already been explored. He therefore eliminates or parodies those traditional devices dealing mainly with obvious, external factors. Beckett speaks admiringly of Proust's contempt for "the literature that 'describes,'" and for "the realists and naturalists worshipping the offal of experience. . . ."[5] Beckett's quarrel with Balzac and other realists centers on this point. In their fiction the characters are classified, stuffed, mounted, and exhibited against a backdrop that simulates their habitat. The more convincing the superficial details, the easier it is to believe the characters are alive. But for Beckett living creatures are complex and mysterious, their deepest thoughts unimaginable, their essential experiences unknown.

An emphasis on the outer reality tacitly suggests that what exists beneath it is unimportant. The psychological insights of writers like Balzac, perceptive as they often are, can be misleading when they imply that the depths of the psyche resemble the surface. A recurring theme in Beckett's works is that little is understood about what it means to be a human being, or about what existence means. The narrator of *Dream* says that he considers it improper "to conjugate *to be* without a shudder."[6]

Beckett's dialogue again violates the traditional rules of novelwriting. His characters' conversations, full of arcane references and drawing-room wit, have little to do with the way people ordinarily speak. In a realistic novel such dialogue might be considered a failure, but in *Dream* it becomes another way of indicating that the characters should not be mistaken for living creatures. Similarly, many of the people in the novel have improbable names: Belacqua, the Smeraldina-Rima, the Alba, Chas, the Syra-Cusa, the Mandarin, the Frica. Some of these characters—like divas or Scottish chieftains—have only surnames preceded by definite articles. Writers like Dickens often gave unusual names to minor characters who epitomized particular qualities (Uriah Heep or Seth Pecksniff, for example). Beckett reverses this technique: the major characters in *Dream* have odd names, while those with more ordinary names, like Lucien and Jem Higgins, are relegated to minor roles.

The narrator, anonymous for most of the novel, casually includes a conversation where he is addressed as "Mr Beckett" (p.

166). Aptly named for his role as the author's principal spokesman, he is in many ways the antithesis of the nineteenth-century unobtrusive narrator. He calls attention to himself, frankly gives his opinions on a variety of subjects, and even argues with the reader. At times he is depicted as a writer, busily working away on the novel in which he appears, pleased with some segments, considering revisions for others. In one passage he shares his concern that the "hyphenation is getting out of hand"; in another he praises an ellipsis: "The dots are nice don't you think?" (pp. 119, 107). The narrator's main criterion for including material is whether or not it bores him (pp. 10, 111, 119). The possibility that these eccentricities might weaken his credibility troubles him very little.

In conventional novels the narrator is often made unobtrusive so that the characters can be portrayed more vividly. Beckett strives for the opposite effect: the narrator of *Dream* keeps insisting that he is more lifelike than the characters. In the following passage, for example, he makes it clear where Belacqua (who is about to develop his aesthetic of inaudibilities) gets his ideas: "What shall we make him do now, what would be the correct thing for him to think for us?" (p. 120). The point of such interjections is to indicate that there is only one mind at work in a novel, the author's. An imagined mind can never attain the amplitude of the mind that created it, and those novelists who pretend that their characters are capable of independent thought can hardly claim to be writing realistically. Beckett refers to his characters as masks and machines; this, in fact, is what they are. The narrator is the author's persona, hence he is given the author's name. What seems at first to be inept characterization turns out to be a parody of the weaknesses of traditional novelistic methods. A similar idea holds throughout the novel: its apparent flaws are usually aspects of some innovative technique.

Many of these innovations are based on Beckett's rejection of the idea—often taken for granted in realistic art—that the distinctions between objects (material entities) and representations (aesthetic entities) should be blurred. Beckett feels that the relationship between objects and representations is subtle and complex. It is distorted by a feedback process in which images garnered from memory are projected onto perceived objects to the degree that the objects seem to possess the attributed qualities innately. This makes it difficult to apprehend the actual differences between material and imaginary entities.

In literature such distortions are even more troublesome because of semantic problems: language tends to direct ideas into predetermined categories. The portion of reality represented by a pre-existent vocabulary begins to seem more vivid than the unnamed portion. Distinctions among entities represented by the same noun are eroded: when an object is perceived as a spoon or a chair, it is commonly treated as a featureless member of a class and whatever unique characteristics it may possess are ignored. This problem could only be overcome by giving every discrete object a different name and eliminating words that lead to classification.[7] The practice of disregarding the differences among similar objects is learned as part of a linguistic process, but it eventually becomes habitual, and is all too readily extended from trivial objects, like spoons and chairs, to human beings.

In attempting to overcome such difficulties the narrator of *Dream* urges his readers to distinguish between objects and representations: "if we could only learn to school ourselves to nurture that divine and fragile Fünkelein of curiosity struck from the desire to bind for ever in imperishable relation the object and its representation, the stimulus to the molecular agitation that it sets up, percipi to percipere. . . ."[8] If objects and representations are no longer equated, the narrator says, we will begin to see reality in a better way, a magical way. How would a familiar object appear if all our memories of similar objects were stripped away? And how would we perceive the idea of an object if we could think of it as totally independent of material reality? (This Berkeleyan alternative is especially appealing to Beckett.) Such questions clear the way for Beckett's attempt to find alternatives to the aesthetics of representational art.

Beckett's approach, however, introduces a problem. Modes of representation differ from genre to genre; what is true for music or painting need not hold for literature. Mimetic representation is rare in music; when it does occur (as in Beethoven's *Wellington's Victory*, for example), it is usually considered weak or eccentric. Though representation was once dominant in painting, today the idea of nonrepresentational art is commonplace. But it may be that this is because the fundamental elements in music and painting, notes and forms, need not in themselves signify anything. Language, on the other hand, has an intrinsic capacity for representation: even an isolated word has some significance. Hence the analogy between literature and other genres seems to break down.

Beckett's way of dealing with this problem is to use figurative language as a way of avoiding direct representation. The mimetic quality of language is strongest in denotative statements; in figurative language, however, one-to-one correspondences are avoided. Metaphor alters the literal meaning of a statement; hyperbole inflates it; irony reverses it. In *Dream* Beckett often demonstrates how figurative language can be used to offset the denotative elements in language. His refusal to give characterizations is based on the idea that factual descriptions falsely suggest that one can depict the essential self of another person. But figurative characterizations—like the following one—hint at these essential qualities without suggesting that they can be defined or circumscribed: "The Syra-Cusa: her body more perfect than dream creek, amaranth lagoon. She flowed along in a nervous swagger, swinging a thin arm amply. The sinewy fetlock sprang, Brancusi bird, from the shod foot, blue arch of veins and small bones, rose like a Lied to the firm wrist of the reins, the Bilitis breasts" (p. 29). The images follow one another rapidly and touch on a variety of subjects—creek, lagoon, horse, bird, song, Bilitis. What representational meaning they contain is undermined by qualification: the creek is dreamt, the amaranth is a mythical flower, the bird is a work of art, and Bilitis (purportedly a classical author) is a hoax.[9] In characterizing the Syra-Cusa, Beckett does not attempt to provide a photographic portrait, to describe the color of her hair or the shape of her eyes; but one gets a sense of her appearance and personality nevertheless. Denotative language tries to capture reality and fails; figurative language, content to observe its quarry from a distance, succeeds somewhat better.

Figurative language is especially appropriate in descriptions of mental reality. Material objects occupy a fixed amount of space; a similar sense of delimited entities characterizes denotative language, which is most useful for dealing with material reality.

Amorphous mental entities, however, are best described in figurative language. In the following passage antithetical metaphors of womb and tomb, prenatal and postmortem existence, suggest the enigmatic, transcendental qualities of Belacqua's mind: "The lids of the hard aching mind close, there is suddenly gloom in the mind; not sleep, not yet, nor dream, with its sweats and terrors, but a waking ultra-cerebral obscurity, thronged with grey angels; there is nothing of him left but the umbra of grave and womb where it is fitting that the spirits of his dead and his unborn should come abroad" (p. 39).

Belacqua's mind is depicted in detail, but the other characters' thoughts are given less attention. The narrator occasionally describes the thoughts of a few of Belacqua's friends and deals with the rest of the people in the novel as if they were mindless puppets. This point of view may seem solipsistic—presumably everyone in the real world has a mind. But, in fact, one has access only to that portion of the outer world which filters through the senses. Beckett accurately depicts what he has experienced: the reality contained in his own mind and the world as it appears when it is reflected in that mind. We have ample knowledge of our own thoughts; the thoughts of a few people—fragments distorted by language—are communicated to us; and we know next to nothing about what the others are thinking. Beckett's portrayals of mental reality conform to this ordering.

The subjective quality of an individual's mental experiences is supposedly rendered in a traditional mode, first-person narrative. But this is a cumbersome device. The first-person narrator is an incorrigible eavesdropper and yet trusted by his friends, who rush to him with their innermost thoughts. He can transcribe lengthy conversations verbatim, yet suddenly becomes forgetful when the author wants to withhold information. The narrator of *Dream* mocks these conventions. He pretends to be limited by the rules of a first-person narrative and then interjects details that he could have known only if he were omniscient. Then, while readers are still puzzling over such inconsistencies, he announces that he is manipulating the characters. This eliminates the bothersome apparatus of both first-person and omniscient narrative. The first-person narrator may be an improbable creature, but the omniscient narrator—with no counterpart in human experience—is utterly impossible. Beckett's narrator, amused or bored by the subject matter, fussing over punctuation marks, is more lifelike than either one. Despite the disadvantages of playing on an unfamiliar court, Beckett often manages to beat the realists at their own game.

Relieved of the obligation of describing the outer world realistically, Beckett devotes himself to an imaginative portrayal of his protagonist's inner life. Belacqua's state of introspection is depicted as an escape into another world where he is liberated from the vicissitudes of day-to-day existence. The people scrambling about him—mindless savants, shameless schemers, heartless sweethearts—recede, and he blissfully retreats into his peaceful sanctuary.

As might be expected, figurative language is dominant in the descriptions of Belacqua's inner world. It is represented as a dark subterranean area, a tunnel, "a country of quiet," a place where "hush and gloom" have replaced the world's "workaday glare." It is also, figuratively, an underworld, where he moves among "shades" in a "Limbo."[10] There, animation is suspended but cerebration is alive: "Torture by thought and trial by living, because it was fake thought and false living, stayed outside the tunnel. But in the umbra, the tunnel, when the mind went womb-tomb, then it was real thought and real living, living thought. . . . The prurient heat and the glare of living consumed away . . . he was in the gloom, the thicket, he was wholly a gloom of ghostly comfort, a Limbo from which the mistral of desire had been withdrawn" (pp. 39–40).

Many of these images link Beckett's inner world with Dante's vision of the afterlife. Like his counterpart in the *Purgatorio*, Beckett's hero is "bogged down in indolence" (p. 108). When the Belacqua of the *Purgatorio* is asked why he has not yet begun his climb toward salvation, he explains that he must wait because he postponed repenting his sins. An excerpt from this comment is quoted in *Dream*: "L'andar su che porta?" ("What is the use of going up?").[11] Beckett seldom borrows from other writers without adding something of his own, and here the original element emerges in his attitude toward lethargy. For Dante, lethargy leads to sin, and it delays one's approach to paradise. Dante, following Christian tradition, sees the will as an agent that permits man to choose between salvation and damnation; volitional strength leads to moral victories. Beckett's Belacqua, however, comes closest to paradise when he surrenders to lethargy. In Beckett's view the effects of the will are harmful and must be countered.[12] The will activates desire, desire demands satisfaction, and this becomes a habitual process that leads to the erosion of freedom. Belacqua, "purged of desire" in Limbo, is liberated from the "will pricks" that torment him in everyday life (pp. 38, 162). Dante's Belacqua, dreaming with his head between his knees, is a symbol of foolish short-sightedness. His namesake, on the other hand, has a clearer view of reality when, "swathed in the black arras of his sloth," he retreats from outer reality (p. 108).

Both Beckett and Dante are concerned with portraying transcendental reality, and some of Beckett's methods are based on Dante's. According to Dante, the "form or method of treating" the subject matter in *The Divine Comedy* is "poetic" and "figurative."[13] Dante suggests that his poem can be understood in a number of ways. On a literal level it can be read as a description of the afterlife; on an allegorical level it deals with a subject—justice—that refers to life on earth. Other medieval allegorists commonly used only a single figurative level, and the importance of the literal level in their works usually diminishes once the figurative meaning has emerged. One mark of Dante's innovative skill is the complexity of his allegory: he worked to sustain three figurative levels in his poem, allegorical, moral, and anagogical.[14] Moreover, the literal level of Dante's poem retains significance even after the figurative meanings have been determined. Beckett admires these qualities to the degree that when Dante's writing does lapse into the simpler type of allegory, he points out the failure and criticizes it.[15]

Dante's way of depicting the intangible qualities of the spiritual world provided Beckett with a precedent for his portrayals of mental reality. Dante's method involves using extended metaphors that expand the circumscribed categories of denotative language. For example, in describing lust a psychologist might refer to the libido, and a conventional allegorist (in this case Bunyan), to a figure named "Wanton." In either case the amorphous idea is represented as a delimited entity. Dante, however, mentions a series of figures—Semiramis, Dido, Cleopatra, Helen,

Achilles, Paris, Tristan, Paolo and Francesca—and he indicates that each one of them represents only some aspect of lust.[16] Even taken together, these figures represent less than the general concept: Virgil explains that there are many other examples of the lustful, and shows Dante "more than a thousand shades, naming them as he pointed."[17] The complexity of this description is further enhanced when Francesca describes the range of emotions that contributed to her seduction.

Beckett uses a similar method. In *Dream* the wanton Syra-Cusa is compared to Lucrezia, Clytemnestra, Semiramide, Scylla, and the Sphinx, among others (p. 44). Beckett sometimes uses crowds of unnamed figures to represent aspects of mental reality, such as the "shades of the dead and the dead-born and the unborn and the never-to-be-born" in Belacqua's Limbo (p. 38). At times aspects of Belacqua's personality are represented by mythological figures, like Echo and Narcissus (p. 107). These figures are similar to the characters in other works who represent emotional forces (the conductor and organist in "Assumption," for example).

Along with *The Divine Comedy*, Beckett used Vico's theory of type-names in formulating his ideas about figurative language. Beckett gives a summary of the theory in his essay on *Finnegans Wake*. According to Vico, in antiquity the name of an outstanding exemplar of a trait was often used as a term for the trait itself. Thus Hercules came to mean hero, and Homer, poet. To Beckett, this kind of primitive language suggests an immediacy and emotional vividness lacking in the abstractions of denotative language, where common nouns refer to classes of objects. In the same essay Beckett uses Vico's theory as a way of establishing the primacy of figurative language over denotative language (which he calls "Metaphysics"):

Before articulation comes song; before abstract terms, metaphors. The figurative character of the oldest poetry must be regarded, not as sophisticated confectionery, but as evidence of a poverty-stricken vocabulary and of a disability to achieve abstraction. Poetry is essentially the antithesis of Metaphysics: Metaphysics purge the mind of the senses and cultivate the disembodiment of the spiritual; Poetry is all passion and feeling and animates the inanimate; Metaphysics are most perfect when most concerned with universals; Poetry, when most concerned with particulars. Poets are the sense, philosophers the intelligence of humanity. Considering the Scholastics' axiom: *"niente è nell'intelleto che prima non sia nel senso,"* it follows that poetry is a prime condition of philosophy and civilization.[18]

Beckett's antithesis goes beyond alternative modes of expression: opposed are different ways of seeing the world. On the one hand, reason, abstraction, metaphysics; on the other, emotion, poetry, aesthetics.[19]

The theme of opposed rational and aesthetic modes runs through Beckett's writing. There is a good example in *Waiting for Godot*, where Vladimir's rational approach is contrasted with Estragon's distrust of rationality. Estragon—seemingly not very bright—at first gives the impression that he could benefit from Vladimir's lectures on where they are and what they are doing. But Estragon's intelligence is in no way deficient: when they discuss the exchange of shoes and hanging themselves, it becomes evident that it is Vladimir who reasons badly.[20] Estragon's aesthetic approach (he was once a poet) is superior: if he avoids rational thought, it is because he understands its limitations. Here, as often occurs in Beckett's works, a point of view that will eventually be undermined is initially presented in a favorable light.

Beckett uses a similar approach in *Dream of Fair to Middling Women*. The novel seems like an inept attempt at social satire, and the narrator's affable readiness to point out its flaws only confirms this impression. One is also put off by Belacqua's self-involvement, and it is easy to agree with his friends when they criticize his eccentricities. But if others think Belacqua is out of step, the converse also holds. To him, their talk is inane, their outlook limited, their existence prosaic. After returning from Limbo, Belacqua finds ordinary life odd and unfamiliar. Eventually, it becomes apparent that the bizarre surface reality in *Dream* is a reflection of the strangeness of the world of ordinary experience.

Dream of Fair to Middling Women is usually considered a failure. It was rejected by so many publishers that Beckett finally gave up trying to get it into print.[21] But few of those who condemned the novel realized that its carnival-mirror distortions of familiar reality could be understood as views of the world as seen from Limbo. *Dream* does have weaknesses; for example, it focuses too much on the world it denigrates and too little on the one it posits as an alternative. In his later fiction Beckett spends less time mocking the world's absurdity because he is preoccupied with descriptions of inner reality. The ineffable nature of this reality presented artistic problems that he would grapple with throughout his career. If he does not dispose of them in *Dream of Fair to Middling Women,* Beckett at least points the way toward the elegant solutions he would later introduce.

Notes

1. Parts of *Dream of Fair to Middling Women* were salvaged and used in *More Pricks than Kicks* (1934; rpt., New York: Grove Press, 1970). "A Wet Night" (pp. 47–84) is a slightly revised version of the conclusion of *Dream* (TS, pp. 178–215); "The Smeraldina's Billet Doux," (pp. 152–57) is a slightly revised version of a similar letter in *Dream* (TS, pp. 49–54). Page references to *Dream of Fair to Middling Women* in this chapter are to the typescript in the Dartmouth College Library, Hanover, N.H. I am grateful to the authorities of the library for permitting me to consult this source as well as Beckett's letter to Axel Kaun.

2. There are other allusions to Chaucer and Tennyson in the novel. The epigraph of *Dream* is taken from the opening of Chaucer's *Legend of Good Women;* there is a reference to the Wife of Bath (p. 195); and one of Beckett's characters is named "the Man of Law" (p. 194). Beckett's phrase, "like Dan the first to warble like a turdus" (p. 186), parodies a reference to "Dan Chaucer, the first warbler," in Tennyson's "A Dream of Fair Women."

3. From Beckett's corrected typescript of a letter to Axel Kaun, dated July 9, 1937, pp. 1–2 (the translation from the German is my own). The typescript is in the collection of the Dartmouth College Library, Hanover, N.H.

4. *Murphy* (1938; rpt., New York: Grove Press, 1957), p. 148.

5. *Proust* (1929; rpt., New York: Grove Press, 1957), p. 59.

6. Page 40. The italics are Beckett's.

7. Beckett touches on this question in *Molloy*. Moran, who knows what a kniferest is, barely notices one he is using; Molloy cherishes his kniferest because he knows nothing of its name and function; see *Molloy* (1951; rpt., New York: Grove Press, 1970), pp. 158, 85. Jorge Luis Borges, in his short story "Funes the Memorious," also explores the problem of the loss of individual characteristics in objects that are perceived as members of a class.

8. Page 142. "Percipi . . . percipere" is an allusion to Berkeley's statement that existence is perceiving or being perceived. See George Berkeley, *Philosophical Commentaries,* ed. A. A. Luce (London: Thomas

Nelson and Sons, 1944), p. 139 (entry 429). Arthur Anston Luce was one of Beckett's professors at Trinity College, Dublin.

9. Pierre Louÿs claimed that a book of his own poems, *Les Chansons de Bilitis* (1894), was the work of Bilitis, a newly discovered contemporary of Sappho's. It was some time before the hoax was discovered.

10. Quoted passages in the description of Belacqua's inner world are from the following pages: "tunnel," pp. 45, 65; "country of quiet," p. 38; "hush and gloom," p. 170; "workaday glare," p. 170; "shades," p. 38; "Limbo," pp. 38, 56, 162.

11. *Purgatorio* 4:127. I have used the translation by John D. Sinclair, *Dante's Purgatorio* (New York: Oxford University Press, 1970), p. 63. The passage Beckett quotes is on p. 126 of *Dream*. There are many other allusions to Dante's Belacqua in *Dream*; see pp. 107, 125, 166.

12. Ruby Cohn makes a similar point about the differences between Beckett's attitude toward Belacqua and Dante's; see *Back to Beckett* (Princeton, N.J.: Princeton University Press, 1973), p. 16. Some of Beckett's ideas about the will resemble Schopenhauer's; see *Proust*, pp. 8–9, where Beckett refers to Schopenhauer in a discussion of willing, habit, and the loss of freedom.

13. Dante Alighieri, "Letter to Can Grande Della Scala," trans. Charles Latham, in *A Translation of Dante's Eleven Letters* (Boston: Houghton Mifflin, 1891), p. 196.

14. On the allegory of justice, "Letter to Can Grande," p. 195; on the three levels of figurative meaning, "Letter to Can Grande," pp. 193–94, and *Dante's Convivio*, trans. William Jackson (Oxford: Clarendon Press, 1909), Tractate II, pp. 73–74.

15. Beckett says that Dante's "purely allegorical figures" are unsuccessful; see *Proust*, p. 60.

16. *Inferno* 5:52ff.

17. *Inferno* 5:68; Sinclair translation, p. 77.

18. "Dante... Bruno. Vico.. Joyce," in *Our Exagmination Round his Factification for Incamination of Work in Progress* (1929; rpt., London: Faber and Faber, 1972), pp. 9–10. The axiom means, "There is nothing in the intelligence that was not first in the senses"; Beckett quotes a Latin version of it in *Malone Dies* (1956; rpt., New York: Grove Press, 1970), p. 43. More pessimistic in the later work, Beckett mocks the axiom as an epistemological truism.

19. While the importance of poetic thought has been stressed by other writers (the New Critics, for example), Beckett is more vehement in his attack on rational and positivistic modes of thought. Schopenhauer is one of the few Western philosophers who similarly insists on the supremacy of artistic thought; see, for example, *The World as Will and Idea*, vol. 1, book iii, section 38. This is a reason why Beckett so often alludes to Schopenhauer; see *Dream*, pp. 55, 75; *Proust*, pp. 8, 66, 70; "Dortmunder," in *Poems in English* (New York: Grove Press, 1961), p. 29.

20. If Estragon's boots were too tight and the new boots are too big, the person who exchanged boots must have had the smaller feet: the boots this person took were smaller than the ones he left behind. Estragon understands this; Vladimir gets it backward. Estragon also wins the debate about who should be first to hang himself. See *Waiting for Godot* (New York: Grove Press, 1954), pp. 43, 45, 12.

21. In the introduction to his anthology of Beckett's writing, Richard Seaver describes Beckett's vain efforts to find a publisher for *Dream*; see *I Can't Go On, I'll Go On* (New York: Grove Press, 1976), p. xxvii.

5

More Pricks than Kicks:
Behind the Glittering Vitrine

Initially, *More Pricks than Kicks* (1934) gives the impression of being a more polished version of *Dream of Fair to Middling Women.* The elaborate digressions and anarchic plot have been replaced by a series of comic episodes presented in orderly chronological sequence. The narrator is less intrusive and eccentric than his predecessor. Belacqua is again the protagonist, and some of his friends make a return appearance, but they have all become more respectable—many of them even have last names. Two excerpts from *Dream* are included in *More Pricks than Kicks* ("A Wet Night" and "The Smeraldina's Billet Doux"); these, however, contain little in the way of stylistic innovation. Nor is much space in the later work devoted to descriptions of Belacqua's mental world; indeed, the narrator does not take Belacqua's references to his inner life very seriously.[1]

Even so, *More Pricks than Kicks* is very different from *Dream,* and also different from what it seems to be in other ways. Its ten sections, each one with its own title, give it the appearance of a collection of short stories; actually, it is more like an episodic novel. The title of the book, *More Pricks than Kicks,* sounds suggestive—this is probably why the Irish censors banned the novel. But *honi soit qui mal y pense:* the title is based on a biblical allusion, and the joke is on the censors.[2]

A clue to the deceptive quality of the novel is given in a footnote where the narrator describes a painting that is exhibited behind glass. Light reflected by the glass makes it difficult to see one of the people portrayed in the painting: "This figure, owing to the glittering vitrine behind which the canvas cowers, can only be apprehended in sections. Patience, however, and a retentive memory have been known to elicit a total statement approximating to the intention of the painter" (p. 87). A similar obser-. vation can be made about the novel itself. Its hard, glittering surface—the satirical level—obscures deeper meanings. But with patience and a retentive memory this difficulty can be overcome. If one recalls and compares widely separated portions of the book, patterns begin to emerge that reveal the underlying themes.

There are a number of other curious footnotes in the novel. These initially seem so frivolous that they are easily overlooked. One footnote, for example, refers back to an accident that occurred in the previous story, but the reminder seems pointless because it comes only four pages after the description of the event (pp. 114, 110). Other footnotes indicate that phrases have been repeated or point out recurring details in different stories. It is not at all clear, however, why the recurring elements should be there in the first place.

Another device whose purpose is initially unclear is based on an odd type of redundancy: rare words and foreign expressions are repeated in different parts of the novel. The device is difficult to detect because the recurring elements are usually many pages apart, but there are numerous examples: objurgation (pp. 53, 90); coenaesthesis (pp. 99, 175); reseda (pp. 102, 177); fanlight (pp. 105, 177); rictus (pp. 61, 185); ebreity (pp. 42, 88); motte (pp. 33, 46); sursum corda (pp. 29, 107). There also are a number of other recurring elements, including allusions (like two passages based on Longinus's comparison of Homer and the setting sun); quotations (a comment of Horace's "limae labor . . . ," is repeated); and references to historical figures (Henry McCabe, a famous murderer, is mentioned in two stories).[3] Some phrases are repeated more than once, a concession to readers with less than perfectly retentive memories. The question "Who shall silence them, at last?" occurs three times (pp. 26, 29, 79), and some rare words are similarly repeated a number of times, like cicisbeo (pp. 65, 102, 103, 113).

One function of the recurring words and phrases is to introduce a sense of unity that belies the fragmented appearance of a book of loosely connected short stories. But this still does not explain why there should be such a profusion of recurring elements, or why the repetition so often centers on particular themes. For instance, many of the women in the novel—especially those who are romantically involved with Belacqua—are described in similar terms. Lucy's hair is swept back to reveal her "fanlight forehead"; the Smeraldina's brow is "reduced to a fanlight" (pp. 105, 177). The Frica's upper lip moves "up and away in a kind of duck or a cobra sneer"; the Smeraldina's upper lip moves "up and back in what you might nearly call a kind of duck or cobra sneer" (pp. 75, 176). Ruby has a "little bird-face"; so does the Smeraldina (pp. 61, 176). Even before Ruby has been formally introduced, one is told that she "had favoured the same taut Sabine coiffure" as the Frica (p. 61). Most of the women who become involved with Belacqua have names with similar endings: Winnie, Ruby, Lucy; Alba, Thelma, the Frica, the Smeraldina. The Frica, Ruby, Lucy, Thelma, and the Smeraldina all have very dark hair; most of them also have very pale skin. They are often compared to works of art: Ruby is like the Magdalene in a Perugino Pièta; Lucy resembles a Signorelli page; Thelma is more memorable than the Venus Callipyge; the Frica is called "a positive gem of ravished Quattrocento"; the Smeraldina has Botticelli thighs and a Pisanello face (pp. 87, 106, 117, 62, 176).

These similarities call attention to another interesting pattern: Belacqua's experiences with these women often are remarkably similar. Beckett hints at this by using recurring phrases to link related episodes. In "Walking Out" the passage "he was as wax in her hands" refers to Lucy's ability to manipulate Belacqua; in "Fingal," an earlier story, Belacqua was as wax in Winnie's hands (pp. 108, 25). The same phrase is used in both stories, and a footnote ("Cp. *Fingal*") calls attention to the repetition (p. 108). This emphasizes an ironic idea in these passages: as eventually becomes apparent, Belacqua is not so much manipulated as manipulative.

Other forms of repetition are used to link "Fingal" and "Walking Out." Both stories are set in the countryside outside Dublin, and both describe how Belacqua abandons a woman who loves him. He tells each of them that he wants to go off for "sursum corda": the same phrase (it is from the Latin Mass, and means "lift up your hearts") is used in both stories (pp. 29, 109). Belacqua tells both Winnie and Lucy that he will go off by himself for a while and arranges to meet each of them later on. The proposed meetings never take place, for reasons related to the unhappy ending in each of the stories.

Still another story, "Love and Lethe," contains details resembling those in "Fingal" and "Walking Out." In "Love and Lethe" Belacqua decides to kill himself, and Ruby, suffering from an incurable disease, amiably agrees to make it a double suicide. They drive into the country and climb a hill from which they can see Dun Loaghaire and Three Rock; the first of these places is mentioned in "Fingal" and the second in "Walking Out" (pp. 95, 26, 101). After admiring the view they change their minds about suicide and make love instead. In "Fingal" Belacqua and Winnie make love on a hilltop and look at the view afterward.[4] In "Walking Out" Lucy is hit by a car and eventually dies of her injuries; Ruby also dies some time after the end of the story, a victim of her incurable disease.

Belacqua is reluctant to become sexually involved with these women; he even hopes Lucy will take a lover after they are married (the repetition of the word "cicisbeo" calls attention to this theme). Moreover, though he is usually depressed after his love affairs, his partners—for reasons that are seldom made explicit— fare much worse. Near the end of the novel the narrator draws up a casualty list: "Thelma née bboggs perished of sunset and honeymoon that time in Connemara. Then shortly after that they suddenly seemed to be all dead, Lucy of course long since, Ruby duly, Winnie to decency, Alba Perdue in the natural course of being seen home."[5] At this point Belacqua marries the Smeraldina and soon afterward he dies, the victim of a carelessly conducted surgical procedure.

These events can be linked with another of the novel's recurring themes, which emphasizes the idea that love and death are analogous. For example, when Belacqua is being prepared for surgery, the narrator says, his "nape was as a bride adorned"; he gets up onto the operating table "like a bridegroom"; and one of his doctors is called "the best man" (pp. 169, 174). All of this occurs moments before Belacqua's death. The narrator often associates women and love-making with death. The word "rictus," used in a description of the Frica's expression, comes up again in a passage about an undertaker's man (pp. 61, 185). Belacqua imagines the Frica as a victim of McCabe, the murderer (p. 76). Ruby calls Belacqua's suicide kit a maternity bag (p. 93). Just as Winnie and Belacqua are about to make love, the narrator gives the following architectural description (which is based on a passage in *Hamlet*): "The tower began well; that was the funeral meats. But from the door up it was all relief and no honour; that was the marriage tables."[6] Thelma, who dies on her honeymoon, marries Belacqua in Glasnevin, famous for its cemetery.[7] All three of Belacqua's weddings are followed by funerals. The last of these funerals, his own, sets the stage for a love affair between Hairy (who was once Belacqua's best man) and his widow, the Smeraldina. The title of "Love and Lethe"—the story about the suicide attempt that ends in love-making—alludes to Keats's "Ode on Melancholy," where love and death are also linked.[8] A similar theme is introduced when a line from Ronsard is quoted at the conclusion of the story: "Car l'Amour & la Mort n'est qu'une mesme chose" ("For love and death are nothing but the same thing").[9]

Belacqua is to some extent responsible for the unhappy events that follow in the wake of his love affairs, though this is not always apparent. The narrator often ends a story without describing the final stages of a relationship, and opens the next one by introducing Belacqua's newest conquest. As soon as Belacqua loses interest in a woman, the narrator seems to forget all about her, and in this way sidesteps embarrassing questions about his protagonist's behavior. At the end of "Fingal" Winnie realizes that Belacqua had deserted her; one never learns if he ever saw her again. In "A Wet Night" Belacqua spends the night at Alba's house; she is next mentioned in connection with his imminent marriage to Thelma. "Love and Lethe" closes with Belacqua and Ruby "together in inevitable nuptial"; at the beginning of the following story he is engaged to Lucy. On the last page of "What a Misfortune" Thelma and Belacqua are en route to Connemara for their honeymoon; on the next page there is a love letter from the Smeraldina to Belacqua.

Despite the narrator's attempts to circumvent the issue, Belacqua's culpability is hinted at in many of the recurring phrases and details. One clue of this sort is the word "motte" (a slang term for "girl"), which is repeated a number of times. The word first occurs when Winnie is waiting—in vain, as it will turn out—for Belacqua to rejoin her. She sees a tower and asks an old man about its history. "You might have heard tell of Dane Swift," says the man, "he kep a motte in it." Winnie does not understand him, but the man only repeats the term: "A motte," he says, "of the name of Stella" (p. 33). In the next story the word is used again. An old woman selling "seats in heaven" urges Belacqua to buy them for "yer frien' . . . yer da, yer ma, an' yer motte" (p. 46). The repeated word serves as a reminder that Winnie, abandoned in the last story, has yet to be mentioned in this one.[10]

The old man's reference to Dean Swift's "motte" introduces another curious theme: a number of parallels are drawn between Swift and Belacqua. Like Swift, Belacqua is a Protestant, a poet, and a resident of Dublin. In his *Journal to Stella* Swift calls himself "Presto"; Beckett's narrator refers to Belacqua as "little fat Presto" (p. 34). Swift often became involved with women who were in bad health and, according to one of his biographers, "a companionship without sexuality or wedlock was probably the deepest satisfying attachment he could form."[11] Belacqua has similar preferences. Swift gave names ending in the letter "a"— Varina, Stella, Vanessa—to the women involved in these satisfying attachments. Alba, Frica, Thelma, and Smeraldina are names that end in "a," and Belacqua renames an attractive nurse Miranda. Belacqua likes women with very dark hair; Swift's Stella had hair "blacker than a raven."[12] Not long before his death Swift was heard repeating, "I am what I am"; Belacqua repeats the same sentence shortly before he dies.[13]

Swift's letters contain many details about the women he loved, but he withheld enough information to leave his biographers frustrated. A single issue—the exact nature of his relationship with Stella—has provoked a scholarly debate of Laputan intensity. Many questions about Belacqua's relationships are similarly left unanswered. Eventually, however, what emerges is that his short-lived love affairs resemble one another, and that his self-involvement seems to leave him unaware of the suffering he has caused.

The women in the novel are sympathetic and warm-hearted, but Belacqua, so often the beneficiary of their kindness, cannot reciprocate. A pair of similar episodes calls attention to this characteristic behavior. After permitting Belacqua to kiss her, Winnie notices that he is suffering from impetigo; disgusted, she wipes her mouth with a handkerchief. Belacqua is afraid that she is about to leave him. Unexpectedly, however, she speaks to him kindly. "This," says the narrator, "came to Belacqua like a drink of water to drink in a dungeon" (p. 25). Shortly afterward Belacqua—who had expected to be abandoned—deserts Winnie.

This episode resembles one in "A Wet Night." Alba, belle of the ball at a Christmas party, is surrounded by admirers. Belacqua arrives, his clothes wet and filthy; embarrassed, he becomes a target for snide comments, one of them from Alba herself. But again there is a sudden reversal. Alba, in "an unsubduable movement of misericord," asks Belacqua to join her. Her invitation, the narrator says, "came to Belacqua like a pint of Perrier to drink in a dungeon" (p. 78). Some time later, when Belacqua is about to marry Thelma, Alba is invited to be bridesmaid. Thelma's father naively wonders whether Alba, "an old flame of the groom," might not turn down the invitation. The other members of Thelma's family greet this question with derisive laughter. Alba is trapped: a refusal would be taken as a public confession that she still cared for Belacqua. It is an intricately cruel maneuver and only Belacqua can save Alba from humiliation, but he does nothing. In the middle of this episode a footnote serves as a subtle reminder that Alba deserves better treatment: "Alba Perdue, it may be remembered, was the nice little girl in *A Wet Night*" (p. 127).

Alba and Winnie are not the only ones victimized by Belacqua's lack of compassion. In "Dante and the Lobster" he self-righteously reviles a grocer for selling him cheese that is not ripe enough. The narrator is careful to point out that the grocer puts up with this treatment not because he needs Belacqua's business but because as a "warm-hearted human man he felt sympathy and pity for this queer customer who always looked ill and dejected" (p. 15). When Belacqua eats his lunch, he discovers that he has made a mistake: the cheese is marvelously overripe. But instead of regretting his rudeness to the grocer, Belacqua smugly concludes that he has learned a valuable lesson in judging the ripeness of cheese.

Another incident in the same story focuses on a similar theme. Belacqua's Italian teacher, Signorina Ottolenghi, suggests that he might do well to study "Dante's rare movements of compassion in Hell" (p. 19). Thinking she has only linguistic instruction in mind, Belacqua responds by quoting from *The Divine Comedy:* "Qui vive la pietà quando è ben morta . . ." ("here pity lives when it is quite dead").[14] Belacqua, carried away by the cleverness of the comment, never considers the unsettling ethical questions it raises. Nor does he realize that by choosing a passage where Dante shows a lack of compassion, he has done the very opposite of what his teacher had requested. He asks the Signorina to agree that it is a great phrase, but she only remains silent. Just then a neighbor enters with a parcel: it contains Belacqua's lobster, which she has saved from her cat. Belacqua does not thank her, and when the woman asks about the contents of the package, he decides that she is a "base prying bitch" (p. 20). The most significant aspect of Belacqua's Italian lesson has unfortunately eluded him.

Signs of Belacqua's self-centeredness are evident throughout the novel. In "Fingal" he steals a bicycle from a man who earlier had given him directions. In "Ding Dong" it takes him a moment to complete a familiar series: "Faith, Hope and—what was it?—Love . . ." (p. 39). In the same story the phrase "round and round" is repeated (pp. 39, 45). It refers both to the movement of the Ptolemaic spheres and to the rotation of Belacqua's "Ego Maximus," which "went nowhere, only round and round" (p. 39). The boundaries of Belacqua's universe do not extend too far outside himself. In *Dream of Fair to Middling Women* a retreat into the self was seen as a cure for the pain of existence; here some of the unpleasant side-effects have become apparent.

Beckett's method in these episodes is to introduce recurring details which call attention to subjects that the narrator tries to avoid. It is as if the narrator's commentary corresponds to Belacqua's conscious thoughts, and the recurring details—like an undercurrent of guilt and remorse—represent thoughts in his unconscious. One example of this method involves a series of stories with a number of recurring elements: expensive automobiles, detached license plates, reckless drivers, traffic accidents, and allusions to Pearse Street, in Dublin. In "Love and Lethe"

Belacqua sets out to pick up Ruby in a rented "swagger sports roadster"—he intends to commit suicide in style. Unworried about his lack of insurance or a driver's license, Belacqua weaves recklessly through the Dublin traffic. On Pearse Street he knocks the wheel off a cab and drives away without stopping to inspect the damage. Later he shows Ruby an old license plate that he has painted over and inscribed with the message "TEMPORARILY SANE" (p. 97). In place of a more conventional suicide note he will use this "palimpsest" (the word hints at Beckett's method of concealing the novel's underlying themes).

There are similar details in another story, "What a Misfortune." Hairy is asked to pick up a borrowed sports car which Belacqua will use on his honeymoon. Hairy needs help in getting the car started and an attendant kindly cranks the engine for him. Suddenly it starts, "most perversely and unexpectedly with a backfire that broke the obliging fellow's arm" (p. 135). Unconcerned about the injured attendant, Hairy speeds away. Again there is a traffic accident: Hairy cuts in front of a bus and knocks off the sports car's license plate.

The connections between these episodes are emphasized by other details. Neither sports car belongs to the driver, and neither driver is the more careful for that. Just as Hairy receives help in starting his engine, Belacqua gets a bystander to help him push his car over a bridge. In each story there are references to the car's dicky (back seat).[15] Both reckless journeys take place just before the events that figure in the love-death theme: a honeymoon that ends with the death of the bride, and a suicide attempt with a honeymoon ending.

These traffic accidents can be linked with another one. In an earlier story, "Ding Dong," Belacqua is taking a walk on Pearse Street.[16] As he watches, a little girl from the slums suddenly darts into the street and is hit by a bus. The accident is witnessed by a group of people waiting to get into a movie theater, but no one tries to help the girl. It is not clear whether Belacqua is affected by this event: he wonders whether the "trituration of the child in Pearse Street had upset him without his knowing it" (p. 43). A later passage, accompanying the description of how he knocks the wheel off the cab on Pearse Street, serves as a reminder of the accident involving the girl from the slums. As Belacqua speeds down "some lowly street or other," says the narrator, "the little children playing beds and ball and other games were scattered like chaff" (p. 90).

Not long after seeing the girl hit by the bus, Belacqua returns to Pearse Street, but he seems to have forgotten entirely about the accident: "Long straight Pearse Street, it permitted of a simple cantilena in his mind, its footway peopled with the tranquil and detached in fatigue, its highway dehumanised in a tumult of buses. Trams were monsters, moaning along beneath the wild gesture of the trolley. But buses were pleasant, tires and glass and clash and no more. Then to pass by the Queens, home of tragedy, was charming at that hour, to pass between the old theatre and the long line of the poor and lowly queued up for thruppence worth of pictures" (pp. 48–49). Belacqua touches on many details associated with the accident: Pearse Street, a highway "dehumanised" by buses, the "poor and lowly" crowded in front of a theater. But he represses his memory of the accident so effectively that he can assure himself that buses are pleasant.

These events set the stage for still another accident. After Belacqua goes off in pursuit of his "sursum corda," Lucy's horse is hit by a "superb silent limousine, a Daimler no doubt, driven by a drunken lord. . . ." Lucy is "crippled for life and her beauty dreadfully marred" (p. 110). The middle-class Belacqua showed little concern about the welfare of lower-class pedestrians; ironically, it is an aristocrat whose careless driving results in his fiancée's injury.

When Lucy dies, the narrator refers back to her accident in a footnote that—if it had seemed superfluous earlier—helps call attention to a series of related incidents in five consecutive stories (p. 114). The slum girl is hit by a bus in the first of these stories. In the next one Belacqua revisits the scene of the accident without remembering what occurred there. He knocks the wheel off the cab and then nearly runs into a crowd of slum children in the third story. Lucy is crippled in the fourth story. The footnote about Lucy's accident comes at the beginning of the fifth story, where Hairy's accidents, involving the injured attendant and the collision of the bus and sports car, are described.

The recurring episodes add a new dimension to the theme of Belacqua's self-involvement. His experience in observing the misery of others is in no way instructive: it does not teach him compassion, or even better driving habits. The only accident that makes an impression on him is Lucy's, because it involves a personal loss. The next time Belacqua is seen behind the wheel his driving is not reckless; significantly, he is troubled by thoughts about Lucy (p. 151). But by now a new series of accidents, involving Hairy, has begun, and Belacqua himself dies as a result of another person's carelessness. Yesterday's witness becomes today's offender and tomorrow's victim. Such cycles of human misery might be interrupted if the witnesses could empathize with the victims and resolve never to become offenders. Yet this seldom occurs. Belacqua's inability to remember the little girl's accident is part of a larger pattern of human failure.

The narrator, referring to a theater not far from where the girl was hit by the bus, twice calls it a "home of tragedy" (pp. 40, 49). This comment raises a question about whether the events Beckett describes are tragic. It has been said that a street accident cannot be understood as an Aristotelian tragedy. But Beckett is concerned about the spectators as well as the victims, and focuses on their need to dissociate themselves from the suffering they have witnessed. Their inability to respond compassionately permits the cycle of human misery to continue uninterrupted; such failures are what make human life tragic.

In "Dante and the Lobster" Belacqua is introduced as a person who seems to be capable of empathy. He cannot understand why Dante is so ready to justify God's harsh retribution against Cain, why there is so little charity in the world and so much vindictiveness. But his concerns are only perfunctory. It never occurs to him that his own behavior might be examined in the light of these high-minded questions. He seldom thinks about the people he has wronged; his feelings of empathy are reserved for McCabe, a person whom he never has met, a convicted murderer. Belacqua is horrified to learn that lobsters are boiled alive, but he makes no attempt to save the lobster his aunt is about to consign to a steaming pot. He tries to persuade himself that the lobster will not suffer; "it's a quick death," he says, "God help us all" (p. 22). The story ends when the narrator contradicts him with an incontestable dictum: "It is not."

For all his apparent interest in crustacean physiopathology,

Beckett's main concern is his protagonist's moral equivocation. He indicates that Belacqua's asides on God and morality are a form of lip-service to ethical commitment which make it easier for him to hedge when personal issues are involved. In the stories that come after "Dante and the Lobster," Beckett begins to introduce the evasive tactics that lead away from questions about the propriety of Belacqua's behavior. The narrator's dispassionate tone and cynical humor make it seem that Beckett himself takes the view that such questions are unimportant. But this is a mask: Beckett is testing his reader's capacity for witnessing the suffering of others and responding compassionately. His narrator cannot be trusted, even when it comes to questions that have nothing to do with ethics. The narrator claims, for example, that his commentary is based on information given him by Belacqua (p. 37). Yet he never explains how he was able to describe events that occurred after Belacqua's death. His ability to depict the characters' thoughts suggests that he is omniscient (pp. 24, 54). But at times—as when he discusses the reasons for Belacqua's desire to commit suicide—he claims to have no knowledge of his protagonist's thoughts (p. 89).

The inconsistency in point of view is only one of the narrator's deceptive practices. Shrewd, evasive, manipulative, he is not above occasional lapses into mendacity. He assures the reader that Belacqua did not show any signs of grief after Lucy's death because he had exhausted his stock of tears: "He could produce no tears on his own account, having as a young man exhausted that source of solace through overindulgence; nor was he sensible of the least need or inclination to do so on hers, his small stock of pity being devoted entirely to the living, by which is meant not this or that particular unfortunate, but the nameless multitude of the current quick, life, we dare almost say, in the abstract" (p. 114). This passage comes only a few sentences after the narrator reveals that Belacqua "tended to be sorry for himself" when Lucy died, and it comes eleven pages before a scene where Belacqua bursts into tears (p. 125). In "A Wet Night" Alba notices that Belacqua is crying; "at it again," she says (p. 79). In "Yellow" Belacqua, about to have a tumor removed, wonders whether laughter or tears would be the more appropriate response. He decides not to cry because the hospital staff might ascribe his tears not "to the follies of humanity at large" but rather "to the tumour the size of a brick that he had on the back of his neck" (p. 164). Such an interpretation, he insists, would certainly be unjust. Shortly afterward, thinking about his toe (which is also to be amputated), he begins to sob. But even so, true to his promise, he sheds no tears on account of the tumor.

During this episode Belacqua recalls a passage about tears and laughter from John Donne's paradox, "That a Wise Man is Known by Much Laughing."[17] One of Donne's observations that is not quoted in the novel is helpful for understanding the narrator's cynicism: "now when our *superstitious civilitie* of *manners* is become a mutuall *tickling flattery* of one another, almost every man affecteth an *humour* of *jesting. . . .*"[18] When unctuous politeness makes conventional responses suspect, laughter retains its authenticity. According to the narrator, after Lucy dies Belacqua is showered with condolences—literally. The mourners, "inarticulate with the delicious mucus of sympathy, disposed in due course of that secretion, when its flavour had been quite exhausted, *viva sputa . . .*" (p. 115). The Smeraldina is no less hypocritical. Belacqua's death leaves her "without thought or feeling," but she assumes an expression of sorrow when she thinks about the friends who will soon be offering condolences (p. 175).

It may seem that expressions of sympathy—even those that are not entirely sincere—are preferable to the narrator's coldness and sarcasm. But the narrative tone is actually an ironic device designed to provoke opposition. Irritated by the narrator's inappropriate responses, the reader begins to question his judgments. At this point it becomes obvious that Belacqua's behavior with women is odious, and that his odious behavior is habitual. One feels sorry for his victims but, as also emerges, Belacqua himself is a victim. He is caught up in a compulsive pattern that finally becomes self-destructive. The narrator's indifferent tone is modeled on Belacqua's mask of indifference, but the repeated passages reveal the feelings behind the mask: guilt, bitterness, misery.

Beckett himself was in a similar emotional state at the time he wrote *More Pricks than Kicks*. To his dismay Joyce's daughter Lucia had fallen in love with him and would not be discouraged. In 1932 it was discovered that she was suffering from schizophrenia; her worsening mental condition intensified Beckett's feelings of guilt.[19] Around the same time he learned that his cousin Peggy Sinclair, with whom he once had been in love, was suffering from tuberculosis; eventually she died. Then, while Beckett was working on the last stories in the book, his father died.[20] This combination of unhappy events affected Beckett deeply. His involvement with Lucia Joyce and Peggy Sinclair (who was the prototype of the Smeraldina) provided a background for the love-death theme in the novel. The satirical descriptions of hypocritical condolences are similarly related to Beckett's reaction to the mourning following his father's death.[21]

During this period of emotional stress Beckett was plagued by a number of painful disorders.[22] These resemble Belacqua's afflictions, though the descriptions of Belacqua's suffering are often exaggerated in order to produce a comic effect. Belacqua has bad eyes, a weak bladder, impetigo, a tumor, and a "tendency to ptosis of viscera" (p. 52). His feet are always sore, and one of his toes must be amputated. He is an incipient alcoholic, a practicing voyeur, and a potential suicide. Troubled by nightmares and depression, he is convinced that he belongs in a mental asylum. The narrator, preserving his mask of indifference, says as little as possible about Belacqua's suffering. He claims not to know how Belacqua felt after the little girl's accident, or why he wanted to commit suicide. He makes contradictory statements about whether Belacqua cries or feels self-pity. Shortly before Belacqua's death the narrator says of a nurse, "Years later, when the rest of the staff was forgotten, she would drift into the mind" (p. 169). This misleadingly suggests that Belacqua will survive the operation, and makes his apprehensiveness about it seem cowardly. In another passage the narrator similarly implies that Belacqua will live for many years: he speaks of a time "when Ruby is dead and he an old optimist" (p. 99).

If little is said about the suffering of Belacqua's victims, the same is true for Belacqua's suffering. Beckett is concerned with two types of compassion. The first, a response to the victims of Belacqua's cruelty, is relatively straightforward. The second, a response to Belacqua's suffering, is more complicated: Belacqua, after all, certainly seems to deserve to suffer.[23] Beckett uses Christ as an archetype of the innocent victim, and Cain as an archetype of the victim who is culpable. The grocer who is upbraided by Belacqua, "instead of simply washing his hands like Pilate," flings out his arms in "a wild crucified gesture of supplication" (p. 14). Later, when Belacqua sees the lobster move, he is startled. "Christ!" he exclaims, "it's alive"; and the narrator describes its position, "exposed cruciform on the oilcloth" (p. 21). But Belacqua—like McCabe, the murderer—is associated not with Christ but with Cain. Belacqua feels sorry for Cain, "with his truss of thorns, dispossessed, cursed from the earth, fugitive and vagabond" (p. 12). He wonders why Cain's stigma, which keeps him alive and preserves his suffering, should be considered a sign of God's pity.

For Belacqua such inquiries may be casual, but not for Beckett, who uses them to question whether Cain's punishment is any less reprehensible than his crime. "The major sin," Beckett has said, "is the sin of being born."[24] Moralists are tenacious in persecuting the wicked and often suggest that God will be offended by the spectacle of unpunished transgressors. But God himself seems to make few distinctions between the innocent and the guilty in meting out punishment. In Beckett's view, human moral dramas become pointless when they are played out before a backdrop of divine indifference.

At the time Beckett began writing *More Pricks than Kicks*, his satire was directed against the follies of humanity: this is the tone in the portions of the novel that were salvaged from *Dream of Fair to Middling Women*. But in the parts that were written later, humanity itself becomes the target of Beckett's satire. Here Beckett is again indebted to Swift. *Gulliver's Travels* opens with attacks on corrupt institutions; Swift presumably hopes they will be reformed. But later in the work Swift seems to be suggesting that the postulates of human life are unalterable, and that reforms are therefore futile exercises. No improvement—social, ethical, or intellectual—can transform Lemuel Gulliver into a Houyhnhnm. Ascending the pinnacles of civilization, humanity only gains a clearer view of the depths of its savage beginnings.

In *Watt* Arsene explains that there are three types of humorless laughter. The first one is a response to "that which is not good, it is the ethical laugh." The second one mocks "that which is not true, it is the intellectual laugh." The third, "the laugh of laughs, the *risus purus* . . . the saluting of the highest joke," is concerned with "that which is unhappy."[25] When Belacqua—yesterday's lady-killer—is transformed into a victim, the response may be an ethical laugh. But the laugh of laughs comes when one empathizes with Belacqua. He causes others to suffer, not because he is wicked but because he is a human being; he himself suffers, not because he has sinned but because he is a human being. Beckett's satire, like Swift's, ends with the bitter laughter of the Yahoo finally coming to terms with what he is.

Relentlessly, Beckett's caustic pessimism works away at suggestions of more hopeful alternatives. This is illustrated by an apparently incongruous incident in "Draff," the last story. After Belacqua is buried, a cemetery groundsman lingers near his grave. As the groundsman stands there musing, he recalls the words "of the rose to the rose . . . 'No gardener has died, comma, within rosaceous memory' " (p. 191). The quotation is an allusion to Diderot's *D'Alembert's Dream,* where a story about roses and a gardener illustrates what Diderot calls "the fallacy of the ephemeral . . . of a transient being who believes in the immutability of things."[26] The roses, knowing they must die, console themselves with the extravagant notion of an immortal gardener. We may smile at their naiveté, but we often are beguiled by similar fantasies. Humanity comforts itself with myths about a world less painful than the one it inhabits, and the myths eventually become beliefs.[27] This illusory world is the one reflected by the polished surface of *More Pricks than Kicks,* but behind the glittering vitrine, Beckett presents a more somber view of reality.

Notes

1. See, for example, the narrator's comments on Belacqua's claim that "He lived a Beethoven pause," and that "he furnished his mind and lived there"; *More Pricks than Kicks* (1934; rpt., New York: Grove Press, 1970), pp. 38 and 161. Subsequent references to the novel will be to this edition.

2. Acts 9:15 and 26:14, where Jesus asks Saul, "Why persecutest thou me? It is hard for thee to kick against the pricks." On the banning of the novel and its effect on Beckett, see Vivian Mercier, *Beckett / Beckett* (New York: Oxford University Press, 1977), p. 38.

3. Homer is mentioned on pp. 49 ("the Homer hour") and 184 ("the magic hour, Homer dusk"). The allusion is to a comment in Longinus's

On the Sublime (sec. 9), that if in the *Odyssey* Homer has lost some of his intensity, still, like the setting sun, he retains his grandeur. "Limae labor et mora" appears on p. 50, and "limae labor" on p. 143; the phrase means "the toil and delay of the file," a reference to the tedium of literary revision. It is from Horace's *Ars Poetica*, ll. 291–92. McCabe is mentioned in "Belacqua and the Lobster" (pp. 10, 11ff.) and in "A Wet Night" (p. 76).

4. Though one is not explicitly told that Belacqua and Winnie make love, this is implied by the narrator's comment that Belacqua was "a very sad animal" (on p. 23; he is again called a "sad animal" on p. 28). Hugh Kenner has identified this as an allusion to Galen's "omne animal post coitum triste est"; see his *Samuel Beckett: A Critical Study* (Berkeley: University of California Press, 1968), p. 40. In Beckett's play *Happy Days* Winnie speaks about "sadness after sexual intercourse" but attributes the idea to Aristotle; see *Happy Days* (New York: Grove Press, 1961), p. 57. In *The Oxford Dictionary of Quotations* the passage is cited in a slightly different form ("post coitum omne animal triste") and attributed to an anonymous postclassical author. See *The Oxford Dictionary of Quotations*, 3d ed. (New York: Oxford University Press, 1979), p. 10.

5. Page 175. The last phrase in this passage introduces a joke based on another recurring detail: twice earlier (on pp. 81 and 144) Alba had asked men to see her home. This was first noted by H. Porter Abbott; see *The Fiction of Samuel Beckett: Form and Effect* (Berkeley: University of California Press, 1973), p. 34.

6. Page 28; and see *Hamlet*, I, ii, 180.

7. Page 122. The cemetery-wedding theme appears again in the French version of *Malone Dies*, where lovers are described "La main dans la main vers Glasnevin"; *Malone Meurt* (Paris: 10:18, Union Generale D'Editions, n.d.), p. 147. A footnote identifies Glasnevin: "Nom d'un cimetière local très estimé." In the English version Glasnevin is not mentioned by name; the lovers go "To the life-long promised land / Of the nearest cemetery"; *Malone Dies* (1956; rpt., New York: Grove Press, 1970), p. 92. Glasnevin is, of course, the scene of Paddy Dignam's funeral in James Joyce's *Ulysses*.

8. "Lethe" alludes to the opening of Keats's "Ode on Melancholy" ("No, no, go not to Lethe . . ."). There is another allusion to Keats and death in *More Pricks than Kicks*: "Take into the air my quiet breath" (p. 22) is from the sixth stanza of "Ode to a Nightingale." Like Keats, Belacqua is a poet who died young.

9. Page 100. This line comes at the end of Book II of Ronsard's *Sonets pour Hélène* (1574); it is from the sonnet that begins, "Je chantois ces Sonets, amoureux d'une Heleine. . . ." This allusion was first noted by John Pilling; see *Samuel Beckett* (London: Routledge and Kegan Paul, 1976), p. 135.

10. The definition of "motte" is from Eric Partridge, *A Dictionary of Slang and Unconventional English* (New York: Macmillan, 1961), p. 534.

The word is also spelled mot, mott, or mort; the last form is listed in the *Oxford English Dictionary*. Beckett may be using the motte-mort link to enforce the love-death idea discussed earlier; he may also be alluding to Madame de la Motte, a French poisoner. Madame de la Motte is mentioned in Beckett's poem "Sanies II," which was published after *More Pricks than Kicks* but written a few years earlier. Raymond Federman makes the interesting point that although Belacqua's "motte" and relatives are offered seats in heaven, no seat is offered to him; *Journey to Chaos* (Berkeley: University of California Press, 1965), p. 36.

11. Irvin Ehrenpreis, *The Personality of Jonathan Swift* (London: Methuen, 1958), p. 9. There are other allusions to Swift in *More Pricks than Kicks*; see Frederik N. Smith, "The Epistemology of Fictional Failure: Swift's *Tale of a Tub* and Beckett's *Watt*," *Texas Studies in Literature and Language*, 15 (1974):649–72.

12. Harold Williams, Introduction to Swift's *Journal to Stella* (Oxford: Clarendon Press, 1948), 1:xxvii. The Smeraldina's hair is "black as the pots" (p. 177); Lucy's is "dark as jet" (p. 105, and see also p. 106).

13. Pages 159–60; on Swift's use of the phrase, see Ehrenpreis, p. 147. "I am what I am" is originally from the Bible (I Corinthians 15:10), but the fact that Beckett repeats it suggests that he had Swift's use of it in mind.

14. Page 19; and see *Inferno* 20:28. The translation is taken from *The Divine Comedy*, trans. John D. Sinclair (New York: Oxford University Press, 1968), 1:251.

15. The word "dicky" is also linked with the love-death theme. On p. 85 Lucy's mother hopes to ride in the car's dicky but instead Belacqua uses it for the suicide kit, which Ruby calls a "maternity-bag" (pp. 92–93). When Belacqua and Thelma, on their honeymoon, drive to Galway (where Thelma will die), the narrator says that the dead Lucy "was *atra cura* in the dicky" (p. 151). "*Atra cura*" ("dark care") is from Horace's *Odes* (Book III, Ode 1, l. 40). A definition of dicky can be found in the *Oxford English Dictionary*.

16. As Ruby Cohn points out, "Ding Dong" is taken from Ariel's dirge in *The Tempest*; see *Back to Beckett* (Princeton, N.J.: Princeton University Press, 1973), p. 20. There is another allusion to death here: Pearse Street is named for Patrick Pearse, who was executed after the Easter uprising of 1916.

17. *The Complete Poetry and Selected Prose of John Donne and the Complete Poetry of William Blake* (New York: Modern Library, 1946), p. 283.

18. *Donne*, p. 284.

19. Richard Ellmann, *James Joyce* (New York: Oxford University Press, 1959); pp. 661–64.

20. Deirdre Bair, *Samuel Beckett: A Biography* (New York: Harcourt Brace Jovanovich, 1978): on Peggy Sinclair, pp. 125–26, 138–39, 165–66; on the death of William Beckett, pp. 167–72.

21. Peggy Sinclair and the Smeraldina, Bair, p. 146; Beckett's feelings about mourners, Bair, p. 168.

22. Beckett's physical disorders, Bair, pp. 125, 128, 159, 165.

23. Beckett does this again in *Waiting for Godot*, when the tyrannical Pozzo is transformed into a victim; Lucky is the innocent victim.

24. John Gruen, "Samuel Beckett Talks about Beckett," *Vogue*, 154 (Dec., 1969):210.

25. *Watt* (1953; rpt., New York: Grove Press, 1959), p. 48.

26. Denis Diderot, *Rameau's Nephew and D'Alembert's Dream*, trans. L. W. Tancock (Harmondsworth: Penguin Books, 1966), p. 177. In *D'Alembert's Dream* the idea is attributed to Fontenelle, who mentions it in his *Entretien sur la puralité des mondes*. Nevertheless, Diderot's discussion of the "fallacy of the ephemeral" indicates that Beckett probably had his version in mind. Moreover, in *Dream of Fair to Middling Women* Beckett mentions *D'Alembert's Dream* and then—a few pages later—refers to the gardener and rose story (TS, Dartmouth College Library, pp. 149, 156). References to the story appear again in Beckett's unpublished sequel to *More Pricks than Kicks*, "Echo's Bones" (TS, Dartmouth College Library, p. 19), and in *Watt* (p. 253).

27. In "Echo's Bones" Beckett describes the experiences of Belacqua's ghost, but the joke is that the afterlife is even more unpleasant than life itself.

6

Learning to Live with Death: "Echo's Bones"

In its original version *More Pricks than Kicks* had not ten but eleven stories. However, an editor at Chatto and Windus (the firm that was about to publish Beckett's novel) decided that the last story, "Echo's Bones," should be dropped.[1] "Echo's Bones" has never appeared in print: the shortened version was used for all subsequent editions of the novel. It is easy to imagine why Beckett's editor—no doubt motivated by the best intentions —found the story objectionable. The setting is unrealistic, the plot improbable, the characters bizarre. The narrator's urbane conceits give way to thighslappers of a lower order (like a joke about an ostrich named Strauss who simply waltzes along). Even the costumes are outlandish: a cemetery groundsman, clad only in truss and boots, has a tattoo with the motto "Stultum Propter Christum" on his stomach.[2]

At the beginning of the story Belacqua—dead, buried, and in most quarters forgotten—makes a return appearance. He may have given up the ghost, but he retains many bad habits—picking his nose in the presence of ladies, for example. He has acquired a taste for cigars, and a stock of them. Death has deprived him of his shadow, and he can no longer see his reflection in a mirror. But he is still a self-centered snob with a love for abstruse conversation.

The narrator presents three episodes as representative examples of Belacqua's postmortem activities. The first one begins with Belacqua sitting on a fence, deep in meditation. Suddenly Zaborovna Privet, an alluring woman with a taste for "sublime delinquencies," emerges from a nearby hedge (Privet from hedge: another thighslapper). Zaborovna introduces herself to Belacqua and, after a long exchange of erudite banter, invites him home. The prospect of collaborating in her sublime delinquencies leaves him cold, but when Zaborovna offers him fried garlic and Cuban rum, he lets himself be persuaded. (Death, so inhibitory to other pleasures, has left Belacqua with an enhanced appreciation of olfactory sensations.) The garlic is prepared, consumed, washed down with rum, but when Zaborovna tries to embrace Belacqua, he vanishes. She is left alone with nothing but "the dream of the shadow of the smoke of a rotten cigar" (p. 7).

The next episode begins with a pensive Belacqua again sitting on a fence. His meditations are interrupted when he feels a sharp pain in his back—Belacqua has been hit by a golf ball. Its owner approaches, putter in hand. He is Lord Gall of Wormwood: landowner, connoisseur, raconteur, inventor; a man of gigantic proportions, distinguished lineage, and unparalleled athletic skill. One tragic circumstance makes Lord Gall as bitter as his name suggests.[3] Because he is childless and impotent, his estate will eventually revert to the Baron Extravas, his archenemy. Not only is the baron degenerate, evil-hearted, reptilian, and a bounder, but the syphilitic condition of Moll, Lord Gall's wife, can be attributed to him.

Lord Gall, his paternal instincts aroused, asks to be permitted to call his new acquaintance Adeodatus (after St. Augustine's illegitimate son). He then takes Belacqua to his aerie, a crow's nest on a great tree, and after a long exchange of recondite discourse proposes that Belacqua father a child on his behalf. The mercurial Belacqua, so recently a fugitive from Zaborovna's embraces, agrees. Unworried about hygienic complications ensuing from Moll's unfortunate illness, he joins Lord Gall on his mount (Strauss, the ostrich) and they gallop off. Belacqua meets Moll, whom he finds boring and repulsive; spends the night with her nevertheless; and proves to be remarkably virile, for a dead man. The episode, until now a blend of fairy tale, dream, and myth, ends as a shaggy-dog story. Moll becomes pregnant, but—alas for Lord Gall and his hopes for an heir—she gives birth to a girl.

Belacqua is again seated at the beginning of the last episode, not on a fence this time but on his own headstone. He encounters a character from "Draff," the cemetery groundsman who introduced the fable of the roses and the gardener. Now the groundsman is given a name, Doyle, as well as the striking truss-and-boots costume mentioned earlier. Doyle carries with him a considerable assortment of tools; as he explains, he plans to steal Belacqua's corpse. Belacqua assures him that such an endeavor would be pointless: he himself is the body. Doyle, however, ignores this as so much hocus-pocus. It may be that he is conversing with the spiritual remnant of Belacqua, but he nevertheless has every expectation of finding the corporal residue in the grave. Belacqua proposes that they bet on the question. After a long, arcane conversation Doyle accepts the bet and they dig down to the coffin and open it. Inside they find a handful of stones.

This incident (as the title, "Echo's Bones," hints) refers to one Ovid describes in the *Metamorphoses:* when Echo is spurned by Narcissus, she wastes away until her bones turn into stone. Nothing remains but her voice; because her chatter once distracted Juno, she is condemned to repeat the last thing she hears. Echo, like many of the figures in the *Metamorphoses,* must endure a form of retribution appropriate to her misdeeds. Belacqua's punishment is based on a similar idea. His conversation has annoyed others; now he cannot remain silent. Once he urged his fiancée to take a lover; in the afterlife he becomes the lover of another man's wife. The narcissistic Belacqua can no longer see his face in a mirror; this, he says, is more agonizing "than all the other pains and aches of the reversion" (p. 13). His expiation, says the narrator, will improve Belacqua: he will become "a trifle better, dryer, less of a natural snob" (p. 1). The drying process leaves Belacqua dessicated, and finally his physical remains, like Echo's, turn into stone.

Dante also describes forms of expiation that correspond to the sinners' vices. In the *Purgatorio* Dante's Belacqua assumes a hunched-over position that symbolizes his moral lassitude. The fence-sitting of Beckett's protagonist is similarly a literal description of a figurative state. Dante's Belacqua must languish in purgatory for as many years as he lived on earth; Beckett's hero must also endure his purgatorial existence for a lifetime.[4] In "Echo's Bones" Beckett's hero yearns for the bliss of nonbeing, but he is forced to return to life because he made such a mess of it the first time around. His resumption of existence is an "atonement for the wet impudence of an earthly state" (p. 7). However, like his counterpart in the *Purgatorio,* he is given a chance to redeem himself. He looks forward to the time when his heart, "drained and dried in this racking guttatim, should qualify at last as a plenum of fire for bliss immovable . . ." (p. 7).

Beckett, like Dante, uses a description of the afterlife to examine moral and psychological aspects of life on earth. Belacqua's expiation in "Echo's Bones" is a form of guilt fantasy, an inner act of contrition that brings relief from the torments of conscience. The purgatory in "Echo's Bones" resembles the inner world in *Dream of Fair to Middling Women* and it also is called a "womb-tomb" (p. 2).

This type of setting reappears in some of Beckett's later works. "Echo's Bones" describes Belacqua's fears that he will never achieve nonbeing, that the "old wound of his life had no intention of healing" (p. 23). He therefore tries to bring an end to consciousness by thinking of his "exuviae as preserved in an urn or other receptacle in some kind person's sanctum . . ." (p. 1). A similar situation occurs in *The Unnamable,* where the pain of a consciousness that persists after death is an important theme; Mahood, whose remains are kept in an urn, longs for oblivion but fears it will never come.[5] When Belacqua is unable to imagine himself in an urn, the narrator speculates about whether his "imagination had perished" when he died (p. 1). A similar question becomes a central theme in *Imagination Dead Imagine.*[6] The narrator of "Echo's Bones" describes the world Belacqua inhabits after his death as a place with "shafts and manholes back into the muck" (that is, leading back into physical existence); these anticipate the tunnels and trapdoors in *The Lost Ones.*[7] Though Beckett was forced to jettison "Echo's Bones," he clearly never lost interest in the themes he had introduced there.

Beckett thought of "Echo's Bones" as the "recessional story" of his novel, and wanted it to serve as the culmination of the action.[8] The Zaborovna episode is related to the earlier stories dealing with Belacqua's love affairs. Zaborovna (like some of the earlier heroines, her name ends in "a") is kind to him. But he finds her sexuality threatening—at one point she takes on the

appearance of a Gorgon—and he makes his getaway. This epito-
mizes his dealings with many of the women in the book: he enjoys their companionship, takes advantages of their generosity,
but vanishes when the relationship becomes sexual.

One reason for this characteristic behavior emerges in the Lord
Gall episode. A passing reference to Belacqua's mother calls attention to the fact that his parents are seldom mentioned in the
earlier stories. Lord Gall, however, in many ways suggests a
mythic father: he towers over Belacqua, takes him by the hand,
even puts him on his shoulders.[9] When Belacqua agrees to sleep
with Lord Gall's wife, the incest theme becomes obvious. This
suggests an underlying reason for Belacqua's behavior with
women: he may seem blasé, but he is torn by an inner conflict
related to his incestuous feelings.

Belacqua becomes more human in other ways. As the narrator
says, he is less of a snob. He is never condescending toward
Doyle, a clownish working-class figure. In the earlier stories he
seemed incapable of accepting criticism; he missed the point of
his Italian teacher's remark about the passages where Dante
shows compassion, for example. But in "Echo's Bones" Belacqua
pays attention when Doyle and Lord Gall complain about the eccentricities of his conversational style.

Another hidden side of Belacqua's personality emerges when it
is revealed that his bones have turned into stone. Belacqua's public side is represented by Narcissus, but inwardly he is more like
Echo. Belacqua suffers because he cannot give up the narcissistic
side of his personality. This situation resembles Ovid's description of Echo wasting away because she cannot give up her love for
Narcissus:

> But still her love clings to her and increases
> And grows on suffering; she cannot sleep,
> She frets and pines, becomes all gaunt and haggard,
> Her body dries and shrivels till voice only
> And bones remain, and then she is voice only
> For the bones are turned to stone.[10]

Belacqua also is haggard and unable to sleep, his body dries and
shrivels, and even after death he keeps up his mindless chatter.

In the *Metamorphoses* Echo suffers because she has been
spurned; Narcissus, because he cannot embrace his reflected

image. Belacqua's unhappiness is related to both dilemmas: Echo represents his need to love another, and Narcissus stands for his inability to give of himself. Love is demanding; narcissism is unrewarding; Belacqua shuttles between these extremes and is left emotionally drained. By the end of the story he is more like Echo than like Narcissus, so parched and shriveled that he is little more than a voice and some stones.

In *Dream of Fair to Middling Women* Beckett used a similar technique—again involving figures from Ovid—to illustrate Belacqua's inner conflicts.[11] There, three aspects of Belacqua's personality are described: "Centripetal, centrifugal and . . . not. Phoebus chasing Daphne, Narcissus fleeing from Echo and . . . neither."[12] Phoebus Apollo represents Belacqua's unfulfilled need for love (Apollo, like Echo, has been rejected). Narcissus again represents the self-involvement that prevents Belacqua from giving of himself. A third category ("neither") negates the first two, and indicates that Belacqua's psychological state is too complex to be defined by a simple antithesis.

In "Echo's Bones" there is no third category; instead, the recurring details are used to enhance the complexity of the narrator's characterization of Belacqua. The most obvious of the recurring elements is a reiterated passage of over one hundred words that appears first in "Draff" and then in "Echo's Bones." The length of the passage (a description of the view from the cemetery where Belacqua is buried) indicates that the inclusion of recurring elements in the novel is not careless but intentional.[13]

Beckett's technique resembles one Ovid uses in the *Metamorphoses*. Though Echo is forced to repeat the last thing she hears, her remarks are not nonsensical. The speeches of Narcissus end with phrases that, when Echo utters them, express her own feelings. The following passage is an example:

"Keep your hands off," he cried, "and do not touch me!
I would die before I give you a chance at me."
"I give you a chance at me," and that was all
She ever said thereafter. . . .[14]

Beckett's echo device is based on a similar principle: the repeated phrases take on a new meaning in a different context. When Belacqua tells Winnie he wants to go off by himself for "sursum corda," the excuse seems plausible; when he later gives Lucy the same excuse, his sincerity is called into question.[15] Other repeated passages emphasize inconsistencies that reveal Belacqua's contradictory impulses: his desire to become involved in a relationship, and his desire to run away.

Ostensibly the narrator identifies only with the narcissistic side of Belacqua: he condones Belacqua's behavior and conceals his faults. But like Belacqua (who is in a sense his alter ego), the narrator has a trait that makes him comparable to Echo: he keeps repeating things.[16] The narrator may pretend that Belacqua is no more than an insensitive egotist, but the recurring passages illuminate the more vulnerable side of Belacqua's personality. The Narcissus theme is emphasized in the content, and depicts Belacqua's mask; the Echo theme is hinted at by the formal devices that suggest what lies behind the mask. In this way Beckett ingeniously preserves a union of form and content.

Clearly, "Echo's Bones" must be considered an integral part of *More Pricks than Kicks*. Beckett wrote to a friend that the deletion of the story, "into which I had put all I knew and plenty that I was still better aware of, discouraged me profoundly."[17] Beckett's complaint is certainly justified: without "Echo's Bones," an essential part of the novel's complex structure is lost. Even editors with the best intentions might think twice before forcing unwanted revisions on unknown authors.[18] *More Pricks than Kicks* is subtle, intricate, brilliant work; the removal of "Echo's Bones" has made it needlessly obscure.

Notes

1. Deirdre Bair, *Samuel Beckett: A Biography* (New York: Harcourt Brace Jovanovich, 1978), p. 162. Bair mentions that the deletion of the story provoked Beckett to write a poem with the title "Echo's Bones"; see pp. 663–64n. The poem appeared in *Echo's Bones and other Precipitates*, published in 1935.

2. "Echo's Bones" (TS, Dartmouth College Library), p. 20. Subsequent page references to "Echo's Bones" in this chapter are to the Dartmouth typescript. I am grateful to the authorities of the Dartmouth College Library for making this source accessible. The Latin motto "Stultum Propter Christum" means "On Account of a Foolish Christ." It may be, however, that "Stultum" is a misprint for "Stultus"; if so, the phrase would mean "A Fool on Account of Christ." On the same page Beckett

speaks of the groundsman as "a sweet dolt on some Christ's account." The "fool on account of Christ" idea, which appears in the writings of Erasmus, Jacopone da Todi, and others, can be traced back to I Corinthians 4:10 ("We are fools for Christ's sake . . ."). I am grateful to my colleague Richard J. Schoeck for pointing out the source of this allusion.

3. The name is from the Bible, where wormwood and gall are mentioned together to epitomize bitterness. See Deuteronomy 29:18, Jeremiah 9:15, 23:15, and Lamentations 3:19.

4. Page 2; and see *Purgatorio* 4:127–34.

5. *The Unnamable* (NewYork: Grove Press, 1958), pp. 73, 117, *et passim*.

6. A question about the death of the imagination is raised at the very beginning of *Imagination Dead Imagine*. See *First Love and Other Shorts* (New York: Grove Press, 1974), p. 63.

7. Page 1. For references to the tunnel and trapdoor, see *The Lost Ones* (New York: Grove Press, 1972), pp. 12, 18, *et passim*.

8. Bair, p. 172.

9. The reference to Belacqua's mother is on p. 10. In some ways Lord Gall resembles Beckett's father. Like Lord Gall, William Beckett was a golfer and a good athlete generally; a tall, brawny man, balding, with a ruddy complexion; and took pleasure in repeating anecdotes. See Bair, pp. 5–6.

10. Ovid, *Metamorphoses*, trans. Rolfe Humphries (Bloomington: Indiana University Press, 1971), p. 69 (Book III, ll. 395ff.).

11. Beckett may have been influenced by Joyce, who used a similar device. In *A Portrait of the Artist as a Young Man* Stephen thinks of himself as a young Daedalus, but at the very end of the book he hints that he may also be the son of Daedalus. A second reading of the novel reveals other connections between Stephen and Icarus, and leads to another way of interpreting the action. Like Stephen, Belacqua is linked with two mythical figures whose story is told in the *Metamorphoses*, and the figures represent antithetical aspects of his personality.

12. *Dream of Fair to Middling Women* (TS, Dartmouth College Library), p. 107. The passage I have quoted is complete; the ellipses are in the original. The Apollo and Daphne story is in Book I of the *Metamorphoses*. In his essay on *Finnegans Wake* Beckett mentions Vico's idea that "every need of life, natural, moral and economic, has its verbal expression in one or other of the 30,000 Greek divinities. This is Homer's 'language of the Gods' "; see "Dante... Bruno. Vico.. Joyce," in *Our Exagmination Round his Factification for Incamination of Work in Progress* (1929; rpt., London: Faber and Faber, 1972), p. 10. By using Ovid's figures to represent psychological forces, Beckett is illustrating a way of applying Vico's idea.

13. The passage, which describes the actions of the cemetery groundsman, begins, "What with the company of headstones . . ." and ends with "He sang a little song . . ."; *More Pricks than Kicks* (1934; rpt., New

York: Grove Press, 1970), pp. 190–91. The corresponding passage (on p. 19 of "Echo's Bones") describes the actions of Belacqua and not the groundsman. This suggests that the groundsman—like some of the other characters in the book—may be an alter ego of Belacqua's, a portion of himself that attends the burial of another part.

14. Ovid, p. 69 (Book III, ll. 390ff.).

15. *More Pricks than Kicks*, pp. 29, 107.

16. A suggestion that Belacqua represents the narrator's alter ego comes when he calls Belacqua "my little internus homo"; *More Pricks than Kicks*, p. 38.

17. Bair, pp. 663–64n.

18. There is another, better-known example of this kind of imposed revision: Anthony Burgess was forced to delete the last chapter of *A Clockwork Orange*, and again the effect was to make the tone of the work seem more cynical than the author had originally intended.

7

"A Case in a Thousand":
Oedipus and the Sphinx

"A Case in a Thousand" (1934) is a short story about an emotionally troubled physician, Dr. Nye.[1] The action begins when a friend of Dr. Nye's operates on a boy with tubercular glands in his neck; after his patient takes a turn for the worse, the surgeon asks Dr. Nye to act as a consultant. Dr. Nye agrees, visits the hospital, and discovers that the boy's mother is Mrs. Bray, his old nursemaid. The doctor then examines her son, and in diagnosing him uses a very odd technique. He lies down on the hospital bed, takes hold of the boy's wrist, and falls into what the narrator calls a "therapeutic trance" (p. 242). When she sees the two of them on the bed, Mrs. Bray is reminded of something that occurred when Dr. Nye was in her care. Thinking about this incident (which the narrator does not describe), she begins to feel ashamed. Upon emerging from his trance Dr. Nye announces his decision: he recommends another operation. The operation is performed, but it is of no help; the boy continues to decline and dies soon afterward. Dr. Nye takes a short vacation and upon his return seeks out Mrs. Bray: he wants to ask her about something that happened while he was in her care. Mrs. Bray obligingly tells him what he wants to know, but the narrator does not say what it is. The two of them then part, and the story ends.

One idea that keeps recurring in "A Case in a Thousand" is that the boy's physical condition and the physician's emotional condition are in some way analogous. When her son is ill, Mrs. Bray keeps a vigil outside the hospital; later, after he dies, she resumes her vigil. This time, presumably, the vigil is for Dr. Nye. The

boy's decline is puzzling: the conventional treatment for his illness is of no help. Dr. Nye, similarly, is troubled "for no reason
known to the medical profession" (p. 241). The title of the story
can refer to Dr. Nye as well as to the boy: each of them is a case in
a thousand.[2] Their ailments correspond to those of Belacqua in
More Pricks than Kicks; Dr. Nye has similar emotional problems,
and the boy similar physical problems (like Belacqua, he dies in a
hospital after an operation on his neck).

Though Dr. Nye's condition seems unchanged at the end of the
story, his fate is hinted at. After seeing his patients he gloomily
concludes, "Myself I cannot save." Like Christ, he is a healer who
cannot alleviate his own suffering.[3] Dr. Nye suspects that his
problem had its origin in his early relationship with Mrs. Bray.
When he sees her at the hospital, he is "troubled to find that of
the woman whom as baby and small boy he had adored, nothing
remained but the strawberry mottle of the nose and the breath
smelling heavily of clove and peppermint" (p. 242). A nurse who
sees him kissing Mrs. Bray lets out a loud giggle. And when Mrs.
Bray reminds Nye that as a boy he had been in a great hurry to
grow up so he could marry her, the narrator notes that she "did
not disclose the trauma at the root of this attachment" (p. 242).

This comment is clearly meant to provoke curiosity—what in
fact is the nature of Dr. Nye's trauma? A number of details seem
significant: Mrs. Bray acted as Dr. Nye's surrogate mother; his
feelings for her are colored by something that occurred in the
past; and this event may be connected with the memory that
makes her feel ashamed. One need not be a psychoanalyst to in-
terpret these details: Dr. Nye seems to be suffering from an Oedipus complex.[4]

No sooner is this idea formulated than its weaknesses begin to
emerge. Freud's ideas had become quite well known by the 1930s;
a story about someone with an Oedipus complex—the common
cold of Freudian psychopathology—hardly deserves to be called
"A Case in a Thousand." Is the narrator splitting hairs about the
difference between medicine and psychiatry when he says that
Dr. Nye is troubled "for no reason known to the medical profession"? Moreover, why does the narrator withhold just those details that might settle whether or not Dr. Nye's problem really is
an Oedipus complex? One learns nothing significant about the

65

memory that makes Mrs. Bray feel ashamed, the basis of Dr. Nye's trauma, or the reason the nurse giggles. The props for the psychological drama, seemingly ready to be brought on stage, are still in the wings when the curtain drops.

The narrator's justification for withholding information about Mrs. Bray's account is disingenuous: "Thereupon she related a matter connected with his earliest years, so trivial and intimate that it need not be enlarged on here, but from the elucidation of which Dr. Nye, that sad man, expected great things" (p. 242). Trivial indeed: the missing details might have provided the story with a denouement. It may be that Mrs. Bray's account is trivial in a different sense, for the narrator hints that Dr. Nye will be disappointed if he expects great things from its elucidation. A similar idea is raised in a passage where the narrator says, "Dr. Nye belonged to the sad men, but not to the extent of accepting, in the blank way the most of them do, this condition as natural and proper. He looked upon it as a disorder" (p. 241).

Dr. Nye apparently feels that his condition can be diagnosed and that Mrs. Bray's story will evoke a memory which will in some way reduce his suffering. His hope for a cure seems to be based on the Freudian theory that an analysis of recollected traumatic incidents can alleviate emotional disorders.[5] The narrator, however, hints that Dr. Nye is naive if he expects any improvement. This is consistent with Beckett's attitude toward Freudian psychotherapy: he is knowledgeable about it without being very optimistic about its effectiveness.[6]

Beckett describes a number of mother-son relationships in his other works, but these never conform to Freud's description of the Oedipus complex. In literary as well as psychoanalytical accounts of Oedipal relationships, the mother is usually an attractive, sympathetic figure (D. H. Lawrence's Gertrude Morel is an example). Beckett's maternal figures, however, are singularly unappealing. One hears about Mrs. Bray's beauty only when the narrator reveals that she no longer possesses it. Moll Gall, in "Echo's Bones," suffers from venereal disease and has a face "like a section of spanked bottom."[7] In "The End," in *Malone Dies*, and in *Company* there are parallel incidents about a little boy who asks his mother a question about the sky; in each of them the mother's reply is unjustifiably caustic.[8] The emotionally repugnant aspects of Molloy's incestuous feelings are reflected in his characterization of his mother: she is a toothless, foul-smelling, senile crone. The portrait is memorable, but the subject is hardly a representative figure in Oedipal fantasies.

Beckett violates the Freudian pattern by introducing protagonists who hate their mothers instead of their fathers—some of them even want to kill their mothers. Molloy contents himself with beating his mother on the head.[9] But the protagonist of *The Unnamable* says, "it's the town of my youth, I'm looking for my mother to kill her. . . ."[10] In "From an Abandoned Work" parricide is mentioned tenuously, but matricide seems to be a foregone conclusion: "My father, did I kill him too as well as my mother, perhaps in a way I did. . . ."[11] Given this pattern, Beckett introduces mythic figures who, unlike Oedipus, are appropriate precursors for his heroes. In *More Pricks than Kicks* Belacqua, who complains that he is pursued by Furies, is called Orestes by the narrator.[12] Incest is the central theme in "Hell Crane to Starling," a poem that appeared in 1931 (the title refers to Dante's description of the carnal sinners).[13] The poem contains references to Hippolytus, whose stepmother fell in love with him; to Lot, who was seduced by his daughters; and to Reuben, who slept with his father's concubine; Oedipus, however, is not mentioned.[14] In *Mercier and Camier* Beckett introduces what may be a first in fictional accounts of incestuous feelings: Mercier describes a dream about being in the woods with a naked woman—his grandmother.[15]

The incestuous relationships in Beckett's works are often described in ambiguous terms. A comment about Molloy's mother has a double meaning: "I took her for my mother and she took me for my father." Molloy confesses that his mother's image is mixed up with memories of sexual encounters with other women; this, he says, "is literally unendurable, like being crucified. . . ."[16] In *Eh Joe* a double meaning is again used to suggest incest. An accusing voice reminds Joe that he tried to put his father out of his mind until his image was laid to rest, and that he tried to do the same with his mother's image, "Weaker and weaker till you laid her too. . . ."[17] Beckett's method is epitomized in an abandoned play where a mother and son appear on stage, "naked under coats."[18]

The most obvious reason for the oblique references to incest—
that Beckett is unwilling to be explicit about material that is
autobiographical—is unconvincing.[19] He could have made the
autobiographical themes more subtle, or he could have eliminated them entirely. Indeed, Beckett must have realized that the
ambiguity in descriptions of incestuous relationships would
arouse curiosity instead of alleviating it. His characters are strug-
gling with repressed feelings; if these are described in ambiguous
terms, it is in order to elicit a similar response from the reader.
When he depicts relationships that come close to conforming to
the Oedipal pattern but never quite do, it is to provoke feelings of
confusion and frustration. This is how Beckett's characters react,
and his method effectively depicts their state of mind.

In "A Case in a Thousand" one is tempted to play psychiatrist
and accept what at first seems self-evident: that Dr. Nye is suffering from an Oedipus complex. But readers who take this bait are
no better at diagnosis than Dr. Nye, who goes into a trance instead of examining his patient. The narrator's comment that Dr.
Nye's ailment is unknown to the medical profession cannot be
disregarded. The problem is mysterious; giving it a name is not
the same as understanding it.

Beckett's refusal to define Dr. Nye's ailment is related to the
idea of reduced significance described by the narrator of "Assumption." The unfamiliar is more disturbing than the commonplace; hence Beckett preserves enigmas instead of explaining
them away. In a book review published four years after "A Case in
a Thousand," Beckett elaborates on this idea. He compares those
who want everything in art to be explained with "Davus and the
morbid dread of sphinxes."[20] Davus, a character in Terence's
comedy Andria, shrugs off difficult questions by protesting that
he is only Davus—not Oedipus.[21] Oedipus challenges the sphinx
and risks his life when he tries to solve her riddle. The word
"sphinx" has come to mean an enigma; oedipe, in French, is a
riddle-solver. Davus, who dreads sphinxes, is the very opposite of
an Oedipus.

The unresolved ending in "A Case in a Thousand" runs parallel
to this attack on the Davus attitude. As Beckett understands, a
diagnosis sometimes brings more relief to the doctor than to the
patient. Psychological literature is a genre that favors the neat

denouement: disorders analyzed, patients cured, science triumphant. The patients with intractable problems—like pilgrims who return from Lourdes on their crutches—receive less publicity.

In "A Case in a Thousand" Beckett introduced a technique he would use later in *Watt* and *Molloy*. These novels are about quests and failures, and Beckett encourages his readers to become involved in the quests in order to experience the failures more sharply. The more effort readers devote to proving that Dr. Nye's problem is an Oedipus complex, the greater their disappointment when they realize they are wrong. Possibilities hover on the perimeter of the story, but enigma is firmly lodged at its center. Those who hunt too eagerly for Oedipus may find themselves being lured into the abode of the sphinx.

Notes

1. "A Case in a Thousand," *The Bookman*, 86 (Aug., 1934):241–42. Page references are to this source.

2. "A Case in a Thousand" in this way resembles Joyce's short story "A Painful Case"; in each story a new perspective emerges with the realization that the word "case" in the title refers to more than one character.

3. See Matthew 27:42: "He saved others; himself he cannot save."

4. In the ensuing discussion I am referring to the definition of the Oedipus complex given in Sigmund Freud's *An Outline of Psychoanalysis*, trans. James Strachey (New York: W. W. Norton, 1969), pp. 44–51.

5. Freud, pp. 40–43.

6. Beckett began his own psychoanalysis in 1934, the year "A Case in a Thousand" was published. He was afraid, however, that his problems were beyond the scope of psychoanalysis, and this pessimism is reflected in the story. See Deirdre Bair, *Samuel Beckett: A Biography* (New York: Harcourt Brace Jovanovich, 1978), pp. 178, 189, 197, 207–8, *et passim*. John Pilling includes a good survey of Beckett's knowledge of Freud's works in *Samuel Beckett* (London: Routledge and Kegan Paul, 1976), pp. 130–31. An indication that Beckett does not take Freud's ideas too seriously comes in a number of playful references to Freudian terminology. Moran says he never saw the "Obidil"—the word is a mirror image of libido; *Molloy* (New York: Grove Press, 1955), p. 222. Moran also blends two of Freud's concepts, the death instinct and the pleasure principle, when he refers to "the fatal pleasure principle"; *Molloy*, p. 135.

7. "Echo's Bones" (TS, Dartmouth College Library), p. 19. The unattractive qualities of Beckett's maternal figures are to some extent a re-

flection of Beckett's feelings about his own mother; see Bair, pp. 16, 23, 88, 202, 205, 210, *et passim.*

8. "The End," in *Stories and Texts for Nothing* (New York: Grove Press, 1967), p. 50; *Malone Dies* (1956; rpt., New York: Grove Press, 1970), p. 98; *Company* (New York: Grove Press, 1980), pp. 10–11.

9. *Molloy*, pp. 22–23.

10. *The Unnamable* (New York: Grove Press, 1958), p. 146. Lawrence Harvey suggests that the poem which begins, "I would like my love to die," probably refers to Beckett's mother; *Samuel Beckett, Poet and Critic* (Princeton, N.J.: Princeton University Press, 1970), p. 229. Krapp sits outside the house where his mother is dying and watches her window, "wishing she were gone"; his vigil, like Mrs. Bray's, takes place near a canal; *Krapp's Last Tape* (New York: Grove Press, 1960), pp. 18–19.

11. "From an Abandoned Work," in *First Love and Other Shorts* (New York: Grove Press, 1974), p. 44.

12. *More Pricks than Kicks* (1934; rpt., New York: Grove Press, 1970), pp. 36–37.

13. "Hell Crane to Starling," in Samuel Putnam *et al.*, eds., *The European Caravan* (New York: Brewer, Warren and Putnam, 1931), pp. 475–76. For the source of the poem's title, see Dante, *Inferno* 5:40–49.

14. Beckett refers to Oedipus in his essay on Proust, but not in connection with incest. He compares one of Proust's characters to King Lear and to "Oedipus, senile and annulled"; *Proust* (1931; rpt., New York: Grove Press, 1957), p. 58.

15. *Mercier and Camier* (New York: Grove Press, 1975), p. 61.

16. *Molloy*, pp. 21, 79. The crucifixion is mentioned in conjunction with Moll, another of Beckett's unattractive maternal figures: she has a tooth carved in the shape of a crucifix; see *Malone Dies*, p. 93. Dr. Nye is indirectly connected with the crucifixion: as was mentioned earlier, his comment, "Myself I cannot save" (p. 241), is based on a biblical passage where the crucified Christ is mocked with the words "He saved others; himself he cannot save" (Matthew 27:42).

17. *Eh Joe*, in *Cascando and other Short Dramatic Pieces* (New York: Grove Press, 1968), p. 37.

18. Richard L. Admussen, "Samuel Beckett's Unpublished Writing," *Journal of Beckett Studies*, 1 (Winter, 1976):72.

19. I disagree with Deirdre Bair, who says that many details in the story are "clumsy attempts to integrate [Beckett's] real-life attitudes towards his mother with his fiction"; Bair, p. 185.

20. "Denis Devlin," *Transition*, no. 27 (Apr.-May, 1938), p. 290.

21. See Terence, *Andria*, l. 194: "Davos sum, non Oedipus."

8

Murphy and the Uses
of Repetition

What is right may properly be uttered even twice.
—Empedocles

Murphy is a novel of great beauty and complexity. These qualities are interrelated: as the work's diverse elements coalesce into a unified pattern, its beauty is revealed. Like *More Pricks than Kicks*, *Murphy* contains many recurring elements that are used to illuminate an underlying level of meaning. One's understanding of the work changes after successive readings: trivial details gain significance, unambiguous statements become mysterious, latent themes emerge. Little of this is immediately apparent, however. In the time since 1938, when *Murphy* first appeared, it has been considered an undemanding work. Beckett himself once said to an interviewer, "it's my easiest book, I guess."[1] But the qualifying phrase is important: if *Murphy* is easier than other works, it is still not an easy book. Nor does Beckett truly believe that it is. In a letter to a friend he called it "slightly obscure," and said that the narrative was "hard to follow."[2]

The apparent simplicity of the novel can be a stumbling block for the unwary reader, or—to use Beckett's term—"gentle skimmer."[3] Unless one is very attentive, the novel's repetitive devices will probably be overlooked. *Murphy* contains many of these devices: reiterated passages, recurring episodes, dual sets of objects, characters with similar traits, and various types of symmetrical configurations. It is tempting, initially, to dismiss the redundancy as a stylistic flaw. But if this temptation is resisted, it becomes evident that there are far too many recurring elements for them to have been included inadvertently.

Recurring Passages

Murphy contains many phrases and sentences that are repeated, some of them more than once. There are more than 400 sets of recurring passages; about 150 of these sets contain more than two items; in all, more than a thousand individual passages are involved in the pattern of verbal repetition. A list of these sets is given in Appendix I.[4]

Many of the recurring passages are short, easy to detect, and relatively unimportant in terms of revealing underlying meanings. This deceptively suggests that the repetition generally is unimportant. But even the more obvious recurring passages have a use: they call attention to others that are subtler. An example occurs in the following excerpt, where Mr. Kelly advises Celia to break off with Murphy:

> Celia made to rise, Mr. Kelly pinioned her wrists.
> "Sever your connexion with this Murphy," he said, "before it is too late."
> "Let me go," said Celia.
> "Terminate an intercourse that must prove fatal," he said, "while there is yet time."
> "Let me go," said Celia.
> He let go and she stood up. (Pp. 24–25)

Mr. Kelly repeats an idea in parallel sentences, and Celia twice says "Let me go": this hardly seems very significant. But in the next chapter Celia again says "Let me go" twice, this time to Murphy:

> She made to rise, he pinioned her wrists.
> "Let me go," said Celia.
> "Is it?" said Murphy.
> "Let me go," said Celia.
> He let her go. She rose and went to the window. (Pp. 40–41)

A comparison of the two excerpts reveals that they contain other recurring elements. The two first sentences each introduce the same archaic terms ("made to rise," "pinioned") and the concluding sentences also are similar ("He let her go . . ."). The repetition occurs in similar episodes: each time Celia is seated near a man who is lying down; when she tries to get up, he takes hold of her wrists; then he releases her and she gets up. In the first of these episodes Mr. Kelly urges Celia to leave Murphy; in the second she tries to follow this advice. Murphy eventually persuades Celia to change her mind and stay with him, but her reiterated "Let me go" suggests that her remark has a figurative meaning: she is asking Murphy to make it easier for her to end their relationship.

Many of the recurring phrases call attention to subtle details that might otherwise be overlooked. In the following excerpt, about Murphy's "recreation" of tying himself into his rocking chair, it seems at first that he is honest and open in his dealings with Celia:

> She knew nothing of this recreation, in which Murphy had not felt the need to indulge while she was with him. He now gave her a full and frank account of its unique features. . . .
> Nor did she know anything of his heart attacks, which had not troubled him while she was with him. He now told her all about them. . . . (P. 30)

The recurring segments in the passage ("while she was with him. He now . . .") indicate that Murphy has been evasive: it is only after she finds out about his activities that Celia is given the "full and frank" accounts. Moreover, Celia is under the impression that Murphy tells her everything—this idea is similarly emphasized by repetition (pp. 13, 20).

Murphy is evasive but Celia has few secrets, even from Mr. Kelly. This becomes apparent when two passages with a recurring phrase ("might give . . . pain") are compared:

> She kept nothing from Mr. Kelly except what she thought might give him pain, i.e. next to nothing. (P. 11)

> "I have not spoken to you of Murphy," said Celia, "because I thought it might give you pain." (P. 12)

The word "nothing," which is repeated in the first of these excerpts, links it to a sentence that appears in the passage about Murphy's "full and frank" accounts:

> She knew nothing of this recreation. . . .
> Nor did she know anything of his heart attacks. . . . He now told her all about them, keeping back nothing that might alarm her. (P. 30)

The last sentence is tricky; it emphasizes not the similarities but the differences between Celia and Murphy. She conceals anything that might be painful; he discloses anything that might be alarming.

The repetitive devices are often used to provide clues about the characters' hidden traits and feelings. Their loneliness is emphasized in a series of related passages, each of which involves a statement about being alone, together with a modification of the original statement. The series begins when Celia says to Mr. Kelly, "You are all I have in the world," and then qualifies her remark: "You . . . and possibly Murphy" (p. 11). Later, when she again tells him, "You are all I have in the world," he tartly responds, "I . . . and possibly Murphy" (p. 18). Echoes of this conversation recur in five other passages:

> Celia, after leaving Mr. Kelly's flat, says to herself: "Now I have no one . . . except possibly Murphy" (p. 25).

> When Celia leaves Murphy, the narrator says: "Now she had nobody, except possibly Mr. Kelly" (p. 35).

> When Murphy makes a disparaging remark about Rosie Dew's dog, the narrator refers to it as "almost all she had in this dreary *en-deçà* . . ." (p. 102).

> When Celia leaves Mr. Kelly, he says: "Now I have no one . . . not even Celia" (p. 115).

> When Neary dismisses Cooper, the narrator says: "Neary also had no one, not even Cooper" (p. 115).

The tone of the qualifying phrases ("except possibly," "not even") seems cynical, but the repetition conveys a sense of despair: most of these characters dread loneliness, and most of them become its victims. Like a leitmotif, the reiterated formula adds significance and intensity to this theme.

Sometimes the repetition is used to reveal idiosyncracies in the narrative method. An example occurs at the end of the first chapter, in a description of Murphy in his rocking chair. Here the redundancy is doubled: a number of phrases recur within the passage, and toward the end of the novel the entire passage is repeated: "The rock got faster and faster, shorter and shorter . . . soon his body would be quiet. Most things under the moon got slower and slower and then stopped, a rock got faster and faster and then stopped. Soon his body would be quiet, soon he would be free" (pp. 9, 252–53). It may seem that the only point of the repetition is to stress that Murphy is rocking more quickly. But one of the reiterated phrases ("and then stopped") calls attention to an apparent paradox: unlike most things in the world, Murphy's rocking chair does not slow down before stopping. The repeated phrase refers to an event that occurs after the chapter ends: Murphy gets the chair moving so quickly that it flips over. He is later found unconscious; how this occurred is hinted at but never explained. The omitted description is alluded to by still another recurring phrase in the passage, "soon his body would be quiet." Ostensibly it suggests that Murphy will shortly go into a trance; actually it anticipates his imminent state of unconsciousness. When the entire passage about the rocking chair is later repeated, other relevant points emerge. Again an important event—Murphy's death—occurs just after the chapter ends, and again the event is not described. The phrase "soon his body would be quiet" ironically refers to the omitted description, just as it did in the earlier episode. The recurring passages finally make it clear that the narrator is intentionally withholding details of the story.

In some instances, even apparently trivial repetitions turn out to be significant. Murphy's fiancée, Miss Counihan, habitually says "—er—" in the middle of a sentence; this she does eleven times in the course of the novel.[5] Her mannerism seems so unimportant that one barely pays attention to it. But if one compares the contexts in which the interjection occurs, a pattern becomes evident: Miss Counihan says "—er—" whenever she is about to utter a euphemism. This is never explained, however; Beckett permits readers to discover it for themselves. Two other characters, Neary and Wylie, appear in an episode where the mannerism is important. Neary, rejected by Miss Counihan, asks Wylie for advice about winning her back. Wylie suggests that Neary tell Miss Counihan that he is "Hers to wipe her—er—feet on" (p. 60). Wylie's joke goes over Neary's head, but readers who have noticed that an "—er—" signals a euphemism will apprehend its deeper meaning.

Another character whose habitual repetition is a sign of hypocrisy is Murphy's landlady, Miss Carridge. Wylie again indicates that he is aware of the meaning of her mannerism by mimicking it.[6] As his name suggests, Wylie is very shrewd; he is sensitive to nuances of speech and uses this skill to his advantage. He understands that if people dissemble, they sometimes also reveal their deeper feelings inadvertently. This idea is related to one of Beckett's techniques: readers are encouraged to learn, as Wylie has, that minor details are often clues to hidden truths.

Cross-references

Another device used to hint at the novel's hidden meanings consists of different types of cross-references that call attention to reiterated passages. When the narrator borrows an aphorism from Neary ("Love requited . . . is a short circuit"), he reminds readers where it originated and in this way also indicates that it has been repeated (pp. 5, 29). Similarly, when the narrator quotes from Murphy's horoscope, he attributes the quotations to Suk, the swami who cast it; this occurs eight times.[7] In some instances quotation marks are used to indicate that passages are being repeated (see, for example, the quotations on pp. 183 and 252). Sometimes the cross-references are themselves repeated, and in this way become part of the pattern of verbal repetition. In the first chapter, when the narrator refers three times to a subsequent chapter, each of his cross-references is the same: "as described in section six" (pp. 2, 7, 9).

Some of the cross-references are more intricate. When Cooper recalls a comment of Wylie's and repeats it verbatim, the narrator says: "It is curious how Wylie's words remained fixed in the minds of those to whom they had once been addressed. It must have been the tone of voice. Cooper, whose memory for such things was really very poor, had recovered, word for word, the merest of mere phrases. And now Neary lay on his bed repeating: 'The syndrome known as life is too diffuse to admit of palliation.' "[8] The comment Neary repeats is, like Cooper's, one originally uttered by Wylie. Neary's feat of memory is perhaps again an effect of Wylie's tone of voice; at any rate, no other explanation is given. Then—in case anyone missed it the first time around—Neary repeats the same trick: a few lines down he quotes still another of Wylie's remarks verbatim (pp. 200–201, 57). At this point overtaxed credulity gives way to skepticism, and one begins to understand that the narrator is being playful. But the joke has an additional purpose as a cross-reference; it emphasizes a number of recurring passages that might otherwise have gone unnoticed.

Repeated Action

Most of the cross-references call attention to verbal repetitions, but some are used in connection with another type of redundancy involving repeated action. It may seem pointless for the narrator to mention that a gesture of Celia's resembles one of Neary's ("She despatched her hands on the gesture that Neary had made such a botch of . . .").[9] But comments like this one call attention to a pattern of reiterated actions. Some actions are repeated many times and are used in conjunction with verbal repetition. When Miss Counihan sits on the edge of Neary's bed, the narrator includes the following cross-reference: "In a somewhat similar way Celia had sat on Mr. Kelly's bed, and on Murphy's . . ." (p. 208). This comment links four episodes: one involving Neary and Miss Counihan, one involving Mr. Kelly and Celia, and two involving Murphy and Celia (pp. 207–8, 24–25, 29, 39). In still other episodes a similar type of action recurs:

> Ticklepenny lies on Murphy's bed; Murphy is seated nearby in his rocking chair (p. 191).
>
> Celia is on her bed; Neary moves his chair to the head of her bed (pp. 232–33).
>
> Murphy lies down on Mr. Endon's bed; Mr. Endon squats on the bed (p. 242).
>
> Murphy, after helping Mr. Endon into bed, kneels down beside the bed (p. 248).

Many of the related episodes are linked by other recurring details. Usually the person in bed is at home; the other person arrives and sits on or near the bed. In most cases the setting (appropriately enough) is a bed-sitting room. In each of the episodes an exchange between the characters redefines some aspect of their relationship, and what emerges is that—as in a royal levee—the person lying down is the more powerful. When Miss Counihan visits Neary and sits on his bed, their positions indicate that their relationship has changed. Previously he had been pursuing her; now he has lost interest and she is pursuing him. Similarly, when Neary moves his chair closer to Celia's bed, the suggestion is that he has fallen under her spell; the narrator later affirms this.

The same pattern holds in the last two episodes on the list. In the first of these Murphy is lying down and Mr. Endon is squatting on the bed. This characterizes the initial stage of their relationship: Murphy, an attendant in the asylum where Mr. Endon is confined, seems to be the dominant person. But in the next scene the situation has changed: Murphy, who wanted to become friends with Mr. Endon, realizes that he has been rejected. At this point he kneels beside the reclining Mr. Endon; as his position indicates, he now is in the inferior role.[10]

A related idea emerges in another set of parallel scenes. Celia, trying to understand why Murphy has left her, pauses as she considers various reasons. The narrator marks these intervals by saying "A rest," as each one occurs (p. 234). Later Murphy pauses in similar fashion when he thinks about why Mr. Endon would not become his friend, and again the narrator keeps repeating "A rest" (p. 250). The reiterated passages and actions point out the similarities in the two situations: Celia and Murphy are unprepared for the rejections and both are hurt by them.

Celia's unhappiness is hinted at in an episode where she emulates the actions of a retired butler known as "the old boy." Once again, both verbal reiteration and repeated action are used to emphasize the parallels. In the first of the two scenes Miss Carridge tells Celia about the old boy's habit of pacing the floor of his room:

> "Hark," she said, pointing upward.
> A soft padding to and fro was audible.
> "The old boy," said Miss Carridge. "Never still." (P. 69)

Soon afterward the old boy cuts his throat: it was presumably because he was thinking about taking his life that he paced the floor. Later Celia moves into the room he had occupied, and when it becomes clear that Murphy has abandoned her, she begins to pace the floor. Wylie calls attention to this in a passage very much like the earlier one:

> "Hark!" said Wylie, pointing upward.
> A soft swaggering to and fro was audible.
> "Mrs. M.," said Wylie, "never still. . . ." (P. 228)

The similarities hint that Celia may be considering following in the old boy's footsteps, figuratively as well as literally.[11] The narrator never says whether Celia is considering suicide, and she herself remains stoically silent. But in Beckett's fiction—as in life—explanations for stoical silence are not always given.

Another series of recurring episodes involves Neary and his cycle of love affairs: as soon as a woman falls in love with him, he goes off in pursuit of someone else. Neary, whose name is an anagram of "yearn," is constantly beset by desire. This emerges in a series of recurring incidents which indicates that his relationships with Miss Dwyer and Miss Counihan are remarkably similar:

Mrs. West loves Neary; he rejects her because he loves Miss Dwyer; she rejects him because she is in love with another man (p. 5).

Miss Dwyer submits to Neary; he rejects her and falls in love with Miss Counihan; she rejects him because she is in love with another man (pp. 48–49).

Neary complains to Murphy, one of his students, about the pain of unrequited love (pp. 4ff.).

Neary complains to Wylie, formerly one of his students, about the pain of unrequited love (pp. 46ff.).

During this conversation Murphy, responding to a question from Neary, admits he finds Miss Counihan physically attractive (p. 6).

During this conversation Wylie, responding to a question from Neary, admits he finds Miss Counihan physically attractive (p. 60).

The story of Dives and Lazarus is used to stress how intensely Neary longs for Miss Dwyer.[12]

The story of Dives and Lazarus is used to stress how intensely Neary longs for Miss Counihan.[13]

Neary's falling in love with Miss Dwyer is explained in terms of the figure-ground concept, a central idea in Gestalt psychology (p. 4).

Neary's falling out of love with Miss Dwyer is explained in terms of the figure-ground concept, a central idea in Gestalt psychology (p. 48).

This comparison is followed by an allusion to Wolfgang Köhler, an important member of the Gestalt movement.[14]

This comparison is followed by an allusion to Kurt Koffka, an important member of the Gestalt movement (p. 48).

Realizing that she has no future with Elliman, Miss Dwyer sleeps with Neary; he thereupon loses interest in her (p. 48).

Realizing that she has no future with Murphy, Miss Counihan submits to Neary's "wishes, or rather whims"; he thereupon loses interest in her (p. 199).

When Neary spurns Miss Dwyer, a new sequence involving Miss Counihan begins: the conclusion of each cycle initiates another one. Neary loses interest in Miss Counihan when he decides to become friends with Murphy; later, attracted to Celia, he forgets about Murphy.

The cyclical movement of Neary's actions also is emphasized by a circular configuration of one-sided love relationships. Neary loves Miss Dwyer at the time she is in love with Flight-Lieutenant Elliman; he loves "a Miss Farren of Ringsakiddy"; she loves "Father Fitt of Ballinclashet"; he loves "Mrs. West of Passage"; she loves Neary (p. 5). Even the place-names in the series suggest circles or movement.

The repetition here and in other episodes introduces the idea that human activity is often mindlessly redundant. This theme is emphasized in a series of scenes where action, settings, and other details recur:

> Two scenes in the novel take place in a rooming house in West Bromp-
> ton. At the beginning of each scene Murphy is alone, tied to his rocking
> chair. Toward the end of each scene he converses with Celia about his
> horoscope (pp. 1–9, 28–31).

> Two scenes take place in Mr. Kelly's flat. In each one Mr. Kelly lies in
> bed, finds it hard to think because of a feeling that parts of his body are
> dispersed, and repairs his kite. At the end of the first of these episodes
> Celia says to herself, "Now I have no one"; at the end of the second
> scene Mr. Kelly tells himself the same thing (pp. 11–25, 114—15).

> Kite-flying is depicted in two scenes. In each one Celia watches a boy
> with two kites yoked in tandem. In the first scene Celia greets the boy,
> who does not respond—he is singing. In the second scene the boy "did
> not sing as he departed, nor did she hail him." Both scenes, which take
> place near the Round Pond in Hyde Park, end when the rangers, crying
> "All out," close the park (pp. 151–53, 276–82).

> Rosie Dew appears in two scenes; both take place in Hyde Park; the
> Long Water (a lake in Hyde Park) is mentioned in each of them. Near the
> end of the first scene Rosie Dew sets out for home after recalling that "A
> boot was waiting for her from Lord Gall . . ."; near the end of the second
> scene she decides to go home after recalling that "A pair of socks was
> waiting from Lord Gall."[15]

> Neary sends Cooper on two missions: to discover where Murphy lives,
> and to dispose of his remains. Each time Cooper passes a supremely
> attractive pub just as it is about to open; forgetting about his mission,
> he remains there drinking until closing time (pp. 120–21, 274–75).

The narrator seldom calls attention to these recurring episodes, and the characters who figure in them seem unaware that they are repeating their actions. It is as if they are unwilling to confront the monotony in their lives, and have insulated themselves from it.

Another form of repeated action is introduced when situations described early in the novel recur toward the end. When she moves in with Murphy, Celia hopes that they will have a "new life" together.[16] She gives up streetwalking, stops visiting Mr. Kelly, and devotes herself to Murphy. The new life, however, does not last very long. This is hinted at when the words "new life" are repeated and then used ironically in a description of dead leaves falling to the ground (pp. 64, 150). Later, when Murphy dies, Celia returns to her old life. Similarly, in the first scene where Celia and Murphy are seen together, she notices that he has a birthmark. In their last scene together she sees the birthmark again: she uses it to identify Murphy's corpse. Such episodes suggest that it is pointless to hope for a new life; only death brings significant changes.

Beckett has said that people usually find change unendurable and use habit, "the guarantee of a dull inviolability," to block it out of their lives.[17] This theme is introduced in the opening sentence of *Murphy* when the narrator, echoing Ecclesiastes, describes the sun shining on the "nothing new." Wylie—in a passage that Neary later repeats verbatim—points out that things "will always be the same as they always were" (pp. 58, 201). Always, always: nothing ever changes, yet everyone seems to think that things are getting better. Beckett challenges his readers with this idea. If the redundancy in *Murphy* goes unnoticed, it may be that they also have insulated themselves from the monotony and repetitiousness of life.

Duality

Another device used to hint at this repetitiousness involves pairs of characters, objects, and locales; there are, all together, about 200 of them in the novel (a list is given in Appendix II).[18] The device is often hard to detect because one of the items in a dual set is more conspicuous than the other. This often occurs with dual sets of characters. Two prostitutes and two landladies are mentioned in *Murphy*, but in each instance one of the two plays an important role and the other one is only mentioned in passing.[19] The novel contains many dual sets of this sort. Among the characters are two coroners, two homosexuals, two waitresses, two fortunetellers, two alcoholics, two Hindus, two alumni of Neary's academy, two scholars who write monographs (both titles are given), two unnamed doctors, two doctors with names, a set of identical twins, two men with tiny heads, and two men with heads that are disproportionately large.[20]

The characters with large heads, Mr. Kelly and Mr. Endon, also have eyes that are similar. Mr. Kelly's eyes "could not very well protrude, so deeply were they imbedded"; Mr. Endon's eyes are "both deep-set and protuberant, one of Nature's jokes. . . ."[21] Nature may be joking here, but Beckett has the last laugh.

The doctors with names, Dr. Killiecrankie and Dr. Fist, have other traits in common. They both are involved in Ticklepenny's cure for alcoholism, they speak with accents (Scottish and German, respectively), and their names contain puns based on German words. Killiecrankie's name suggests that he kills the sick—*krank*, in German, means sick—and *Faust* is the German word for fist. Dr. Fist, "more philosophical than medical, German on his father's side," may well be a distant relative of Goethe's famous doctor (p. 88).

Some sets of characters are used to suggest double-dealing in amorous transactions. Wylie is attracted to Celia as well as to Miss Counihan, they are both in love with Murphy, and Murphy abandons both of them. Neary, who also yearns for Miss Counihan and for Celia, has been involved with two other women in Ireland and has deserted two wives in other countries. Celia's parents died "clinging warmly to their respective partners in the ill-fated *Morro Castle*" (p. 12). Ticklepenny, Bim's minion, flirts with Murphy. Cooper's only experience with women came when he loved two of them, "simultaneously as ill-luck would have it" (p. 206). Even minor characters like Flight-Lieutenant Elliman, Miss Dwyer, and Ariadne Cox participate in two relationships.[22]

Some of the characters involved in these dual sets again have traits in common. Both Miss Counihan and Celia are remarkably beautiful, eager to marry Murphy, and determined to transform him into a wage-earner. Both of them later complain—using similar expressions—when his hunt for a job delays the marriage.[23] But the parallels finally serve to emphasize an essential difference. Celia, ostensibly a whore, is innately faithful; Miss Counihan is the very opposite.

Some of the characters in the novel are associated with dual sets of objects or undergo similar experiences. Celia interprets two events as omens suggesting that she should leave Murphy. Miss Counihan is vulnerable in two areas, "her erogenous zones and her need for Murphy." The old boy had two seizures before he died, "one on Shrove Tuesday, the other on Derby Day," and he ate two meals daily.[24]

Some of the dual sets, like the following examples, have common elements that link them together into pairs of doubles:

Rosie Dew offers the sheep in Hyde Park two heads of lettuce; these are twice mistaken for cabbage (pp. 101–2, 106).

Murphy divides jokes into two categories; he has two favorite jokes, both about stout (pp. 65, 139).

Murphy sends Celia two letters; she calls him on the telephone twice (pp. 22–23).

Neary receives two similarly phrased telegrams from Cooper; he sends two similarly phrased letters to Wylie and Miss Counihan (pp. 57, 199).

At times the narrator introduces the idea of duality by using the word "second" in a context where one would logically expect to find the word "first." After consoling Neary, Wylie feels purer "than at any time since his second communion" (p. 51). Dr. Killie-crankie and the coroner have a polite quarrel at the door of the mortuary about which of them would "pass second" (p. 259).

There are many dual sets involving places: every important locale in the novel figures in some set. As the following list indicates, many of the dual sets are linked by still other common elements:

The action of the novel takes place in two countries, Ireland and England. There are two main settings in Ireland, Cork and Dublin: two scenes are set in Dublin, two flashbacks take place in Cork. The rest of the action takes place in England, in London and at the Magdalen Mental Mercyseat.

Two rivers figure in the novel. One is Irish (the Lee, into which Neary throws two keys). The other is English (the Thames, where Celia sees a coupled tug and barge).

Two London parks are used as settings, Hyde Park and Battersea Park. Rosie Dew, Celia, Murphy, Cooper, and the boy with tandem kites all appear in parallel scenes that take place in Hyde Park. Battersea Park is mentioned twice in the novel (pp. 16, 106).

During the course of the novel two characters, Miss Counihan and Neary, move from Cork to Dublin; both are in pursuit of Murphy. In Dublin each one stays first at Wynn's Hotel and then moves to another, unnamed hotel.

In London, Murphy lives in two rooming houses. Both of his landladies agree to "cook" the bill and overcharge Mr. Quigley, his uncle. Mr. Quigley lives in two cities, Amsterdam and Scheveningen.

Among the furnishings in Murphy's second rooming house are "Two massive upright unupholstered armchairs, similar to those killed under him by Balzac"; there are two references to these armchairs (pp. 63, 228).

When Celia moves into a new room at Miss Carridge's rooming house, she takes two suitcases with her. The second room is "half as big . . . half as high, twice as bright" as the first one she occupied (p. 148).

Murphy has lived in two cities in continental Europe, Paris and Hanover. A route he travels daily in London is compared to one he used to take in Paris, and his garret at the Magdalen Mental Mercyseat is compared to one he occupied in Hanover. The narrator says that the second garret is "not half, but twice as good as the one in Hanover, because half as large" (p. 162).

The Magdalen Mental Mercyseat (or M.M.M.) is copiously endowed with dual entities. The asylum has a counterpart in Ireland which, like the M.M.M., is named for a religious figure: John o' God's. The M.M.M. is outside of but not far from London; the Irish asylum is outside of but not far from Dublin. Two chapters are set at the M.M.M.; John o' God's is mentioned twice in the novel.[25]

The M.M.M. is "situated in its own grounds on the boundary of two counties" (p. 156). It has two staff houses and two convalescent houses. The mortuary at the M.M.M. has double-decker refrigerators and its walls are covered with two types of climbing plants; these are described twice (pp. 165, 258). Murphy's supervisors at the M.M.M. are the identical twins, Thomas "Bim" Clinch and Timothy "Bom" Clinch. It is two o'clock when Murphy begins his first shift as an attendant; his last shift ends during his second week at the M.M.M., after his second round of visits to the patients. Murphy works in Skinner's House, a building shaped like "a double obelisk"; it has two stories, two sections (for men and for women), and its wards "consisted of two long corridors" (pp. 165, 166).

The dual sets are used to emphasize two parallel themes: body versus mind, and sanity versus insanity. Murphy, a dualist in the Cartesian tradition, believes that reality has a physical component ("the big world") and a mental component ("the little world"). After arriving at the M.M.M., Murphy persuades himself that insanity is nothing more than full-time residence in the little world. If the inmates at the M.M.M. seem bizarre, it is because they are being judged by the rules of a world they have abandoned. The psychiatrists are the only ones whose behavior is irrational: they condemn the pleasures of the little world without having sampled them. The patients rightly refuse to be rehabilitated; they are happy enough as "microcosmopolitans," citizens of the little world (p. 240).

The dual images suggest that the M.M.M. represents a no-man's-land between the big world and the little. Convinced that the asylum will provide him with a crossing point into the realm of mental activity, Murphy tries to become friends with the patients. He is particularly fond of the catatonic Mr. Endon, whose condition, he feels, is closer to a philosophical breakthrough than a psychological breakdown. A solipsist manqué, Murphy hopes to study the fine points of introversion under Mr. Endon's tutelage. It never occurs to him that a veteran solipsist might have reservations about giving instructions to a figment of his own imagination.

Murphy wants to communicate with Mr. Endon in order to learn how to emulate him, but solitude is a condition for withdrawal into the self. Murphy is unwilling to give up other enjoyable activities in the big world; this "deplorable susceptibility," says the narrator, forestalls his transition into the little world (p. 179). Suk also notes Murphy's tendency to equivocate: "There has been persons of this description," he says, "known to have expressed a wish to be in two places at a time" (p. 32).

As Murphy grows fonder of Mr. Endon, his ability to endure isolation diminishes and his capacity for withdrawal is weakened by "vicarious autology" (p. 189). Murphy remains on the border between two worlds, hoping to experience the best of both. But this is impossible; as the narrator says, "He could not have it both ways, not even the illusion of it" (p. 189).

Reiterated Allusions

Another type of redundancy, similar to that of the dual sets, is based on repeated allusions. Two figures who epitomize Murphy's self-involvement and indolence are Narcissus and Belacqua; both also were important in Beckett's earlier fiction. There are two references to Narcissus in *Murphy*, and two passages about Belacqua. In each of the passages Belacqua is portrayed lazily watching the sky, just as he does in *The Divine Comedy*, and his name occurs twice in each passage.[26] References to two of Homer's heroines, Helen and Penelope, call attention to Celia's outstanding atttributes, beauty and fidelity (pp. 176, 149). Miss Counihan, on the other hand, is compared to Dido and Jezebel (pp. 195, 199).

Another form of duality is suggested when Beckett introduces pairs of figures who are traditionally linked, like Jacob and Esau, Dives and Lazarus, or Ixion and Tantalus.[27] In one paragraph the narrator mentions two classical sculptors, Phidias and Scopas; two sculptors from more recent times, Puget and Barlach; and a matched set of caryatids, the work of Puget (pp. 238–39). Beckett sometimes varies this technique by using pairs of allusions that have similar sources. Murphy, making parallel points, cites two quotations from the New Testament.[28] The narrator uses descriptions of sleep taken from two Shakespeare plays in two successive sentences.[29] Celia remembers two couplets she heard as a child; both are from Elizabethan songs.[30] When Neary complains about the pain of unrequited love, he alludes to two passages from the third chapter of Job.[31]

Some of the recurring allusions are concealed. A phrase that is twice attributed to Neary, "the big blooming buzzing confusion," actually is from an essay by William James.[32] According to James, the physical world would seem incoherent if not for the mental patterns that organize one's experience of it. A person responding directly to sense impressions would apprehend only the world's "big blooming buzzing confusion." Beckett uses this concept in stressing the differences between the big world and the little.

Murphy contains many philosophical allusions, and a number of them are involved in the pattern of duality. Often, when Beckett refers twice to the same philosopher, one of the references is much easier to detect than the other, usually because the source is given. This creates the type of dual set in which one item is more prominent than the other. The following is a list of some of the more easily identified allusions:

Pythagoreanism: Murphy is eager to learn about "what Neary, at that time a Pythagorean, called the Apmonia" (Apmonia, or *Harmonia*, is a state of attunement which the Pythagoreans considered a prerequisite for good health).[33]

Democritus: Murphy experiences "the Nothing, than which in the guffaw of the Abderite naught is more real" (Democritus of Abdera is known as the laughing philosopher—hence the guffaw).[34]

Descartes: The floor of Murphy's room is covered with "dream of Descartes linoleum" (that is, its wild pattern is associated with Descartes' famous dream of November 10, 1619).[35]

Geulincx: Murphy's conclusion that he is not of the big world is justified by a quotation: "In the beautiful Belgo-Latin of Arnold Geulincx: *Ubi nihil vales, ibi nihil velis*" ("want nothing where you are worth nothing").[36]

Berkeley: Neary says, "I don't wonder at Berkeley. . . . He had no alternative. A defence mechanism. Immaterialize or bust" (Neary is suggesting that Berkeley's immaterialism is a response to the harshness of existence).[37]

For the most part, these allusions deal with well-known concepts that illuminate the philosophical issues introduced in the novel. But one can compile another list of allusions where, if the sources are the same, they are less easily identified. Here Beckett introduces ideas that are more obscure—and sometimes more bizarre:

Pythagoreanism: Neary tells Wylie, "betray me . . . and you go the way of Hippasos." According to Neary, Hippasos was "Drowned in a puddle" because he divulged secrets such as "the incommensurability of side and diagonal" (p. 47).

Democritus: Mr. Endon stares at "some object immeasurably remote, perhaps the famous ant on the sky of an airless world" (p. 248).

Descartes: Neary says to Murphy, "your conarium has shrunk to nothing" (p. 6).

Geulincx: Wylie says that he heeds "the voices, or rather voice, of Reason and Philautia" (p. 216).

Berkeley: After explaining that Murphy's mind "excluded nothing that it did not itself contain," the narrator adds, "This did not involve Murphy in the idealist tar" (pp. 107–8).

The first item on the list refers to a story about Hippasos, a member of the Pythagorean order. Pythagoras held that number was the underlying principle of nature. This doctrine could not be reconciled with the discovery that the ratio between the side and diagonal of an isosceles right triangle is not expressible as a rational number. The Pythagoreans tried to keep the discovery secret: they were willing, in other words, to suppress the truth when it conflicted with the teachings of their founder.[38]

The "famous ant" in the next excerpt is one mentioned by Democritus. According to Aristotle, Democritus maintained that small objects were in theory visible at any distance: if not for the intervening air, "one could distinctly see an ant on the vault of the sky."[39] Not only is this a faulty theory of vision—Democritus also seems to have believed that the sky was solid and that insects crawled on it.

Neary's remark about the conarium (the organ that translates mental impulses into physical responses) refers to a problem in Cartesian philosophy. Descartes claimed that the function of the pineal gland was to permit the interaction of mind and body. But despite numerous challenges, he was unable to prove his theory, or even to explain how the process of interaction worked.[40]

In the next excerpt Wylie equates "Reason" and "Philautia." "Philautia" means self-love: it is a transliterated Greek word (Beckett, using the same license that permitted it to be Latinized, Anglicizes it).[41] The unscrupulous Wylie admits that reason and self-love speak to him with the same voice. Geulincx, however, arrives at a very different conclusion. Four cardinal virtues are described in his study of moral philosophy, the *Ethica,* and all are aspects of Reason. Among these virtues are Diligence, the voice of Reason, and Humility, a disdain for oneself ("contemptio sui"). These virtues can be contrasted with Philautia ("amor sui"), which Geulincx says repudiates the voice of Reason and encourages sinful behavior.[42] Wylie's assertion, then, is actually a cynical reversal of Geulincx's concept.

The idealist tar in the last excerpt alludes to one of Berkeley's hobbyhorses: he wrote a book on tar-water, which in his time was considered a cure-all. Given his doctrine of immaterialism, Berkeley's willingness to endorse a nostrum for physical ailments seems somewhat extravagant.[43]

As these summaries indicate, when the allusions are easily identified, Beckett seems to be taking the ideas he cites seriously; when they are not, he introduces a sardonic note. Beckett enjoys a bit of fun at the expense of the philosophers, but his satire is mainly directed against his own characters, Murphy in particular. If the concepts of thinkers like Berkeley or Descartes sometimes seem far-fetched, what can be said for Murphy, whose ideas are a pastiche of theirs?

Dozens of novelists have explored the depths of philosophy; Beckett's side-trip to the shallows is no less instructive. The irony in the obscure allusions is his tool for avoiding the didactic solemnity that often creeps into philosophical fiction. Beckett is interested in philosophy, but for him art takes precedence over ideas. He is less concerned with either side of an intellectual argument than with the way both sides can contribute to a symmetrical aesthetic structure.[44]

Symmetry

Many of these symmetrical configurations are part of a larger pattern that emphasizes balance in both the form and the content of the novel. Dual sets are sometimes used to suggest balanced alternatives. Celia, for example, has "two equally important reasons" for insisting that Murphy find a job; Neary's gesture can be concluded in "two equally legitimate ways" (pp. 65, 4). The narrator demonstrates that subtle truths can be lodged in balanced contradictions: "There seems really very little hope for Neary, he seems doomed to hope unending" (p. 201). At times the narrator even equates antithetical ideas: "Yes or no?" he refers to as the "eternal tautology" (p. 41).

Beckett occasionally does favor a particular point of view, especially when that point of view is pessimistic. But in most cases what seems like advocacy is part of a larger scheme in which opposing ideas are presented elsewhere in the novel. In this way the symmetry is preserved. Astronomy and astrology, for example, are treated as equally valid sides of a debate. In one passage, sounding very knowledgeable about astronomy, Beckett speaks about "Mr. Adams" and his "beautiful deduction of Neptune from Uranus."[45] Neptune and Uranus are also mentioned in Suk's horoscope—though this is easily overlooked because Uranus is called by an old name, Herschel (p. 33). The reference to Herschel establishes a link between the passages about astronomy and astrology. In one, John Couch Adams, a discoverer of Neptune, is mentioned; in the other, there is an allusion to Sir William Herschel, the discoverer of Uranus.

Astronomy and astrology also figure in two passages in which the moon's position is given:

> The moon, by a striking coincidence full and at perigee, was 29,000 miles nearer the earth than it had been for four years. (P. 26)

> The moon twenty-three degrees of the Serpent promotes Great Magical Ability of the Eye. . . . (P. 32)

Portions of both of these passages are later repeated, which makes the similarities between them easier to notice.[46]

Another type of symmetry is introduced by rhetorically balanced sentences. In a gracefully formed sentence silence is defined as "that frail partition between the ill-concealed and the ill-revealed, the clumsily false and the unavoidably so" (p. 257). The narrator, more concerned about symmetry than nutrition, gives the following description of Murphy's lunch: "Twopence the tea, twopence the biscuits, a perfectly balanced meal" (p. 80). The mind-body theme presents the narrator with many opportunities to use symmetrical sentences:

> There was the mental fact and there was the physical fact, equally real if not equally pleasant. (P. 108)

> The mind felt its actual part to be above and bright, its virtual beneath and fading into dark. . . . (P. 108)

> He neither thought a kick because he felt one nor felt a kick because he thought one. (P. 109)

> As he lapsed in body he felt himself coming alive in mind, set free to move among its treasures. The body has its stock, the mind its treasures. (P. 111)

For Murphy, mental activity is enhanced by physical passivity. In passages that deal with this theme, form and content work together to depict the balanced opposition of mind and body, as the last of these excerpts suggests.

In some cases symmetry is achieved by using word-play involving antitheses. Mr. Quigley is called "a well-to-do ne'er do well" (p. 17). Murphy, punning on a Latin word, says that his feelings for Miss Counihan are not "cordial" but "precordial."[47] Miss Counihan is observed "stepping out of her step-ins" (p. 204). Miss Carridge finds the old boy with "a cut-throat razor clutched in his hand and his throat cut in effect" (p. 134). A similar type of word-play involves foreign terms. Neary praises Wylie for his "savoir ne pas faire" as well as for his "savoir faire" (p. 116). Rosie Dew, who has few friends in the "en-deçà," communicates with spirits in the "au-delà" (pp. 102, 99). The narrator distinguishes between "voyeur" and "voyant" and, alluding to Berkeley, between "percipere" and "percipi."[48]

The idea that life and death form a balanced antithesis often occurs in the novel. It is introduced by a series of symmetrically opposed terms: "spermarium" and "crematorium"; "vagitus" (a child's cry) and "rattle" (a death rattle); "gas" (which sustains life) and "chaos" (which destroys life); "dozing" and "dying"; "Sleep" and "Sleep's young brother" (Death).[49] The series culminates in a comment made by the coroner after Celia recognizes the birthmark on Murphy's corpse: "How beautiful in a way," he says, "birthmark deathmark, I mean, rounding off the life somehow . . ." (p. 267).

The opposing terms of some antitheses are often separated by many pages, and readers must rely on their memories to connect them. In one passage the narrator says that Murphy "had set out to capture himself, not with anger but with love. This was a stroke of genius that Neary, a Newtonian, could never have dealt himself . . ." (p. 201). To discover what Newton has to do with capturing oneself, it is necessary to recall a passage where Murphy, retreating into his mind, enjoys the pleasure of being "caught up in a tumult of non-Newtonian motion" (pp. 112–13). Neary believes only in the reality of physical motion; a prisoner in a world governed by Newtonian law, he must endure the torments of physical desire. Murphy, on the other hand, recognizes the existence of purely mental—that is, non-Newtonian—motion, governed by different laws. In this way he succeeds in minimizing some of the frustrating effects of desire.

Another type of balanced antithesis involves character traits; Murphy and Cooper are symmetrically opposed in this way. Murphy loves to sit and never wears a hat; Cooper—the victim of a strange compulsion—is unable to sit or to remove his hat. Murphy is loquacious, erudite, and never drinks; Cooper is a taciturn, semi-literate alcoholic. Murphy favors thought over action; Cooper, the reverse. Murphy's name suggests form (the meaning of the Greek word *morphe*); Cooper's suggests content, in the sense of a thing that envelops a form (*cooperire* in Latin means to envelop). Another symmetrical connection between the two characters becomes apparent when Cooper is liberated from his compulsions after Murphy's death. At this point, in an exuberant expression of triumph, Cooper crushes his hat by sitting on it.

Symmetry also plays an important role in the sanity-madness theme. Murphy, observing the lunatics at the M.M.M., is certain that insanity is bliss. But the narrator points out that Murphy has prejudged the issue: "The frequent expressions apparently of pain, rage, despair and in fact all the usual, to which some patients gave vent, suggesting a fly somewhere in the ointment of Microcosmos, Murphy either disregarded or muted to mean what he wanted" (p. 179). Murphy has a good knowledge of psychology. He alludes, for example, to the work of the Würzburg psychologists, and mentions some prominent members of this group: Oswald Külpe, Karl Marbe, Karl Bühler, Henry J. Watt, Narziss Ach.[50] Given his background, it is surely impulsive—after only a day in the asylum—to renounce sanity and pay homage to catatonia. As the narrator says, the sanity-madness issue is "lovingly simplified and perverted by Murphy" (p. 178). Murphy's problem is not that he is unbalanced mentally: it is his judgment that is unbalanced. He differs markedly from the narrator, for whom every issue must be balanced and, whenever possible, described in symmetrical terms.

Aside from the narrator, the only person in the novel who is properly appreciative of symmetry is Mr. Endon. In his chess game with Murphy Mr. Endon abandons the usual rules: his goal is not to win but to arrange his pieces in pleasing patterns. Murphy misinterprets this. He takes Mr. Endon's nonaggressive style as a friendly gesture and then, gratified, tries to reciprocate. He imitates fifteen of Mr. Endon's moves—which introduces still another kind of recurring action—but succeeds only in making a mess of his side of the board. Later Mr. Endon plays another game involving symmetry when he works through the permutations of a switch and indicator turned on and off. Murphy interrupts him before he finishes: he has again failed to understand the significance of Mr. Endon's games.

These games are less frivolous than they may appear. They illustrate a central principle of the novel, one that explains why the narrator is so fond of symmetry. The principle is introduced when Murphy is about to eat his lunch, an assortment of biscuits. It occurs to him that the order in which he eats the biscuits is determined by his preference for certain varieties. If he could rid himself of this partiality, says the narrator, "the assortment would spring to life before him, dancing the radiant measure of its total permutability. . . ." In order to enjoy the assortment of biscuits fully, Murphy must learn "not to prefer any one to any other" (pp. 96–97). But Murphy is interrupted just as he begins to understand the implications of this idea, and he forgets about it.

The concept Murphy forgets has to do with desire and indifference. Desire involves an exercise of the will and the need to possess an object; it leads to momentary gratification which soon is replaced by the need for a new object. Neary's cycle of endless yearning illustrates the frustrating result of unchecked desire. An alternative to desire is a detached receptiveness, which leads to aesthetic enjoyment. Symmetry encourages this kind of receptiveness by presenting objects in configurations instead of emphasizing their intrinsic values. Appreciating such configurations permits one to enjoy objects without possessing them; in this way the aesthetic process removes one from the realm of volition and its frustrations. Aesthetic pleasures may be less intense than those of volition, but they result in an indifference that brings freedom from unfulfilled desire and from the renewed yearning which accompanies the gratification of desire.

Mr. Endon and the narrator understand that indifference can lead to freedom; Neary will never understand it; Murphy, contemplating his assortment of biscuits, is on the verge of understanding it. As the narrator says in an elegantly balanced passage: "The freedom of indifference, the indifference of freedom, the will dust in the dust of its object, the act a handful of sand let fall—these were some of the shapes he had sighted, sunset landfall after many days. But now all was nebulous and dark . . ." (p. 105). Murphy, after many days at sea, glimpses a distant shore, but darkness falls and he is adrift once again.

After failing, finally, to understand the importance of indifference, Murphy returns to an old concern: his search for a path into the remote recesses of the self. He renounces "all that lay outside the intellectual love in which alone he could love himself"; but this, as the narrator says, "had not been enough and showed no signs of being enough" (p. 179). Murphy's attempt to escape from the world of desire fails because it still leaves him vulnerable to demands that originate from within himself. The "intellectual love in which alone he could love himself" is not really that different from his love for Celia or for a particular type of biscuit. It involves a preference for one entity to the exclusion of all others. Loving oneself precludes true indifference; it leads to an exercise of will and prevents Murphy from achieving liberation.

Beckett's idea about freedom and indifference is related to a concept in Schopenhauer's *The World as Will and Idea*. The will, says Schopenhauer, is a fundamental force at the very root of the character. If this is not widely understood, it is because philosophers like Descartes and Spinoza, who assumed that the will was an attribute of the mind, paid little attention to it. The will is actually an attribute of the body; the mind's function is only to transmit impulses that originate in the will. Freely exercising the will leads to perpetual desire: its demands can never be satisfied or modified. Only by abnegating the will—admittedly a difficult task—can one attain freedom. The best way of achieving this is by engaging in deep aesthetic contemplation. This, says Schopenhauer, shifts one's focus from the self to more impersonal concerns, and eventually leads to a denial of the will.[51]

Murphy, withdrawing into his mind, does not understand that he has still not liberated himself from willing. He enjoys visiting the little world because—as the narrator twice points out—it gives him pleasure (pp. 2, 113). He has not escaped desire; he has only changed the object of his desire. He hopes to gain freedom by focusing attention on himself but, according to Schopenhauer, a very different approach, "the forgetting of self as an individual," is necessary for self-liberation.[52]

A number of Murphy's ideas are based on the philosophy of Descartes and Spinoza. In the *Meditations* Descartes argues that the reality of experiences in the physical world must be questioned, but the validity of the mental processes engaged in such questioning is taken as a foregone conclusion.[53] Murphy similarly rejects physical reality without sufficiently inquiring into the mental processes he has used to reach this conclusion. The epigraph of the chapter on Murphy's mind, "Amor intellectualis quo Murphy se ipsum amat" ("the intellectual love in which Murphy loves himself"), is based on a passage in Spinoza's *Ethics*. Spinoza, however, says that it is God who is the object of his own intellectual love.[54] Murphy starts out using Cartesian philosophy to justify his withdrawal from the physical world, but when he is equated with Spinoza's God it becomes evident that egotism is an equally important source of his solipsistic ideology.

Murphy's theories can be contrasted with Mr. Endon's actions. In a brilliant transformation Mr. Endon turns chess—a contest of wills—into an aesthetic diversion. His manipulation of the switch and indicator, says the narrator, "seemed haphazard but was in fact determined by an amental pattern as precise as any of those that governed his chess" (pp. 246–47). Much as he may enjoy these games, however, Mr. Endon uncomplainingly permits them to be interrupted: indifference, and not pleasure, is his ultimate goal.

It is true, of course, that Mr. Endon is mad, but his is a special type of madness. Unlike Murphy, the narrator understands very well that lunacy is an unhappy condition; even so, he considers Mr. Endon's state an enviable one. An important aspect of Mr. Endon's good fortune, he says, is his ability to remain indifferent—to inner directives as well as to those originating outside himself (p. 248). Schopenhauer, describing how aesthetic contemplation counters the effects of the will, says that complete indifference to volition can be achieved only by geniuses. But these geniuses, he adds, "may exhibit certain weaknesses which are actually akin to madness."[55] Here again Beckett makes use of a balanced configuration. Mr. Endon's madness, the eccentric progeny of Schopenhauer's concept of genius, is offset by Murphy's solipsism, the monster offspring of Descartes' introspective method.

Mr. Endon's approach seems superior to Murphy's; hence, to preserve the symmetry, Murphy's views are given more emphasis. The narrator includes extensive discussions of Murphy's theories and spends a chapter describing what, as he says a number of times, Murphy's mind "pictured itself" to be (pp. 107, 110). Mr. Endon's side of the argument is advocated wordlessly; he is always silent and his thoughts are never described.

The symmetry here involves disparate types of behavior—Murphy's talk versus Mr. Endon's action—as well as opposed ideas. There are other examples of this technique: elegant manners accompany shabby behavior; unbalanced people utter beautifully balanced sentences. A common feature in this kind of antithesis is an opposition of form and content. Again and again, descriptions of chaotic events are embodied in a style that emphasizes balance and symmetry.

Many of the antitheses in *Murphy* are part of an elaborate pattern linking three sets of opposed themes: symmetry versus asymmetry, mental reality versus physical reality, and form versus content. The novel's symmetry is emphasized by formal devices; its asymmetry, by the content. The symmetry reflects the mind's tendency to impose orderly patterns on whatever it perceives; the asymmetry is a reflection of the world's blooming, buzzing confusion. The human imagination continually conjures up visions of order and integrity, but these are countered by experiences in a world where (according to the laws of thermodynamics) disorder rules. Murphy seeks respite from the world's chaos in his mind; the narrator, in his style. But there can be no respite: disorder, no less than order, is a part of existence. This is what is finally suggested by the duality in *Murphy*. The style whispers about the perfection of what might be; the content grumbles about the chaos of what was; and together, irreconcilable, they reveal what is.

Notes

1. "Talk of the Town," *New Yorker*, 40 (Aug. 8, 1964):23.

2. Deirdre Bair, *Samuel Beckett: A Biography* (New York: Harcourt Brace Jovanovich, 1978), p. 243. Beckett's comments are from a letter written to George Reavey on Nov. 13, 1936, before the novel was published.

3. *Murphy* (1938; rpt., New York: Grove Press, 1957), p. 84. Subsequent page references in the text are to this edition.

4. The recurring elements include repeated segments of various lengths (from a short fragment to a series of sentences); some are repeated verbatim and some have similar phrasing; see Appendix I.

5. Miss Counihan says "—er—" on pp. 52 (twice), 54 (twice), 55, 126, 129, 219, 227, and 272 (twice). The passage about "the bogs" and "the—er—fens" (p. 272) contains an allusion to Milton's *Paradise Lost* (II, 621). Beckett is suggesting that Ireland resembles Milton's Hell.

6. On p. 136 the narrator says "not a penny out of pocket, not one penny" in a description of Miss Carridge's reaction to the old boy's death. Miss Carridge repeats "the principle of the thing" on p. 147 and says, "I haven't a doubt, not a doubt" on p. 227. Wylie mimics her mannerism when he repeats "you are quite sure" on p. 227. The significance of Miss Carridge's repetitions will be discussed in the next chapter.

7. The horoscope appears on pp. 32–33. Excerpts from the horoscope are attributed to Suk on pp. 63, 82, 87, 93, 138, 164, 182, and 183.

8. Wylie originally made the remark on pp. 123–24; Cooper remembers it verbatim on p. 198; the narrator's comment comes on pp. 199–200.

9. Page 35; Neary's gesture is described on pp. 4–5.

10. This idea is also suggested in a description of Clarke, who "would repeat for hours the phrase: 'Mr. Endon is *very* superior' " (p. 193). When Murphy kneels next to the bed he is "stigmatised" in Mr. Endon's eyes (p. 249). Murphy's position suggests that Beckett has in mind the Greek word from which "stigmatized" is derived: στιγμᾶτίας (one who has been branded a runaway slave). Mr. Endon's name, as a number of critics have pointed out, is derived from ἔνδον (within), which suggests that he has withdrawn into an inner world.

11. A few other details hint that Celia may be contemplating suicide: a rambling speech (pp. 229–30) in which she keeps mentioning words that rhyme with "death," and Neary's assumption that Cooper is referring to Celia when he says, "she is dead" (pp. 272–73).

12. Neary speaks of the love that "craves for the tip of her little finger, dipped in lacquer, to cool its tongue" (p. 5). This passage is based on Luke 16:24, where after his death Dives asks Father Abraham to "send Lazarus, that he may dip the tip of his finger in water, and cool my tongue. . . ." This allusion has been noted by Hugh Kenner; see *A Reader's Guide to Samuel Beckett* (New York: Farrar, Straus and Giroux, 1973), p. 60.

13. Neary's "relation toward" Miss Counihan is "that post-mortem of Dives to Lazarus, except that there was no Father Abraham to put in a good word for him" (pp. 48–49). This again (see n. 12) is an allusion to Luke 16:24.

14. After Neary explains his love in terms of Gestalt psychology concepts, Murphy asks, "And then. . . . Back to Teneriffe and the apes?" (p. 5). This is an allusion to the work of Wolfgang Köhler. Köhler, interned on Teneriffe during World War I, spent a number of years studying apes at the

Anthropoid Research Station established there by the Prussian Academy of Sciences. One result of this work was his landmark study, *The Mentality of Apes* (first published in 1917; translated into English in 1925). It is likely that Beckett knows this book: the plot of *Acts Without Words I* is based on experiments Köhler describes there.

15. Rosie Dew is a medium and Lord Gall is her patron: she plans to use these objects to establish contact with Lord Gall's father (pp. 103, 278). Lord Gall is the same as the character in "Echo's Bones."

16. When Celia and Murphy first meet, they gaze at each other and then fall in love (p. 14). This suggests that the references to "the new life" (repeated three times on p. 64) are allusions to Dante's *La Vita Nuova* (and perhaps to the beach scene at the end of the fourth section of Joyce's *A Portrait of the Artist as a Young Man,* also based on Dante's work). References to a new life occur again on pp. 130 and 150, but the hope for a new life is refuted in the opening sentence of the novel, when the sun shines "on the nothing new" (p. 1; and cf. Ecclesiastes 1:9).

17. The idea that things never change is central in *Waiting for Godot.* Beckett's comments on habit are from *Proust* (1931; rpt., New York: Grove Press, 1957), p. 8, and see also pp. 7–12.

18. This total includes repeated incidents, pairs of objects, recurring character traits, and dual sets involving locales; see Appendix II.

19. Prostitutes, Celia and the former occupant of Murphy's room (p. 7); landladies, Miss Carridge and Murphy's first landlady (p. 7). The unnamed prostitute rented a room from the unnamed landlady; Celia rents a room from Miss Carridge (p. 146).

20. Coroners, pp. 145 and 259ff.; homosexuals, Ticklepenny and Bim (p. 156); waitresses, Cathleen (p. 46) and Vera (p. 81); fortunetellers, Suk and Rosie Dew; alcoholics, Cooper and Ticklepenny; Hindus, Suk (called a swami on p. 23) and the "Hindu polyhistor" (p. 196); alumni of Neary's academy, Murphy and Wylie; scholars, the polyhistor, author of *The Pathetic Fallacy from Avercamp to Kampendonck* (p. 196), and Neary, author of *The Doctrine of the Limit* (p. 50); doctors without names, an obstetrician (p. 71) and the doctor who attends the old boy (p. 135); doctors with names, Dr. Killiecrankie and Dr. Fist (p. 88); twins, p. 165; Cooper and Wylie have "tiny heads" (p. 131); Mr. Endon and Mr. Kelly have unusually large heads (pp. 186, 276).

21. Mr. Kelly's eyes, p. 11; Mr. Endon's, p. 248.

22. Flight-Lieutenant Elliman loves Miss Farren (p. 5) and Miss Dwyer (p. 48); Miss Dwyer is involved with Neary and Elliman (p. 48); Ariadne Cox, after being deserted by Neary, falls in love with Sacha Few, who also abandons her (p. 272).

23. Celia says, "Now it was September . . . and their relationship had not yet been regularised" (p. 17). Miss Counihan says, "It was August and still she had no news of Murphy" (p. 53). A recurring episode also links these characters: Celia, at an upstairs window, watches Murphy's depar-

ture in a scene that resembles one in which Miss Counihan (also at an upstairs window) watches Wylie (pp. 142–43, 131).

24. Omens, the coin (p. 28) and the broken mirror (p. 30); Miss Counihan's vulnerability, pp. 126–27; the old boy's seizures, p. 145; the old boy, who "never left his room," is given food by Miss Carridge "twice daily" (p. 69).

25. John o' God's is mentioned twice on p. 43; chapters nine and eleven are set at the M.M.M. It seems odd that the Magdalen Mental Mercyseat should have a three-word name; this may be why Beckett expanded it in the French translation, where it became La Maison Madeleine de Miséricorde Mentale, or M.M.M.M.

26. Narcissus, pp. 186 and 228; Belacqua, pp. 78 and 112. Beckett's Belacqua watches "the dayspring run through its zodiac" (p. 78), and "the dawn break crooked" (p. 112). Dante's Belacqua comments on the sun's position in *Purgatorio* 4:119–20.

27. Jacob and Esau, p. 23; Dives and Lazarus, p. 48; Ixion and Tantalus, p. 21. At times Beckett, emphasizing another form of duality, mentions members of these sets a second time. The word "tantalus" is used to describe a pub that tempts Cooper (p. 121), and the name Lazarus also occurs a second time (p. 180). It should be noted that while there are two references to the Lazarus mentioned in Luke 16 (as explained in an earlier note), the allusion on p. 180 is to a different Lazarus, the one who was raised from the dead, mentioned in John 11 and 12.

28. These are (p. 22) "The hireling fleeth because he is an hireling" (John 10:13), and "What shall a man give in exchange for Celia?" which is based on "What shall a man give in exchange for his soul?" (Matthew 16:26, Mark 8:37).

29. The quotations are on p. 239; "nature's soft nurse" is from *2 Henry IV*, III, i, 5; "knit up the sleave . . ." is from *Macbeth*, II, ii, 36: "Sleep that knits up the ravell'd sleave of care."

30. Page 235; the songs are "Sephestia's Song to her Child," by Robert Greene, and "What Thing is Love?" by George Peele.

31. The allusions to Job (p. 46) are "cursed . . . the day in which he was born . . ." (based on Job 3:3), and "why . . . is light given . . ." (Job 3:24).

32. The phrase occurs on pp. 4, 29, and 245; it is attributed to Neary on pp. 29 and 245. Its source is "The World We Live In," in *The Philosophy of William James* (New York: Modern Library, 1953), p. 76. The phrase did not really originate with James: he says it was first used by another, unnamed person. I am grateful to Professor Lawrence Graver for help in identifying the source of this quotation. In an interview Beckett referred to the world as "this buzzing confusion"; see Tom Driver, "Beckett by the Madeleine," *Columbia University Forum*, 4 (Summer, 1961):21.

33. "Apmonia" is repeated three times (pp. 3–4). There is a joke here: άρμονία (*harmonia*) is Greek but looks like an English word when it is written in capital letters. "APMONIA" appears as a page heading in a

The Development of Samuel Beckett's Fiction

book Beckett used for background material on the Pythagoreans: John Burnet's *Greek Philosophy*, pt. I (London: Macmillan, 1924), p. 45. This source was noted by Sighle Kennedy in *Murphy's Bed* (Lewisburg, Pa.: Bucknell University Press, 1971), p. 302n. The words Neary uses as synonyms for "Apmonia," "Isonomy" and "Attunement" (p. 4) are also mentioned by Burnet (p. 50). Neary's master's "figure of the three lives" (p. 90) refers to Pythagoras's division of humanity into levels represented by those who buy and sell at the Olympic games, those who compete, and those who observe (the highest level); see Burnet, p. 42. Other allusions to Pythagorean philosophy in *Murphy* are probably also based on material from Burnet's book, including the Hippasos story (p. 47; Burnet, pp. 55–56), the reference to the tetrakyt (p. 5; Burnet, p. 52), and the doctrine of the limit (p. 50; Burnet, p. 44).

34. Page 246. This idea is attributed to Leucippus and Democritus by Aristotle; see *Metaphysics* 985b. It is clear that Beckett has Democritus and not Leucippus in mind because he refers to "the guffaw of the Abderite," and Democritus is known as the laughing philosopher. In *More Pricks than Kicks* (1934; rpt., New York: Grove Press, 1970) Democritus is identified as the laughing philosopher (p. 162), and laughter is again associated with "the Abderite" in *The Unnamable* (New York: Grove Press, 1958), p. 170. "*Nothing is more real than nothing*" (the italics are Beckett's) appears in *Malone Dies* (1956; rpt., New York: Grove Press, 1970), p. 16.

35. Page 140. Descartes' description of his dream is lost, but its paraphrased version is given in Adrien Baillet's *Vie de Monsieur Des-Cartes*, 1 (Paris, 1691):81–85. Beckett is familiar with this work: see Lawrence Harvey, *Samuel Beckett, Poet and Critic* (Princeton, N.J.: Princeton University Press, 1970), pp. 8n, 20, *et passim*; John Fletcher, *Samuel Beckett's Art* (London: Chatto and Windus, 1967), pp. 126–27. For a discussion of Descartes' dream and its importance in the development of his philosophy, see Jacques Maritain, *The Dream of Descartes*, trans. Mabelle Andison (Port Washington, N.Y.: Kennikat Press, 1969).

36. Page 178. My translation is based on Beckett's, which is given on p. 179. According to Geulincx, because man enjoys true freedom only in the mental world, he would do best to abstain from desiring the things of the physical world; see Arnold Geulincx, *Metaphysica, Opera Philosophica*, 2 (1891–93; facsim. rpt., Stuttgart: Friedrich Frommann Verlag, 1965): 155. Beckett drops a word, *etiam*, when he quotes the passage; the original reads, "*Ubi nihil vales, ibi etiam nihil velis.*" The passage is italicized both in the original and in *Murphy*. For more material on the influence of Geulincx, see Samuel Mintz, "Beckett's *Murphy:* A 'Cartesian' Novel," *Perspective*, 11 (Autumn, 1959):156–65.

37. Page 58. Berkeley's doctrine of immaterialism is expounded in his *Principles of Human Knowledge* and *Three Dialogues*.

38. It is likely that Beckett used Burnet's *Greek Philosophy* here. Neary's comments about Hippasos (pp. 47–48) are very much like those

in Burnet's book (pp. 56–57). However, Burnet (like other commentators) says that Hippasos was drowned at sea, not in a puddle. The significance of this discrepancy will be discussed in the next chapter. That the Pythagoreans cared more for their doctrine than for the truth is again illustrated in another allusion, Neary's "unction of an *Ipse dixit*" (p. 102). According to Cicero, when they were assured that Pythagoras himself had said something ("Ipse dixit"), the Pythagoreans would accept a statement with no other proof; Cicero, *De Natura Deorum*, I, 10.

39. Aristotle, *De Anima*, 419a. The passage I have quoted is from the translation by J. A. Smith in *Introduction to Aristotle*, ed. Richard Mc-Keun (New York: Modern Library, 1947), pp. 190–91. Beckett uses the word "famous" in connection with the ant (p. 248) to indicate that the passage is based on an allusion, and (introducing another dual set) he does the same thing with a second allusion. The narrator's comment that Cooper "experienced none of the famous difficulty in serving two employers" (p. 197) is based on Matthew 6:24 and Luke 16:13.

40. Descartes describes the pineal gland as the locus of the mind-body interaction in *Les Passions de l'Ame*, première partie, article XXXI. He refers to the pineal gland as the *conarium* in letters to Mersenne dated Apr. 1, July 30, and Dec. 24, 1640, and Apr. 21, 1641; see also Kenner, pp. 60–61. The idea of the conarium shrinking to nothing may also refer to the shrinking skin in Balzac's *La Peau de Chagrin*.

41. *Philautia*, which occurs only rarely in Latin (it is listed in few Latin dictionaries), is derived from the Greek word φίλαυτος (self-loving, selfish). The Latin form does appear in Robert Estienne's *Thesaurus Linguae Latinae* (Basil: Thurnisiorum Fratr., 1741), where it is defined as "Amor sui ipsius."

42. At the very beginning of the *Ethica*, Geulincx defines ethics as a study of virtue, and says a number of times that virtue is the love of reason; *Opera Philosophica*, 3:9, 12, 14, 15, *et passim*. According to Geulincx, "*Philautia* is love of oneself; such love is distant from virtue based on reason; indeed, it leads to sin" (3:13). Philautia is "*amor sui*," love of oneself; humility is "*contemptio sui*," disdain for oneself (3:28).

43. Tar-water is an infusion of tar and water. Berkeley's *A Chain of Reflexions and Inquiries Concerning the Virtues of Tar-Water* appeared in 1744.

44. Beckett once told Harold Hobson, "I am interested in the shape of ideas even if I do not believe in them.... It is the shape that matters"; see Harold Hobson, "Samuel Beckett, Dramatist of the Year," *International Theatre Annual*, no. 1 (London: John Calder, 1956), p. 153.

45. Page 280. John Couch Adams (1819–92), studying irregularities in the motion of the planet Uranus, concluded that they were caused by an undiscovered planet. He is one of two astronomers who predicted its position (Leverrier is the other one); in 1846 it was observed and named Neptune.

46. "Moon . . . serpent," repeated on pp. 93, 182, 183; "great magical

ability," repeated on pp. 39, 80, 157, 183; "moon . . . coincidence," repeated on p. 121. Both statements about the moon are unreliable; this will be discussed in the next chapter.

47. Page 6. The common definition of "precordial" (situated on or occurring near the heart) does not explain Beckett's joke. In Latin *praecordia* means stomach or midriff; by mentioning Miss Counihan in conjunction with a lower anatomical area, Murphy is suggesting that he values her more as a bedmate than as a soulmate. This definition is enforced on p. 216, where Wylie covers his "praecordia." There is a similar joke in the French version of *Murphy*.

48. Pages 90, 246. According to Berkeley, "Existence is percipi or percipere . . ."; it is impossible, he says, that "any thing besides that *wch* thinks & is thought on should exist"; *Philosophical Commentaries*, ed. A. A. Luce (London: Thomas Nelson and Sons, 1944), pp. 139, 140. Beckett referred to *percipi* and *percipere* in *Dream of Fair to Middling Women* (TS, Dartmouth College Library, p. 142), and used "Esse est percipi" as the epigraph of *Film*.

49. Spermarium etc., p. 78; vagitus etc., p. 71; the etymological links between gas and chaos are mentioned on p. 175; air and illuminating gas sustain life, but chaos is associated with death (pp. 175, 253); dozing etc., p. 281; Sleep etc., p. 207. Sleep and Death are brothers in Hesiod (*Theogeny*, 212) and in Homer (*Iliad*, 16:671ff.). Beckett refers to Neary's "smattering of Greek urns, where Sleep was figured with crossed feet, and frequently also Sleep's young brother . . ." (p. 207). This is an allusion either to G. E. Lessing's essay "Wie Die Alten den Tod Gebildet" ("How the Ancients Represented Death") or to Lessing's "Laokoon." In "Laokoon" Lessing mentions in a note that in antiquity Death and Sleep were represented as twin brothers, often with their feet crossed; see G. E. Lessing, *Werke* (Munich: Winkler-Verlag, [1969]), 2:74–75 ("Laokoon," Ch. 11, n. 1). In "How the Ancients Represented Death" this point is discussed extensively, and line drawings of the allegorical figures are included; see *Werke*, 2:167ff.

50. Pages 80–81. Murphy refers to the group as the "Külpe school"; it is also known as the Würzburg school. This movement was a forerunner of Gestalt psychology. As was explained in an earlier note, Murphy seems familiar with the figure-ground concept, which is important in Gestalt psychology, and with the work of Wolfgang Köhler, a founder of the Gestalt movement. Beckett's many references to closed systems may be based on an allusion to a work by a member of the Würzburg school, Henry J. Watt's *Psychology* (1913; rpt., London: T. C. and E. C. Jack, n.d.). In the foreword to this book Watt argues that "experience is at least a part of a closed system—analogous to that of chemistry" (*Psychology*, p. iii). Watt is mentioned on p. 81 of *Murphy*, and there are references to closed systems on pp. 57, 102, 109, 117, 182–83, and 200. It is also possible that Beckett is familiar with Watt's *The Sensory Basis and Structure of Knowledge* (London: Methuen, 1925). Here Watt admits that psycholo-

gists have yet to provide a satisfactory solution for the mind-body problem (p. 159), and disagrees with Berkeley and Kant when they argue that the outer world is a construct of the mind (pp. 234–35). Watt sees mind as a "vast sphere of activities that is surrounded on all sides by the rest of the universe, acting and reacting upon its parts" (p. 231). Beckett may be parodying this idea in the following passage: "Murphy's mind pictured itself as a large hollow sphere, hermetically closed to the universe without" (p. 107).

51. In *Proust* Beckett refers to "the wisdom of all the sages, from Brahma to Leopardi, the wisdom that consists not in the satisfaction but in the ablation of desire . . ." (p. 7). On the next page Beckett mentions Schopenhauer and discusses his idea that the world is a projection of the individual's will. My summary of Schopenhauer's ideas is based on the following passages in *The World as Will and Idea*, trans. R. B. Haldane and J. Kemp (1883; rpt., London: Routledge and Kegan Paul, 1957), vol. 1: on assertion and denial of will, pp. 349ff.; connections between will and the body, pp. 130–41, esp. p. 132; refutations of Descartes and Spinoza, pp. 377, 385; will as the basis of character, p. 377; difficulty of redirecting the will, pp. 379–80; aesthetic contemplation, pp. 253 *et passim*. Neary's cycle of perpetual yearning may be based on Schopenhauer's comments about the cycle of yearning (*The World*, 1:253–54).

52. The forgetting of the self is a part of the process of aesthetic contemplation that leads to abnegation of the will and freedom from desire; see *The World*, 1:257.

53. That is, Descartes' skeptical method is never used to examine the phenomenological and epistemological questions raised by the *cogito* in *Meditations on First Philosophy* (see Meditation II).

54. *Murphy*, p. 107; a loose translation of the passage is given on p. 179: "the intellectual love in which he alone could love himself. . . ." My translation is based on this one. Spinoza's original reads, "Mentis amor intellectualis erga Deum est ipse Dei amor, quo Deus se impsum amat . . ." ("The intellectual love of the mind toward God is the very love with which God loves himself"); *Ethices*, V, prop. 36, and see also prop. 35.

55. *The World*, 1:238–59; the passage about genius and madness is on p. 246. There can be little question that Beckett is familiar with this idea. Schopenhauer writes, "Poetical inspiration has been called a kind of madness: *amabilis insania*, Horace calls it (Od. iii 4), and Wieland in the introduction to 'Oberon' speaks of it as 'amiable madness' " (*The World*, 1:246). The end of this passage, in the original, reads, "*ambilis insania* nennt sie Horaz (Od. iii 4) und 'holder Wahnsinn' Wieland im Eingang zum 'Oberon' "; Arthur Schopenhauer, *Sämtliche Werke* (Wiesbaden: F. A. Brockhaus, 1961), 2:224 (*Die Welt als Wille und Vorstellung*, Book II, par. 36). In *Proust* Beckett alludes to this passage without referring to its source. "The Proustian stasis is contemplative," he writes, "a pure act of understanding, will-less, the 'amabilis insania' and the 'holder Wahnsinn' " (p. 70).

9

Duality and Duplicity: Unreliable Narrative in *Murphy*

In some of Beckett's early works the narrator's commentary is occasionally untrustworthy; in *Murphy* the unreliable narrative becomes an important structural device. Many of the narrator's seemingly plausible statements are in some way misleading or inconsistent. For example, he twice says that Murphy is "a strict non-reader," but he also reveals that Murphy is familiar with works by Fletcher, Swift, Wordsworth, Dante, Campanella, and Bishop Bouvier, among others.[1] A possible way of resolving this problem is given in a passage where the narrator describes how Murphy was forced to sell some of his possessions: "He thought of the rocking-chair left behind in Brewery Road, that aid to life in his mind from which he had never before been parted. His books, his pictures, his postcards, his musical scores and instruments, all had been gradually disposed of in that order rather than the chair" (p. 189). It may be, then, that Murphy gave up reading when he was forced to sell his books, but calling him a strict nonreader is nevertheless somewhat misleading. Moreover, if this explanation resolves one contradiction, it introduces another. Earlier the narrator had assured the reader that Murphy's rocking chair "never left him"; here the narrator includes a reminder that it had been "left behind in Brewery Road."[2]

Another problem involving the rocking chair arises in the opening pages of the novel. The narrator says that Murphy uses seven scarves to bind himself to the chair and then, enumerating them, mentions only six (p. 2). According to some critics (A. Alvarez, for example), this is an inadvertent error.[3] But Beckett is careful about small details. If the error had been an oversight, it would probably have been eliminated when Beckett translated his novel into French. However, the inconsistent enumeration of scarves, the assurances that Murphy is a nonreader, and other misleading statements are retained in the French version. Moreover, Beckett's other novels have inconsistencies of this sort; John Mood has discovered twenty-eight of them in a single work, *Watt*.[4]

One of the ways Beckett uses unreliable material is illustrated in an exchange between Bim Clinch, the head male nurse at the Magdalen Mental Mercyseat, and Ticklepenny. Bim hires Ticklepenny as an attendant and promises him a salary of five pounds per month. After ten days among the lunatics Ticklepenny has had enough; he persuades Murphy to take over his job, and asks Bim to pay him for the time he has worked. Bim, who has "a fancy for Ticklepenny not far short of love," agrees to this arrangement (pp. 156–57). But he adds a stipulation: "you will get your one-six-eight," he says, "as soon as your Murphy has given a month's satisfaction and no sooner."[5] Ticklepenny accepts this offer without realizing that after working ten days he is owed a third of five pounds, or one-thirteen-four (one-six-eight is a third of four pounds). The exact value of Bim's fancy not far short of love may be difficult to compute, but it is clearly less than six shillings eightpence.

There is another bit of legerdemain in this episode. When Ticklepenny offers Murphy the job, he says nothing about his relationship with Bim. Yet Murphy predicts that he will not be hired if Ticklepenny is involved in "a liaison with some high official, the head male nurse for example."[6] How does Murphy manage to guess the truth so accurately? Either he has become uncharacteristically perceptive or—more likely—the narrator is sharing a joke with the reader. For, despite the premonition about the head male nurse, Murphy (who thinks that the liaison will hurt his chances for employment) still has managed to get things backward.

Many of the inconsistencies in the novel become apparent when one compares related details in widely separated passages. One example involves two appearances of the word "whinge" (to whine or whimper). According to the narrator, "All the puppets in this book whinge sooner or later, except Murphy, who is not a puppet" (p. 122). This suggests—or seems to—that whatever forms of expression will be elicited from Murphy, the whinge is not among them. But some pages earlier the narrator had described how Murphy "threw his voice into an infant's whinge" (p. 37). Nor can the narrator's statement be taken to mean that all the minor characters in the book whinge and are puppet-like, but that Murphy (who also whinges) is not puppet-like. There are other characters, notably Mr. Endon, who never whinge.[7]

Murphy's horoscope introduces a number of other inconsistencies. Some of Suk's predictions, like those about fits and quadrupeds, are accurate; many others are not.[8] Suk indicates that Murphy possesses "great Magical Ability of the Eye, to which the lunatic would easy succumb" (p. 32). When Celia threatens to leave unless he looks for work, Murphy fixes his gaze on her "with great magical ability"; the only result is that he is forced to seek employment (p. 39). Later on the narrator notes that the M.M.M. is ideally suited for Murphy to take advantage of the "great magical ability of the eye to which the lunatic would easy succumb" (p. 183). Attempting to achieve rapport with Mr. Endon, he stares into his eyes; again, Murphy is the one who is defeated.[9] Murphy loves to talk, but Suk claims that silence is one of his highest attributes. Like the narrator, Suk has his playful moments: shortly after praising Murphy's silence he says, "Avoid exhaustion by speech" (p. 32). Celia twice quotes this admonition back to Murphy after he engages in long-winded monologues.[10]

According to the narrator, Suk was told the day and year of Murphy's birth but not the time (p. 23). Yet the opening words of the horoscope are, "At time of Birth of this Native four degrees of the GOAT was rising . . ." (p. 32). Suk could not have given the position of a zodiacal constellation this accurately without knowing the time of birth to within a few minutes. [11] Again, a repeated word is used to call attention to the inconsistency. The narrator says that Suk would be able to prepare Murphy's horoscope without being told "the precise moment of vagitus" (birth cry); later the word "vagitus" appears twice in a passage about Murphy's birth (pp. 23, 71). The narrator seems to know when Murphy was born—he describes what occurred in the delivery room—but this knowledge is never shared with the reader. Hence it is impossible to determine whether some of the details in the horoscope are reliable.

There is a way, however, of estimating roughly when Murphy was born, and this points to another inconsistency. The action of the novel takes place in 1935, and Murphy is called young (twice) and a young man (twice on the same page).[12] Assuming that Murphy is at least sixteen but no more than fifty (to take the extreme cases), the year of his birth is between 1885 and 1919. Suk says that when Murphy was born, Neptune was in Taurus and Uranus was in Aquarius.[13] Neptune was in Taurus from 1874 until 1889; Uranus was in Aquarius from 1912 to 1920. Hence one of Suk's statements could be true if Murphy were forty-six or over; the other one, if he were twenty-three or under; but both of the statements cannot be true. In fact there is no time in the nineteenth or twentieth centuries when Neptune and Uranus are in the designated positions simultaneously.[14]

With characteristic evenhandedness, Beckett makes certain that the astronomy in *Murphy* is as unreliable as the astrology. If the comment about the moon promoting magical ability is misleading, so is the statement that is its counterpart, "The moon, by a striking coincidence full and at perigee, was 29,000 miles nearer the earth than it had been for four years" (p. 26). On the night in question (September 11, 1935—the date can be calculated from details given in the novel) the moon was in fact full.[15] Perigee, however, was not reached until the next evening; since the moon is full and at perigee about once a year, the coincidence is not so very striking.[16] On September 12 the moon was well over 29,000 miles nearer to the earth than it had been only thirteen days earlier, when it was at apogee. Nor was it closer to the earth than it had been for four years: when it was at perigee on April 20, 1932, the lunar distance was less by ten miles. Indeed, unless someone tampers with its orbit, the moon never can be "29,000 miles nearer the earth than it had been for four years"; the difference between the average and minimum perigee distances is less than 5,000 miles.[17] It is remarkable how much error the narrator has packed into a single sentence; yet his information is so plausible, his tone so self-assured, that it seems almost rude to check on the data.

Another error in astronomy is introduced when the narrator explains why Murphy can see no stars from the window of his garret: "when it was not too cold to open the skylight in the garret, the stars seemed always veiled by cloud or fog or mist. The sad truth was that the skylight commanded only that most dismal patch of night sky, the galactic coal-sack, which would naturally look like a dirty night to any observer in Murphy's condition, cold, tired, angry, impatient and out of conceit with a system that seemed the superfluous cartoon of his own" (pp. 188–89). But if Murphy had wanted to see more than the coal sack, he only needed to wait a bit and the area framed by the skylight would have changed: this is one of the many salutory effects of the earth's diurnal motion. Moreover, if the coal sack seems dark in contrast to nearby regions of the Milky Way, it can hardly be called dismal, and it does contain visible stars.[18] A more likely explanation for Murphy's inability to see the stars is given at the end of the quoted passage: he is "out of conceit" with the celestial system.

According to the narrator, Murphy starts out believing in two systems: that of the heavenly bodies (astrology), and that of his own mental processes (pp. 22–23, 75–76). But the narrator notes "a certain disharmony between the only two canons in which Murphy can feel the least confidence."[19] Murphy begins to think of his own system as the superior one: "The more his own system closed round him, the less he could tolerate its being subordinated to any other" (pp. 182–83). He becomes more and more convinced that his mind is "a closed system, subject to no principle of change but its own . . ." (p. 109). The stars he had believed in as an influence on his life become the "stars he commanded" and "his stars"; finally Murphy thinks of astrology as "a system that seemed the superfluous cartoon of his own."[20]

Ironically, Murphy's repudiation of astrology is predicted in the epigraph of his horoscope, which is a passage taken from Shakespeare's *Romeo and Juliet: "Then I defy you, Stars."*[21] Murphy, like Romeo, can defy the stars, but neither hero can escape his destiny, which is to die a short time afterward. There is another quotation from *Romeo and Juliet*—again about stars—in *Murphy:* "Take him and cut him out in little stars . . ." (p. 86). This passage is from a speech of Juliet's in which the imminent death of Romeo is foreshadowed:

> Come, gentle night, come, loving, black-brow'd night,
> Give me my Romeo; and, when he shall die,
> Take him and cut him out in little stars,
> And he will make the face of heaven so fine
> That all the world will be in love with night. . . .[22]

The remains of Romeo will be transformed into stars: this idea nicely offsets Murphy's notion that the astral system can be subsumed into his own.

Murphy's separation from the outside world is symbolized by his diminishing ability to see the stars. A related theme occurs in two works that are important influences on *Murphy: The Divine Comedy* and *The World as Will and Idea.* In *The Divine Comedy* Dante loses sight of the stars when he descends into the underworld. Only when he emerges does he see them again; this is described in the last verse of the *Inferno.*[23] There is also a reference to the stars in the last sentence of *The World as Will and Idea.* Describing the insubstantiality of the physical world, Schopenhauer says, "to those in whom the will has turned and has denied itself, this our world, which is so real, with all its suns and milky ways—is nothing."[24] The universe that we believe exists outside ourselves is actually projected from within. In *Proust* Beckett refers to this idea: the outer world is "a projection of the individual's consciousness (an objectivation of the individual's will, Schopenhauer would say). . . ."[25] A similar concept is introduced when Murphy decides that his own system has taken precedence over the celestial system: "They were *his* stars, he was the prior system. He had been projected, larval and dark, on the sky of that regrettable hour as on a screen, magnified and clarified into his own meaning. But it was *his* meaning."[26]

The struggle for priority between the two systems leads to a new way of understanding the errors and inconsistencies in the novel. If Murphy's is the prior system, there is no need for the narrator's descriptions of celestial phenomena to be in accord with those of the almanac. Indeed, strict conformity to astronomical data would suggest that the system of the novel is subordinate to the system of the outer world. The narrator, however, indicates that the world of the novel is a closed system, and one with priority over other systems.

A related idea emerges in still another passage about the moon. According to the almanac, the moon was visible before dawn on October 21, 1935, and it set long after sunrise.[27] But the narrator, using a balanced sentence, disagrees: "An hour previously the moon had been obliged to set, and the sun could not rise for an hour to come" (pp. 250–51). Symmetry is the controlling factor here, and not the almanac. Once Murphy has repudiated the outer system, the narrator no longer feels compelled to follow it. He himself is perhaps the one who "obliged" the moon to set. Soon after this passage he describes the "starless" and "abandoned" sky; presumably it is starless because Murphy has abandoned it.

Other events in the novel do conform to the laws of the external world, but this is part of the narrator's strategy for credible mendacity. Most of the time, fallacious material is introduced sparingly and is surrounded by easily verified facts. To gain the reader's confidence, the narrator even calls attention to possible errors: "The next day," he says at one point, "was Saturday (if our reckoning is correct) . . ." (p. 149). As might be expected, in this instance the date has been calculated accurately.

When Ticklepenny claims that he once saw Murphy drunk, the narrator finds it necessary to set the record straight: "Now the sad truth was that Murphy never touched it" (p. 86). This, so far as one can tell, is in fact "the sad truth." But this phrase later resurfaces in a less reliable context: "The sad truth was that the skylight commanded only that most dismal patch of night sky, the galactic coal-sack . . ." (p. 188).

One factor that makes the errors hard to discover is that many of them are based on obscure facts. Not too many readers will know that Hippasos was drowned at sea and not (as Neary claims) in a puddle.[28] Another subtle error is introduced in a passage about "Barbara, Baccardi . . . Baroko . . . Bramantip" (p. 16). These are medieval mnemonic terms that represent different types of syllogisms—all of them, that is, except for Baccardi, which has been substituted for a legitimate term, Bocardo.[29] The device resembles an intelligence-test problem where one must discover the item that does not belong in a series. Baccardi also appears in the French version of *Murphy*.[30] Beckett wittily uses the spurious term to allude to a beverage that might provide some respite from the rigors of medieval logic.

A similar sense of playfulness emerges in other unreliable passages where author and reader are involved in a battle of wits. The chess game hints at this idea: Murphy, naturally enough, takes it for granted that the game will be played in the conventional way, but Mr. Endon has introduced new rules. Beckett's readers will probably also begin by assuming that the conventional rules of novel-writing are being followed. Discovering that the rules have changed is part of the challenge, but it would be unsporting to introduce the new rules without any warning. Hence Beckett includes errors that are relatively easy to detect, like the faulty enumeration of scarves; these make it easier for readers to discover other unreliable passages.

Many of the recurring passages are similarly used to hint at the pattern of unreliability. The narrator reveals that he has been taking liberties with the dialogue by saying three times that a character's remarks have been "expurgated, accelerated, improved and reduced" (pp. 12, 48, 119). Cleverly, Beckett reveals that the dialogue has not been transcribed verbatim by repeating the disclosure verbatim.

Repetition is often used to underscore ironical passages. Neary's letters to Wylie and Miss Counihan both begin with the same sentence: "I can never forget your loyalty" (p. 199). Neary means, of course, that he will long remember their treachery. The narrator refers four times in as many pages to Murphy's success in achieving rapport with the mental patients (pp. 180–83). This ironically foreshadows Murphy's failure with the only patient he really cares for, Mr. Endon.

Utilizing a technique he introduced in *More Pricks than Kicks*, Beckett calls attention to unreliable statements by repeating them. The following are among the misleading ideas that are reiterated:

That Murphy is a strict nonreader (pp. 162, 234).

That silence is one of Murphy's highest attributes (pp. 32, 39, 164).

That Murphy possesses great magical ability of the eye (pp. 32, 39, 157, 183).

> That it is a striking coincidence for the moon to be full and at perigee (pp. 26, 121).

Beckett's method involves using a formal device, repetition, to counter the errors in the subject matter. In this way, even when the content flirts with the truth, the style remains faithful to it.

In some instances a series of repeated passages is used to offset a misleading idea. It may seem, for example, that Miss Carridge's most offensive quality is her overwhelming body odor; actually, she is even more odious than malodorous. She agrees to cheat Murphy's uncle while mouthing pieties about "the principle of the thing, the principle of the thing" (p. 147). The narrator calls attention to her eavesdropping by repeating that it is facilitated by darkness rich "in acoustic properties" (pp. 155, 233). Whenever Miss Carridge brings Celia tea, the narrator points out that this uncharacteristic generosity comes only on days when her other transactions have been profitable (pp. 67–68, 132, 143). Twice the narrator says that only cupidity can fire Miss Carridge's feeble imagination, and twice that her charity knew no bounds but alms (pp. 144, 148, 143, 154).

Miss Carridge crosses the line between casual frugality and dedicated avarice when she discovers that the old boy has cut his throat. Her first impulse is to call a doctor but, inspired by mercenary logic, she summons the police instead (whoever calls the doctor foots the bill).[31] In describing the ensuing events the narrator repeats the word "arrived" to call attention to the delay caused by Miss Carridge's maneuver: "The police arrived and sent for a doctor. The doctor arrived and sent for an ambulance. The ambulance arrived and the old boy was . . . put into it. This proved that he still lived . . ." (pp. 135–36). The old boy dies on the way to the hospital and the narrator—imitating Miss Carridge's habit of repeating phrases for emphasis—says, "Miss Carridge was not a penny out of pocket, not one penny."[32] Unconcerned about whether the old boy could have been saved, the narrator cynically praises Miss Carridge for having "carried off the whole affair in splendid style" (p. 136).

When she is faced with the problem of renting the old boy's room, Miss Carridge lets it be known that he suffered a seizure while shaving and accidentally cut his throat. She reasons that accidental death, more acceptable socially than suicide, will be less of a liability in the housing market. When she describes the accident, the narrator—self-righteously indignant at her perversions of the truth—repeatedly contradicts her: "A lie. . . . A lie. . . . Lies. . . . All lies" (pp. 144–45). The coroner is equally skeptical and rules that the old boy's death was a suicide.

This incident, seemingly no more than a digression, contains a number of recurring details that link it to a more important episode. When Murphy dies there is another inquest, and again an unnamed coroner must determine the cause of death. The second coroner thinks he can easily explain how Murphy died: "My function perhaps it is part of my duty to inform you is to determine, one, who is dead, and two, how. With regard to the latter matter, the latter matter, happily it need not detain us . . ." (p. 261). Here again form and content are ingeniously juxtaposed to suggest contradictory ideas: when the coroner repeats "the latter matter," the issue he considers unimportant is emphasized. Moreover, he does the same thing twice again. After discussing whether Murphy's death was caused by burns or shock, he says, "So much for the *modus morendi*, the *modus morendi*."[33] Later, insisting that the death was accidental, he refers to "the matter of the manner of death. The matter of the manner of death" (p. 263). Each of the reiterated passages contains a rhyme or an alliterative phrase: these underscore the redundancy and hint at an obsessive quality in the coroner's assurances. If he is so certain that the matter has been settled, why does he keep harping on it?

The coroner seems to have questions about the cause of death, but he also has reasons for avoiding them. The inquest has come at a most inopportune time; if Murphy had done the decent thing—expired in a different county—the coroner would now have been on the links. Golf is the coroner's joy, his passion. Admitting that Murphy's death was not accidental would raise the possibility of suicide and prolong an inquiry he is desperately eager to conclude.

Dr. Killiecrankie agrees with the coroner's verdict, and he also has an ulterior motive. One of his greatest concerns, as resident physician at the M.M.M., is to prevent suicides among the patients; this is emphasized in a reiterated passage.[34] Dealing with the gossip about an attendant who took his life would be unpleasant: like Miss Carridge, Dr. Killiecrankie is afraid that the news of a suicide might threaten the economic well-being of his establishment.

Despite the efforts made to suppress them, questions about whether Murphy took his life finally emerge when Murphy's will is read (this is why Killiecrankie holds on to it until the coroner has given his verdict). The will, in the form of a letter to Celia, contains instructions for the cremation of "these my body, mind and soul" (p. 269). If Murphy had written the will shortly before his death, it could be taken as evidence that he had intended to commit suicide. But as luck would have it, the will is charred in the very corner where one might expect to find a date. Even so, Neary seems skeptical about the verdict of accidental death, and Wylie hints that Murphy's last wish must have been to take his own life (pp. 262–63, 270).

There are, however, questions about the will's authenticity. It contains no instructions for the disposal of Murphy's posses-sions—his clothing, his suitcase, and his rocking chair. The will is unsigned. The narrator twice repeats an excerpt from it about the "body, mind and soul" (pp. 271, 275). This serves as a re-minder that if Murphy often referred to his mind and his body, he never spoke about his soul in conjunction with them. Moreover, the will specifies that Murphy's body, mind, and soul are to be "burnt and placed in a paper bag," implying that all three are equally vulnerable to being reduced by cremation. Such an idea reflects a materialistic point of view inconsistent with Murphy's dualistic philosophy.

The will is found in an envelope with "the name Mrs. Murphy and the address in Brewery Road, pencilled in laborious capitals" (p. 258). Murphy was not married to Celia, never referred to Celia as Mrs. Murphy, and never before had any problems with his handwriting. Would Murphy, who was so obsessed with mental reality, have left a will entirely given over to instructions for the disposal of his body? Is the text of the will written in the same laborious capitals as those on the envelope? Such questions are never raised.

Celia could comment on the authenticity of the handwriting; she has received letters (two, as it happens) from Murphy. With-out calling the will a forgery she reveals what she thinks of it when she starts to tear it in two. She checks herself, however, when she realizes that other people are watching her. The narrator says that when Celia was given the will, she "grasped it to tear it across"; the same phrase is used in an earlier chapter when Murphy, about to rip up his horoscope, stops when he realizes that others are watching him (pp. 269, 93). The parallel incidents raise another question. According to the narrator, Murphy always kept his horoscope with him (pp. 74–75). If he did not destroy it, he must have had it with him when he died. Dr. Killiecrankie, however, claims that aside from the will, no papers were found with Murphy's body (p. 258). It seems unlikely that the will would have survived after an explosion that left Murphy's body completely charred and no trace of the horoscope.

Some of the anomalies in an earlier episode now become relevant. Miss Carridge's story about the old boy's accidental death is patently implausible; yet the narrator says (and repeats) that she can be very imaginative when inspired by cupidity. It is possible that Miss Carridge's story is in fact extremely clever: she may have wanted it to provoke skepticism. The coroner, distracted by its improbability, dismisses it. The narrator (who is hardly someone to be throwing stones) keeps repeating that she is lying. But the point of Miss Carridge's story may have been to divert questions about her own culpability in the affair. The coroner never realizes that she called the police while the old boy was still alive, the question of criminal negligence is never raised, and Miss Carridge is never punished or even reprimanded. This, as her name suggests, is a miscarriage of justice.

At the second inquest similar alternatives, suicide and accidental death, are the only ones ever considered; again, questions about another person's culpability are never raised. Yet there is reason to think that Murphy might have been the victim of foul play. The coroner seems to understand this intuitively, and almost says "accused" when he asks about "the identity of the ac—the deceased."[35] The coroner's verdict is based on the theory that gas had accumulated in Murphy's garret before he arrived home, and had exploded when he lit a match upon entering.[36] But the narrator gives a different description of the relevant events. He says that Murphy returned, lit his candle, "and tied himself up in the chair, dimly intending to have a short rock and then, if he felt any better, to dress and go . . . back to Brewery Road, to

Celia . . ." (p. 252). Murphy's last wish, according to the narrator, was not to commit suicide but to return to Celia.

The coroner takes it for granted that it was Murphy who opened the gas tap, but the narrator makes it clear that a tap in the bathroom was turned on after Murphy had tied himself to his chair (p. 253). Who then did turn on the gas? One possibility is that it was someone fumbling in the dark for the toilet valve, but on two other occasions the tap is manipulated by an unnamed person just after Murphy returns to his room. When Ticklepenny installs Murphy's radiator, he cannot get it to work; then Murphy arrives and asks him whether the gas tap is open. Ticklepenny assures him that it is: he opened it only minutes before. Murphy, however, insists that he go downstairs to check. When Tickle-penny gets to the bathroom, he is amazed to find the tap closed. "Well that beats all," he says. "Well that beats everything. . . . Well that beats the band" (pp. 173–74). The narrator, echoing the reiterated phrase, then explains: "What beat all was how the tap, which he really had turned on, came to be turned off" (p. 174). A few days later Murphy, returning to the garret, looks to see if there is anyone in the bathroom. After assuring himself that it is empty, he goes upstairs. Soon afterward the gas is again mysteriously turned on: "It was night when he reached the garret with the chair, having satisfied himself on the way up that no one was about, least of all in the w.c. Almost at once gas, reminding him that he had forgotten to turn it on, began to pour through the radiator" (pp. 190–91). Murphy never inquires into this strange occurrence; grateful that he has been saved a trip downstairs, he lights his radiator.

Murphy remains unperturbed about these incidents, but Tick-lepenny, who feels that Murphy is in some sort of danger, gives him three similarly phrased warnings: "You want to watch yourself. . . . You want to mind your health. . . . You want to take a pull on yourself."[37] A third term is added to mind and body in the will; three mysterious events involve the gas tap; Ticklepenny gives Murphy three warnings. Just as duality is associated with symmetry, the number three is associated with chaos—especially the kind of chaos that accompanies exploding gas.

Ticklepenny's warnings suggest that Murphy might have been murdered, but who could have killed him? There is no lack of suspects. With Murphy dead, Wylie can marry Miss Counihan; Neary can pursue Celia; Bim's fancy for Ticklepenny can flourish; Cooper's nemesis is destroyed; and the staff of the M.M.M. will no longer be scandalized by the presence of a humane attendant. Among the suspects are some who protest that they are Murphy's friends—his very dear friends. But this phrase is repeated so often that its irony becomes obvious.[38] As Celia says, Murphy has no friends (p. 8).

Ticklepenny's warnings make it seem that Bim may indeed have been jealous of Murphy. But if Bim did kill Murphy, it is unlikely that he could have forged the will: its author is familiar with Lord Chesterfield's letters and has visited the Abbey Theatre in Dublin.[39] This may disqualify Bim but Ticklepenny, formerly a poet and recently a resident of Dublin, could have been enlisted as an accomplice. According to the narrator, Ticklepenny is the "merest pawn in the game between Murphy and his stars, he makes his little move, engages an issue and is swept from the board" (p. 85). But Ticklepenny is still on the board after Murphy has been removed, and it may be that his "little move" involves a little forgery.

Wylie and Neary also have their reasons for wanting Murphy out of the way. Either one might have paid Cooper, a "ruthless tout," to do the dirty work (p. 54). Cooper thinks of Murphy as "his quarry, therefore his enemy" (p. 121). Wylie seems to understand the mechanism behind Cooper's strange compulsions and assures him, "in a short time you will be sitting down and taking off your hat and doing all the things that are impossible at present" (pp. 123–24). Cooper remembers what Wylie tells him: this is the comment he later repeats verbatim (p. 198). Possibly, then, Wylie also indicated that Cooper would be liberated from his compulsive behavior after Murphy's death. Wylie and Neary are both Irish, both well read; hence either one could have forged the will. The Brewery Road address written in laborious capitals on the envelope may have been Cooper's finishing touch—the narrator pointedly notes that Cooper had memorized this address.[40] Still another detail implicates Wylie: Murphy is often compared to Christ, and Wylie in one passage is called a Judas.[41]

Yet Wylie, Neary, and Cooper all have alibis. The narrator lists them among the lodgers who did not leave Miss Carridge's rooming house for "two days and three nights," a period covering the time of Murphy's death.[42] But there is (as usual) a loophole in the narrator's statement: the time of Cooper's arrival at the rooming house is never specified. He could have turned on the gas at the M.M.M. and then joined the others at Miss Carridge's on the first of the three nights.[43]

These hypotheses are all rather inconclusive. There may have been a conspiracy involving some, or all, of the suspects. It is possible that the narrator's description of Murphy's last hours is no more reliable than some of his other assertions. Murphy, yielding to a suicidal impulse, may have made no effort to save himself when the gas was turned on. It is unlikely but not inconceivable that the coroner was right, and that the death was an accident. The gas could have been turned on by mistake; Murphy might not have noticed it go on; or he might not have been able to untie himself quickly enough to escape. According to the maxim known as Murphy's Law, everything that can go wrong eventually does.

It is hardly necessary to try to answer every question about Murphy's death. In "Assumption" Beckett argues that mystery is essential in art. In *Dream of Fair to Middling Women* he mocks the idea that it is necessary to resolve the action. In "A Case in a Thousand" he refuses to include a denouement. Here the mysterious death leads to questions about other problematical elements in the novel. An important function of the mystery is to indicate that the novel cannot be understood after only a single reading. Once this idea emerges, questions about murder or accidental death become superfluous: if readers keep returning to the novel, Murphy's immortality is assured.

Notes

1. *Murphy* (1938; rpt., New York: Grove Press, 1957); subsequent references will be to this edition. "A strict non-reader," pp. 162, 234. This discrepancy has been noted by Ruby Cohn; see *Back to Beckett* (Princeton, N.J.: Princeton University Press, 1973), p. 33. References to Fletcher, p. 49; Swift ("Lilliputian wine" etc.), p. 139; Wordsworth, p. 100; Dante ("Antepurgatory" etc.), pp. 77–78; Campanella, p. 17; Bishop Bouvier, p. 72. According to Hannah Copeland, Bouvier's book is an example of the "imaginary works" in *Murphy*; see *Art and Artist in the Works of*

Samuel Beckett (The Hague: Mouton, 1975), p. 63. In fact Jean-Baptiste Bouvier's *Dissertatio in sextum Decalogi praeceptum, et Supplementum ad Tractatus de Matrimonio* was published in Le Mans in 1827, and went through a number of editions.

2. On p. 1 the narrator says of the chair, "it never left him"; on p. 189 he refers to the chair as "that aid to life in his mind from which [Murphy] had never before been parted." Even so, the original statement is misleading.

3. A. Alvarez calls the passage about the scarves one of the two places he knows of in Beckett's works "where his arithmetic lets him down"; *Samuel Beckett* (New York: Viking Press, 1973), p. 9.

4. John Mood, " 'The Personal System'—Samuel Beckett's *Watt*," *PMLA*, 86 (Mar., 1971):255–65. Mood writes, "The mistakes were certainly planned. If there had been one or two, we could write it off as someone's error. Twenty-eight mistakes clearly indicate a deliberate strategy at work, particularly when linked to the many other mistakes pointed out by the text itself" (p. 263).

5. Ticklepenny says he was promised five pounds a month on p. 89; he is offered one-six-eight on p. 157. The irony in the phrase "a fancy not far short of love" emerges when it is repeated (pp. 156, 157). In the French version of *Murphy* references to currency are usually converted from sterling to francs (e.g., Murphy's fourpenny lunch); here, however, the currency remains unchanged and the passage is translated with the same figure as in the English version. Beckett preserved the miscalculation, and wanted it to remain subtle: the difficulty of computing in the old British system is what makes Bim's maneuver hard to detect. See *Murphy* (Paris: Les Editions de Minuit, 1965), pp. 69 ("cinq livres par mois") and 116 ("une livre six shillings et huit pence").

6. Page 92. A phrase related to Murphy's prediction, "Murphy was inclined to think . . . ," is repeated on p. 92; this calls attention to the passage about the head male nurse.

7. Mr. Endon, who never whinges, may not be a puppet, but he is called a "figurine" (p. 241).

8. The predictions about fits and quadrupeds are on p. 32; Murphy's fit of laughter, "more like one of epilepsy," is described on pp. 139–40; the warning about quadrupeds is justified when the dog Nellie eats Murphy's biscuits, p. 100.

9. According to the statement in the horoscope, the moon's position at the time of Murphy's birth "promotes great Magical Ability of the Eye, to which the lunatic would easy succumb" (p. 32). The reference to the moon may indicate "the lunatic" is really Murphy. Murphy stares into Mr. Endon's eyes on pp. 248–49 and he concedes defeat on p. 250.

10. Celia says, "Avoid exhaustion by speech" on p. 37, repeating a line from the horoscope. Later Celia, "in weary ellipsis of Suk," practices what she preaches and says only "Avoid exhaustion" when she urges Murphy to remain silent (p. 138).

11. Page 32. Suk is giving the position, in degrees, of the constellation that was rising when Murphy was born (the constellation is "THE GOAT," or Capricorn). Unless Suk invented the figures in the horoscope, he would have needed to know the time of Murphy's birth to within a few minutes: it takes about four minutes for a degree of longitude on the celestial sphere to traverse the horizon. Another unlikely proposition is given on the same page: according to Suk, at the time of Murphy's birth Mars had "just set in the East."

12. Murphy is twice called a "young man" and twice a "young aspirant" (p. 53). On p. 75 the narrator indicates that in a year it will be 1936, and the dates he gives (e.g., he refers to Thursday, September 12, and to Friday, October 11, on p. 114) occur in 1935.

13. According to Suk, Neptune is in "the Bull" (Taurus), and "Herschel" (Uranus) is in Aquarius (p. 33). As was explained in Chapter 8, Herschel is an old name for Uranus, and later the two planets are mentioned again (p. 230). The repetition serves as a clue to the unreliability in the horoscope passage.

14. The sidereal period of Neptune is 163.9 years. If Neptune is in Taurus between 1874 and 1889, it would not return to that constellation in the twentieth century; and it would not have been there more than once in the nineteenth century. Information on the zodiacal positions of the planets is taken from Grant Lewi, *Astrology for the Millions*, 4th ed. (New York: Bantam Books, 1978), pp. 268, 259.

15. On p. 114 the narrator says that Celia's triumph over Murphy "was gained about the middle of September, Thursday the 12th to be pedantic. . . ." The triumph (which is described on p. 41) comes "in the morning" (p. 29); the narrator says that the moon was full and at perigee on the night before (p. 26). This would be September 11, 1935.

16. The moon was at perigee at about 6 P.M. on September 12, 1935. This and other data about the moon's position are from editions of Joseph Whitaker's *Almanack* (London) for the years 1931–35. According to the astronomer Fred L. Whipple, the moon is full and at perigee about once a year; see *Earth, Moon and Planets* (Philadelphia: Blakiston Co., 1946), p. 106.

17. The moon's average perigee distance is 225,757 miles and the smallest perigee distance is 221,463 miles. The maximum variation in perigee distances would be about twice the difference between these figures, or some 8,500 miles. It should be pointed out that such a figure represents an extreme: monthly variations in perigee distance are far smaller than this. Information about lunar distances is taken from Charles M. Huffer *et al.*, *An Introduction to Astronomy* (New York: Holt, Rinehart and Winston, 1967), pp. 145–46.

18. Coal sacks, also known as dark nebulae, are clouds of dust that obscure the stars beyond them; but some stars, closer to earth than the clouds, still are visible in front of them. The most prominent coal sack in the northern hemisphere is in the constellation Lynx. For an observer in

London (the M.M.M. is near London) only an object at the celestial north pole would seem to remain fixed in the sky. But there is no dark nebula in the immediate vicinity of the celestial pole, and a fairly bright star, Polaris, is located about a degree from the pole.

19. Other passages suggest that the diminishing importance of the stars is a sign that Murphy is withdrawing into himself. The second time the narrator says that Murphy has confidence in only two systems (p. 76), he adds: "So much the worse for him, no doubt." The narrator's attitude is like Suk's: both are skeptical about Murphy's theories. Suk advises Murphy to "Resort to Harmony" (p. 32); this comment runs parallel to the narrator's observation about the "disharmony" in Murphy's two systems (p. 76).

20. The "stars he commanded," p. 175; "his stars," pp. 76, 85, 93, 183; "superfluous cartoon," p. 189. Murphy's comments about "his stars" can be compared to one about "his own dark" (p. 91). This last phrase suggests that Murphy cannot see the stars from his garret because they are obscured by his own dark.

21. The epigraph (p. 32) is from *Romeo and Juliet,* V, i, 24; the italics are Beckett's.

22. *Romeo and Juliet,* III, ii, 21. The two quotations about stars form a matched set with two quotations about sleep, also from Shakespeare; these were discussed in Chapter 8.

23. See Dante, *Inferno* 3:23, 16:83, 34:139.

24. Arthur Schopenhauer, *The World as Will and Idea*, trans. R. B. Haldane and J. Kemp (1883; rpt., London: Routledge and Kegan Paul, 1957), 1:532. (The subsequent volumes of this work contain supplements to the first; hence the end of the first volume can be considered the conclusion.) In German the end of the passage quoted in the text reads, "deise unsere so sehr reale Welt mit allen ihren Sonnen und Milchstrassen—Nichts."

25. *Proust* (1931; rpt., New York: Grove Press, 1957), p. 8. For Schopenhauer's comments on "objectivation of the will," see *The World*, 1:123ff., esp. pp. 140, 219; 3:48ff.

26. Page 183. The italics are Beckett's.

27. The date can be established as follows: on p. 235 the narrator says that it is the afternoon of October 20; the comment about the moon having set refers to the next dawn. Information about sunrise and moonset is taken from Whitaker's *Almanack* (London, 1935), pp. 110, 114. It is possible to detect this inconsistency even without an almanac. The moon in its third quarter rises in the middle of the night and sets in the middle of the day; see Stanley Wyatt, *Principles of Astronomy* (Boston: Allyn and Bacon, 1974), p. 133. The narrator says that there was a full moon on October 11; hence, eleven days later, on the night of the 20th-21st, the moon is just past its third quarter and sets well after sunrise. This corresponds to the information in Whitaker's *Almanack* for October 21, 1935: moonrise, 2:10 A.M.; moonset, 2:36 P.M.; sunrise, 6:34 A.M.

28. Page 47. Beckett's account of the drowning of Hippasos is probably based on a passage in John Burnet's *Greek Philosophy*, pt. I (London: Macmillan, 1924), pp. 55–56. Beckett's use of this work was discussed in Chapter 8. The wording in Burnet's version of the story resembles Beckett's, but Burnet makes it clear that Hippasos was drowned at sea. The joke is preserved in the French version of *Murphy:* Hippasos is drowned in a sewer ("égout"); *Murphy* (Paris, 1965), p. 40.

29. The distortion is greater than it seems to be, because the change of vowels in the Baccardi-Bocardo substitution completely alters the significance of the term. The terms Beckett refers to are the first four in a series of nineteen; each one represents a different type of syllogism. A description of the system can be found in *The Encyclopedia of Philosophy* (New York: Macmillan and the Free Press, 1967), 5:69.

30. *Murphy* (Paris, 1965), p. 18.

31. The narrator says that when Miss Carridge found the old boy, it was "exactly what she would have expected, and must therefore at some time or other have imagined . . . ," but a few lines down he says that "she could never have imagined" the details she observed (p. 135). The contradiction forces readers to re-examine the passage and reveals the irony in the situation. The old boy dies, probably because Miss Carridge wanted to save the doctor's fee, but when it becomes known that the room was occupied by a suicide, she has difficulty renting it. So Miss Carridge may really have defeated her own purpose.

32. Page 136. Miss Carridge habitually repeats concluding phrases; this also occurs on pp. 227 ("a doubt") and 147 ("the principle of the thing").

33. Page 262. *"Modus morendi"* (manner of dying) is a play on *modus vivendi* (manner of living), a legal term, or on *modus operandi* (manner of operating), a common term in criminology. This again suggests that the coroner may have suspected that foul play was involved in Murphy's death.

34. The concern about suicide is discussed on pp. 184–86, and is emphasized by a repeated passage, "any other available means," in descriptions of different types of suicide.

35. Page 263. In the French version of the novel (p. 188) the coroner asks about "l'identité de l'ac—du décédé."

36. This becomes evident when the coroner reveals that he does not know that the candle was lit before the explosion: he sarcastically asks about the kind of match that set off the explosion, "a Brymay safety" or a "wax vesta" (p. 263). The two kinds of matches introduce a dual set which calls attention to this detail.

37. Page 194. Since (as will be pointed out) Murphy is associated with Christ, and the number three comes up several times in connection with his death, this may be an allusion to Jesus' comment, "This night, before the cock crow, thou shalt deny me thrice" (Matthew 26:34).

38. "His very dear friends," pp. 226, 258 (twice), 267; "His dearest

friends," p. 267; "Bosom friends," p. 229. The irony is underlined by the narrator's reference to "The very dear friends" (p. 264).

39. There is a reference in the will to "what the great and good Lord Chesterfield calls the necessary house . . ." (p. 269). Lord Chesterfield describes a man who managed his time so well "that he would not even lose that small portion of it which the calls of nature obliged him to pass in the necessary-house, but gradually went through all the Latin poets in those moments"; letter dated Dec. 11, 1747, *Letters to His Son* (London: Dent, 1963), p. 38.

40. On p. 153 Cooper sees Celia enter the Brewery Road rooming house and concludes, "She let herself in, therefore she lived there." Then, says the narrator, he "hastened away as soon as he had made a mental note of the number." On p. 120 Cooper watches as Murphy enters the West Brompton rooming house and decides, "He let himself in, therefore he lived there." The narrator then says, "Cooper made a mental note of the number and hastened back the way he had come. . . ." As was noted earlier, the number three is associated with Murphy's death, and Cooper is "triorchous" (p. 54).

41. Wylie is called "Judas" on p. 199. The thirty shillings it costs to cremate Murphy can be associated with Judas's thirty pieces of silver (p. 271). Murphy turns the other cheek and is in a crucified position on p. 28. Murphy's "long climb home" is a kind of calvary: it involves "the toil from King's Cross" (p. 73). There are other comparisons between Murphy and Christ: see S. C. Steinberg, "External and Internal in *Murphy*," *Twentieth Century Literature*, 18 (Apr., 1972): 95; Cohn, p. 33.

42. Page 256. They all leave Miss Carridge's before noon on Wednesday, October 23, for the inquest (p. 254). If they had not left for two days and three nights before that, they were at Miss Carridge's during the nights of October 20–21, 21–22, and 22–23. Murphy died on the first of these nights, some time before dawn on October 21. One possible function of the repeated comments indicating that the time of Murphy's birth cannot be established (these were noted earlier) could be a subtle suggestion that it might be more useful to try to establish the time of his death.

43. Miss Counihan, Wylie, and Neary arrive at Miss Carridge's rooming house on the afternoon of October 20 (pp. 224–26, 235). Cooper is not with them at that time, nor is he a member of the group that listens to Celia's story, which she finishes after it has grown dark (p. 233). At some time during that night he arrives and is given a place to sleep by Miss Carridge (p. 256). If he arrived shortly after Murphy died, he could still be included in the group that never left Miss Carridge's "For two days and three nights" (p. 256). Another detail that implicates Cooper is a repeated passage about how Cooper (p. 119) and the gas (p. 174) "came to be turned off." This passage can be linked to Cooper's recurring complaint, "I do be turned off" (p. 118 and twice on p. 119).

10

Watt and the Philosophers

Samuel Beckett says in interviews that he knows little about philosophy—but his little could easily be another person's abundance. Different critics say he has borrowed from (among others) Pythagoras, Heraclitus, Democritus, Plato, Archimedes, Augustine, Aquinas, Duns Scotus, Dante, Bruno, Campanella, Descartes, Pascal, Geulincx, Schopenhauer, Kierkegaard, Mauthner, Bergson, Heidegger, Wittgenstein, and Sartre; he has been called a dualist, an occasionalist, an existentialist, a Taoist, a Buddhist, a Christian, a skeptic, a nihilist, and a solipsist.[1] From this it may be inferred that Beckett's reading is wider than he admits; that some of the influences claimed by critics are cursory or peripheral; and that if he is a solipsist, he has an atypical interest in others' ideas.

Creative writers occasionally stumble on philosophical ideas by themselves, sometimes even before philosophers get around to explicating them. In this way Dostoevsky stole some of Nietzsche's thunder. Like Dostoevsky, Beckett is familiar enough with important streams of thought to arrive at a position associated with a particular philosopher without necessarily having read that person's works. When Beckett claims he knows little about philosophy, he probably is being modest; when he says he has not been influenced by a particular book, he probably is telling the truth.

In his early works Beckett often included references to writers he borrowed from. Dante's ideas are central in the first story in *More Pricks than Kicks,* and its title is "Dante and the Lobster." In his essay on Proust, Beckett refers to a number of Schopenhauer's ideas and mentions him by name three times.² These writers are again important in *Watt*. Watt's journey metaphorically represents an inner experience, and Beckett's source for this type of metaphor is Dante. On a philosophical level the novel presents a critique of rationalism that is similar to Schopenhauer's. However, these writers are not mentioned by name in *Watt*; instead, Beckett includes quotations from their works.³

The type of rationalism which is attacked in the novel can be associated with that of Descartes. Beckett's interest in Cartesian philosophy goes back at least to the time when he was a university student.⁴ An early poem, *Whoroscope*, is based on his reading of works by and about Descartes; like the poem, *Watt* contains references to Descartes' life as well as to his ideas. After years of travel Descartes retired to a stove-heated room and there spent his time in solitary contemplation. "This succeeded much better, it seemed to me," Descartes writes, "than if I had never departed either from my country or my books."⁵ Watt, an "experienced traveller," also decides to lead a more sedentary, meditative life (p. 20). His travel, like Descartes', was not very useful: "for all the good that frequent departures out of Ireland had done him, he might just as well have stayed there."⁶ Descartes often chose intelligent men as his servants, and trained them in mathematics and philosophy (one of them, a valet named Gillot, is mentioned in *Whoroscope*).⁷ This perhaps explains why the well-educated Watt is so eager to work as a servant in Mr. Knott's house. Upon arriving there, he settles down near a stove and experiments with a light and glowing coals (two of Descartes' early works, *The World* and *The Dioptrics*, deal with the nature of light).

Watt is in many respects a model Cartesian. He has great faith in rational inquiry and considers it useful for solving every kind of problem. At times Watt proceeds as if he had memorized Descartes' *Rules for the Direction of the Mind* and resolved to follow its precepts literally. This leads to a parody of the Cartesian rules; Watt applies them so rigorously that their weaknesses soon become manifest. One of Descartes' rules specifies that second-hand information should not be trusted: he urges his readers to rely only on what they "can clearly and perspicuously behold."⁸ Watt complies and never seeks help from others, even with the problems he finds most difficult. Erskine could probably tell him about the function of a bell he is curious about; Art and Con might be able to answer his questions about the procedures for feeding their dog; but Watt refrains from asking.

Another of Descartes' rules specifies that one should pay attention to "the most insignificant and most easily mastered facts, and remain a long time in contemplation of them. . . ."[9] Few people ever labored longer, or with more insignificant facts, than Watt; few ever made a more earnest attempt to follow the Cartesian dictum to "traverse in a systematic way even the most trifling of men's inventions. . . ."[10] By limiting himself to modest problems, careful observations, and logical deductions, Watt demonstrates how easily even the simplest inquiries can be transformed into confusion.

In one of Descartes' later works, the *Discourse on the Method of Rightly Conducting the Reason,* he again describes his method and promises that it will yield information about "all those things which fall under the cognizance of man." So long as the rules are properly applied, he says, "there can be nothing so remote that we cannot reach to it, nor so recondite that we cannot discover it."[11] Descartes seems persuaded that he has discovered the philosophical aqua regia, and will shortly dispose of every problem previously considered insoluble. Watt is taken in by this claim. When his investigations are fruitless, he only becomes more certain that some fine point of the logical method has eluded him. He clings to the belief that his setbacks are temporary. "All this will be revealed," he assures himself, "in due time" (p. 119).

In his *Objections and Replies* Descartes recorded difficulties raised by his arguments and then methodically refuted them. Watt lists objections and solutions when he attempts to solve the intricate "problem of how to bring the dog and food together" (p. 93). The harder he works on it, the further he gets from an answer: the proposed solutions increase arithmetically, but the possible objections increase geometrically.[12]

Upon arriving at Mr. Knott's house, Watt is pleased because, as Arsene says, he is certain that "he is in the right place, at last" (p. 40). Watt seems to think he has reached an arena of skeptical inquiry, an appropriate place for expressing the *dubito* that will be (as it was for Descartes) the preamble to a *cogito.*[13] But the skepticism at Mr. Knott's house is all-embracing and threatens to leave none of his positive values intact. Watt's investigations begin to yield conclusions that resemble the result of dividing by zero: surds and arbitrary figures. The skepticism he had welcomed as a stepping stone to knowledge finally leaves him mired in a pool of doubt.

For Descartes and the thinkers who followed him, such paradoxical conclusions were less disturbing: they could be taken as timely reminders of the differences between the human intellect and the divine. The phrase "God only knows" in its literal sense was a satisfactory formula for dealing with enigmas. Pascal's derivation of scientific principles from God's truth, Leibniz's metaphysically necessary principles, Newton's infinite universe created by an infinite God, Malebranche's theological solution of the mind-body problem: such concepts reasserted the cosmological proof of God's existence and at the same time disposed of irksome intellectual difficulties.

Watt, however, is closer to a modern generation of rationalists whose agnosticism precludes such an approach; he seems unaware of the important role that theistic belief played in the rationalism of the Enlightenment. The long chains of reasoning recommended by Descartes, unless they begin with the idea of God as prime mover, stretch back toward an incomprehensible infinity.[14] Descartes himself admits this in the *Meditations:* "if I were ignorant of the facts of the existence of God ... I should have no true and certain knowledge, but only vague and vacillating opinions."[15] Lacking a theistic core, Watt's skepticism is transformed into an intractable nihilism that leaves him intellectually destitute. He does not believe in God, but retains his faith in rationalism; he is skeptical about everything he learns, but never questions the viability of his method. The ironic aspects of this situation never occur to him.

Some critics have suggested that Beckett was influenced by modern analytical philosophers, Ludwig Wittgenstein in particular.[16] But Beckett's sense of the shortcomings of the Cartesian method led to a distrust of methods primarily based on skepticism, logical analysis, and the imitation of mathematical models. Such methods, to be sure, are effective in a limited arena. But even modern analytical philosophers have been unable to fulfill

Descartes' promise that there would eventually be "nothing so remote that we cannot reach to it, nor so recondite that we cannot discover it."[17] The philosophical satire in *Watt* is directed against this kind of naive optimism.

Despite the attempts of Voltaire and others to undermine it, the optimism of the Enlightenment survived and—nurtured by nineteenth-century positivism—even flourished. By the late nineteenth century, however, some of the problems of the analytical approach had surfaced, and by the twentieth the optimism began to give way to despair. Such despair is evident in Beckett's novel, and one of his sources is Schopenhauer, who describes the weaknesses in Descartes' method and the emptiness of his promise of universal knowledge.

Schopenhauer, deeply influenced by Kant, criticized the rationalism of the Enlightenment in an early work, *On the Fourfold Root of the Principle of Sufficient Reason*. Schopenhauer begins by arguing that there is a logical error in Descartes' proof of the existence of God. Descartes considers God the cause of causes, the starting point of the causal chains used to explain all other phenomena. For him, the immensity of the universe implies a greater immensity, God's, as its cause. But Schopenhauer finds the idea of a cause of causes absurd. Descartes, he feels, blurs the distinctions between reasons (which refer to logical procedures) and causes (which refer to processes in space and time). God's immensity is not, properly speaking, a cause: it is a reason. "Descartes," says Schopenhauer, "met the demands of the inexorable law of causality, which reduced his God to the last straits, by substituting a reason instead of the cause required, in order thus to set the matter at rest." Descartes resorts to what Schopenhauer calls a "sleight of hand trick": he begins with an a priori belief in God's existence and then offers his faulty proof "in majorem Dei gloriam."[18]

In Schopenhauer's major work, *The World as Will and Idea*, he argues that an understanding of metaphysical reality cannot be derived from investigations of the material world. Again following Kant, he questions whether an understanding of causality can yield information about anything but phenomena, events in time and space. Metaphysical entities are almost impermeable to the human understanding because they exist outside time and space in the world of noumena. Material objects have a different appearance in the world of noumena; because we so easily perceive the material aspects of objects, we accept these as the only reality. But the reality of time and space is illusory; it blocks out our ability to apprehend the noumenal reality, the reality of the thing-in-itself. It is in the noumenal world, with its things-in-themselves, that the ultimate reality resides.

Causal investigations, says Schopenhauer, pertain only to material reality; metaphysical questions, to things-in-themselves. This is why investigations of causes are inadequate for questions about the existence of God, or of a cause of causes. A point of view that takes into account only material reality leads the mind into a maze of paradoxes: "With naturalism, then, or the purely physical way of looking at things, we shall never attain our end; it is like a sum that never comes out. Causal series without beginning or end, fundamental forces which are inscrutable, endless space, beginningless time, infinite divisibility of matter . . . constitute the labyrinth in which naturalism leads us ceaselessly round."[19] This precisely is Watt's dilemma: his intricate causal chains lead only to muddles and paradoxes.

A good illustration of this comes when Watt investigates a problem involving the sequence of servants employed at Mr. Knott's house, "a chain stretching from the long dead to the far unborn" (p. 134). Whenever a new servant arrives, another servant leaves; ostensibly, one of these events has caused the other. Watt, pursuing this line of reasoning, makes a determined effort to find the causal connections in the series. But Beckett—carefully, deliberately, exhaustively—makes it clear that the series is not causally determined. No servant is ever summoned to Mr. Knott's house; no servant is ever dismissed; they arrive and depart in arbitrary fashion; and yet they replace one another in an orderly way. Arsene also has difficulty in understanding the "purposelessness" in the servants' actions (p. 58).

Frustrated in his attempts to define the sequence as a causal chain, Watt decides that it is based on "the notion of a pre-established arbitrary."[20] But here Watt can be accused of using a sleight-of-hand trick: either the sequence is arbitrary (undetermined) or it is pre-established (determined). As he mulls over the problem, Watt imagines a series of servants, "Tom, Dick, Harry and another," who succeed one another at Mr. Knott's house (p. 134). He inspects every step of the sequence for evidence of causality but is forced to admit that there is none: "for Mr Knott was a harbour, Mr Knott was a haven, calmly entered, freely ridden, gladly left" (p. 135). Why then do the servants arrive and leave when they do? "Because," says the narrator, "Tom is Tom, and Dick Dick, and Harry Harry, and that other that other, of that the wretched Watt was persuaded" (p. 134). Watt then asks himself, "But why Tom Tom?"—that is, why should the statement "Tom is Tom" serve in lieu of a cause? The answer to this is, "Because Dick Dick and Harry Harry": Tom does what he does because, like Dick or Harry, he is who he is (p. 135). Every human being possesses a capacity for volition isolated from the mechanical predictability of physical laws, untouched by cause and effect.

Watt's error, in terms of Schopenhauer's philosophy, is to use rational methods (investigations of causality) in trying to understand the effects of a thing-in-itself (the ultimate basis of the decision-making process). One's first glimpse of noumenal reality, says Schopenhauer, comes when the inner nature of the self is investigated.[21] This eventually reveals that a person's aspect as a thing-in-itself, which is unaffected by causality, is the center of the essential qualities of the self. Beckett is familiar with this idea, and refers to it in *Proust.*[22]

When Watt begins to recognize the importance of the "because Tom is Tom" concept, he is on the brink of a discovery. He has found a problem where causal explanations are inadequate; if he could understand the principle behind the example, he might be able to discover the weaknesses of his rational method. But he never reaches this point; instead he persuades himself that the question is irrelevant. The narrator explains why:

> And the reason why Watt for the moment had no need for this conception was perhaps this, that when one's arms are full of waxen lilies, then one does not stop to pick, or smell, or chuck, or otherwise acknowledge, a daisy, or a primrose, or a cowslip, or a buttercup, or a violet, or a dandelion . . . but treads them down, and when the weight is past, and past the bowed head buried blinded in the white sweetness, then little by little under the load of petals the bruised stems straighten, those that is that have been fortunate enough to escape rupture. (Pp. 135–36)

Watt, distracted by the "white sweetness" of the artificial flowers, is unaware that he is crushing real flowers underfoot. The
waxen lilies represent the glittering and obtrusive illusions of the
material world; the living flowers, things-in-themselves. Watt
has lost an opportunity to apprehend the underlying reality that
phenomena, like artificial flowers, only mimic.

Having dismissed the "because Tom is Tom" concept (which
suggests that the locus of volition is outside space-time reality),
Watt makes another error: he begins to analyze the sequence in
terms of its "then-Tomness, then-Dickness, then-Harryness" (p.
136). Watt has removed the thing-in-itself from an atemporal context and put it into a time frame. The result is that he reverts to
the conventional way of seeing the servants: as creatures in time
and space, the empty husks of things-in-themselves.

Soon afterward Watt wearily returns to the "ancient labour" of
his rationalistic thinking. He focuses on a less interesting series:
three frogs croak at different rates; if they croak simultaneously,
how many intervals will it take until they croak together again?
The solution to the problem—the list of intervening croaks—is
given in its entirety (pp. 137–38). The problem has little to do
with how frogs behave in the real world: unless every frog main-
tains the beat precisely, the ability to predict when they croak in
unison is lost. But the list of croaks is useful in a different way; it
provides an Aristophanic chorus that mocks Watt's investigative
methods.

A related theme is illustrated by an incident that occurs when
Watt first arrives at Mr. Knott's house. Looking at a grate, he notices that the ashes seem to glow when he covers a lamp with his
hat; when he uncovers the lamp, the glow seems to diminish.
Finally the coals die, and Watt can no longer perform the experiment (pp. 37–39). Beckett, like Descartes (and many other authors), often uses illumination as a metaphor for thought.[23] On a
figurative level Watt's experiment concerns the ability of the
mind to know itself. The glowing coals represent the mind as
object (the entity being investigated); the lamp represents the
mind as subject (the entity conducting the investigation). Watt's
experiment suggests that epistemological inquiries are ultimately
futile: the more light one directs toward the mind, the more difficult it becomes to discern its inner glow. Human frailty eventu-

ally makes even this activity impossible: the glow flickers, dims, and disappears.

Similar points about the limitations of the human intellect are made in other passages. The narrator says that the appearance of Mr. Graves "at the backdoor, twice and even three times every day, should be gone into with the utmost care, though there is little likelihood of its shedding any light on Mr Knott, or on Watt, or on Mr Graves" (p. 69). Hackett wants to know all about Watt, but Mr. Nixon adamantly refuses to provide biographical details: "I tell you nothing is known," he says. "Nothing" (p. 21). The clearest statement about human knowledge is made by Arsene: "What we know partakes in no small measure of the nature of what has so happily been called the unutterable or ineffable, so that any attempt to utter or eff it is doomed to fail . . ." (p. 62).

This theme again is related to an issue introduced by Descartes and disputed by Schopenhauer in *The Fourfold Root.* Descartes assumes that the mind can know itself, and some of his subsequent proofs are based on this idea. The *Meditations* begins with the premise that examining one's own thoughts can reveal the nature of outer reality, and the existence of the world is derived from the proposition "I think therefore I am." Schopenhauer finds this reasoning faulty. The mind, he says, is divided into that which knows (Subject) and that which is known (Object). Because it can never be Subject and Object simultaneously, the mind can never know itself. "There can therefore be no *knowledge of knowing,*" says Schopenhauer, "because this would imply the separation of the Subject from knowing, while it nevertheless knew that knowing—which is impossible."[24] Schopenhauer's conclusion resembles the one illustrated by Watt's experiment with the light and glowing ashes.

In Schopenhauer's philosophy aesthetic activity is presented as an alternative to intellectual activity. Rational inquiry supplies information only about the world of phenomena, but aesthetic contemplation, says Schopenhauer, hints at the reality of the thing-in-itself. Great art can suggest alternatives to the superficial reality of the material world, both to those who are engaged in creative activity and to their audiences; this again is an idea Beckett mentions in *Proust.*[25] For Schopenhauer, artistic activity is important not only for the insights about things-in-themselves but also because it brings freedom from desire.[26]

The characters in *Watt* discover that artistic activity can lead to a sense of being liberated. Arthur finds relief from the "fixity" of Mr. Knott's house by telling the story of Louit. Arthur's audience also benefits: Watt enjoys listening to the story of Louit "more," the narrator says, "than he had enjoyed anything for a long time" (p. 198). When Arsene is depressed by the subject matter of his discourse, he tells a story or recites a poem. Erskine and Mr. Knott seem to have given up conversation almost entirely but they do, on occasion, sing songs. The description of Watt's experiences at Mr. Knott's house is a story Watt tells Sam; the novel itself can be considered one of Sam Beckett's stories. At times, these stories entertain the reader; when they are boring, they provide overdoses of ordinary reality that turn the mind away from its habitual concern with phenomena. In this sense, storytelling becomes the kind of artistic activity that anesthetizes the rational faculties and stimulates a deeper level of the understanding. As Watt learns, the attempt to resolve metaphysical or teleological questions by rational means leads to constant frustration.

Schopenhauer deals with this issue in similar terms. He describes how man, developing from a brutish creature into an intelligent being, began to speculate about the purpose of his existence. "With this reflection and wonder," says Schopenhauer, "there arises therefore for man alone, the *need for a metaphysic;* he is accordingly an *animal metaphysicum.*"[27] A need for metaphysical knowledge has driven man to develop the most absurd theories, as a disinterested examination of the world's religions demonstrates: "Temples and churches, pagodas and mosques, in all lands and in all ages, in splendour and vastness, testify to the metaphysical need of man, which, strong and ineradicable, follows close upon his physical need. Certainly whoever is satirically inclined might add that this metaphysical need is a modest fellow who is content with poor fare. It sometimes allows itself to be satisfied with clumsy fables and insipid tales."[28] In personifying man's metaphysical need and in noting the resultant satirical possibilities, Schopenhauer anticipates the philosophical humor in Beckett's novel. Watt, endlessly asking questions in an attempt to satisfy his hunger to know, is a modern version of the *animal metaphysicum.*

According to Schopenhauer, the need to know—like any other desire—originates in the will; attempts to satisfy such needs are always frustrating. Paradoxically, on the rare occasions when human desires are satisfied, the suffering increases when one is left with a terrible sense of ennui: "The wish is, in its nature, pain; the attainment soon begets satiety: the end was only apparent; possession takes away the charm; the wish, the need, presents itself under a new form; when it does not, then follows desolateness, emptiness, ennui, against which the conflict is just as painful as against want."[29] In *Watt* Arsene points out that the satisfaction of desire leads to unhappiness; "it is useless not to seek, not to want," he says, "for when you cease to seek you start to find. . . ." Finding can be worse than seeking: "The glutton castaway, the drunkard in the desert, the lecher in prison, they are the happy ones. To hunger, thirst, lust, every day afresh and every day in vain, after the old prog, the old booze, the old whores, that's the nearest we'll ever get to felicity. . . ."[30]

Beckett uses long lists and tedious descriptions of minutiae to illustrate the ennui and emptiness described by Schopenhauer. The narrator initially appears to be a literal-minded exponent of realism who feels obliged to include even the most trivial details. But Beckett's underlying purpose is to demonstrate that there is an inherent emptiness in the world's profusion of things. Ennui is a part of existence, and is more difficult to endure than the arid lists in *Watt:* there one can skip over the boring stretches.

Beckett, like Schopenhauer, is dismayed by the unsatisfactory alternatives existence offers: the misery of unfulfilled desire on the one hand, the boredom of satiety on the other. Thus it is in the nature of living things, says Schopenhauer, to swing "like a pendulum backwards and forwards between pain and ennui"; Beckett often echoes this concept.[31] The minor characters in *Watt* cannot accept this idea; they believe in an idealized view of existence and block out whatever is unpleasant in order to preserve it. The novel opens with a description of people at a tram-stop; soon afterward the action shifts to a railroad station. In these scenes ordinary people are depicted in a relatively plain (if somewhat satiric) style. When Watt begins his journey to Mr.

Knott's house, the style becomes difficult, so as to suggest the unusual nature of his experiences. Later, after arriving at the asylum, Watt seems even further from day-to-day reality and the style—as in the inverted passages, for example—is even more obscure.

Then, near the end of the novel, there is an abrupt reversion to the style and subject matter of the opening section. Again, the setting is a railroad station and, again, ordinary citizens are depicted discussing mundane topics. At first this ordering suggests that Beckett, after exposing his readers to a disconcerting *Walpurgisnacht*, is making amends by ending with order and sanity restored. The impression that the conclusion represents a return to normalcy is strengthened by Beckett's technique of alluding to themes introduced in the opening section. There are references to policemen, financial transactions, newspapers, literature, marriage, and motherhood in both the opening and closing sections, as well as a number of casual conversations quite different from the unconventional dialogue in other portions of the novel.[32]

The recurring themes call attention to the repetitiousness and habitual actions that screen out a sense of what life really is like. Oblivious to the illusory qualities of the material world, dismissing the evidence of unhappiness that surrounds them, most people still believe in the goodness of life, the beauty of nature, and the mercy of God. At the close of the novel Watt, after being knocked down and injured, is covered with blood and filth. Mr. Gorman and Mr. Case turn away from this unsavory spectacle. Raising his hands in a reverent gesture, Mr. Gorman says, "life isn't such a bad old bugger" (p. 245). Mr. Case, taking his cue from Mr. Gorman, reasserts his belief in God. This purification ceremony effaces memories of their distasteful encounter. The novel then ends with a description of the landscape, which "made as pretty a picture, in the early morning light, as a man could hope to meet with, in a day's march."[33]

Schopenhauer points out that the beauty of the world is hardly enough to compensate for the misery of existence: "an optimist bids me open my eyes and look at the world, how beautiful it is in the sunshine, with its mountains and valleys, streams, plants, animals, &c. &c. Is the world, then, a rareeshow? These things are certainly beautiful to *look at*, but to *be* them is something quite different."[34] Schopenhauer's comment brings to light the irony in the closing description of the landscape. Watt has given up the world of ordinary values in which pretty landscapes are consoling. The ordinary world is associated with trams and trains because their restricted movements suggest the limited freedom of creatures governed by physical laws. This idea is expressed in a limerick by Maurice Hare which Beckett liked enough to commit to memory:

> There was a young man who said, "Damn!
> I suddenly see what I am,
> A creature that moves
> In predestined grooves,
> In fact not a bus but a tram."[35]

Watt's name is usually interpreted as a reference to his role as a questioner, a man who asks "what?"[36] But he can also be thought of as a *wattman* (a French term for "tram-driver"): physical laws, like rails, direct his movements. In *Proust* Beckett speaks of "wattmen," as if the word were English; in *Waiting for Godot* the names Puncher and Wattman (in Lucky's speech) jokingly refer to a ticket-taker and a tram-driver.[37]

In the closing pages of the novel Watt tries to escape from his *wattman* existence. He asks for a ticket to "the end of the line" (p. 244). His experience at Mr. Knott's house has altered his way of seeing reality, and he wants to leave the conventional world. For him the end of the line turns out to be an insane asylum, but his perception of reality is more acute than it was before, and he finally becomes Sam's mentor, just as Arsene once instructed him.[38]

One of Watt's first experiences with this new type of perception comes when he leaves Mr. Knott's house: having departed from the arena of skepticism, he can again accept new ideas. He walks down the road toward the station and sees a mysterious figure. Though it seems to be approaching, it comes no closer, grows no larger; Watt, curious about it, tries to discover what it is. The figure's odd gait is very much like Watt's, which suggests that he may be seeing an image of himself. Watt does not notice the resemblance, nor is he interested in the essential qualities of the figure. "Watt's concern," says the narrator, "deep as it appeared, was not after all with what the figure was, in reality, but with what the figure appeared to be, in reality" (p. 227). Watt wants to know about the sex of the figure, its size, its clothing—in Schopenhauer's terms, about its qualities as a phenomenon rather than a thing-in-itself.[39] He clings to an approach that focuses on the outer world; as the narrator says, "since when were Watt's concerns with what things were, in reality?" (p. 227).

But there has been an improvement: Watt is dissatisfied with his old way of thinking. He finds it "mortifying" that he is "forever falling into this old error, this error of the old days when, lacerated with curiosity, in the midst of substance shadowy he stumbled" (p. 227). This passage, like the one about the real and artificial flowers, refers to the mask of appearances which obscures a deeper reality. When Watt speculated about the series of servants at Mr. Knott's house, his mistake (another "error of the old days") was to focus on their temporal qualities. Watt's questions about the apparition center on its material qualities, and he is again unable to apprehend its deeper reality.[40] This time, however, all is not lost: Watt is struck by his experience with the apparition and thinks of it as "possessing exceptional interest" (p. 228).

Later, in the waiting room of the railroad station, Watt tries to negate the vivid impression of the material world conveyed by his senses. He puts his hat over his face: the only solution for the "problem of vision," he decides, is "the eye open in the dark" (p. 232). Watt's last thoughts about time-space reality, significantly, have to do with a train.[41] Then, says the narrator, "suddenly he ceased, as suddenly as he had begun, to think" (p. 232). Watt then spends the night in the waiting room—figuratively the starting point for his journey inward.

Beckett has said that as a prelude to writing he sometimes engages in long periods of contemplation, and his descriptions of such experiences resemble those he depicts in the novel. When Watt feels himself losing touch with the outer world, he begins to hear faint sounds: "In his skull the voices whispering their canon were like a patter of mice, a flurry of little gray paws in the dust" (p. 232). In a conversation with Lawrence Harvey, Beckett spoke about his own sense of "getting below the surface, concentrating, listening, getting your ear down so you can hear the infinitesimal murmur. There is a gray struggle, a groping in the dark for a shadow."[42] Beckett described this as a search for an inner self that exists beneath the superficial self of the day-to-day world. Referring to "the attempt to find this lost self," he said that "the encounter was like meeting oneself."[43] Watt's experience with the apparition seems to be based on such an encounter.

The events which occur at the railroad station indicate that Watt is making progress in his journey toward the inner world. But Beckett's description of the journey is not without irony: the moment of transition is marked by Watt's discovery that "he felt no need, nay, no desire, to pass water." When this desire—the "last regular link with the screen"—leaves him, he begins to look forward to the "eventual rupture" of the screen itself (p. 232). By calling the outer world the "screen," Beckett emphasizes its role in obscuring the deeper level of reality. When it begins to break down, Watt loses the last of his desires. Even the desire to urinate can be thought of as a link with the world of phenomena (unlikely as it may seem, this idea is consistent with Schopenhauer's philosophy).[44]

Watt spends much of the night listening to the voices in his mind, experiencing "soliloquy, under dictation" (p. 237). In the morning, when a porter unexpectedly unlocks the door of the waiting room and kicks it open, Watt is knocked down. "Now I am at liberty," he says, "I am free to come and go, as I please" (p. 238). Watt is free to leave the waiting room; more important, he has achieved the freedom of indifference. Having given up the last of his desires, he does not protest when he is knocked down, for he is experiencing the sense of liberation that accompanies the absence of volition.

Lying on the floor of the waiting room, Watt gazes at its ceiling and undergoes another important experience when he is struck by its intense whiteness. This episode resembles one at the end of *The Divine Comedy*, when Dante looks upward toward a light "so far exalted above mortal conceiving" that he finds it difficult to describe. This is the Eternal Light "into which," he says, "it is not to be believed that any creature should penetrate with so clear an eye." Moved by this vision, Dante feels himself "drawing near the end of all desires."[45] Watt sees the ceiling of the waiting room "with an extreme distinctness"; it is "of a whiteness that he would not have believed possible, if it had been reported to him."[46]

An ironic note in Beckett's description emerges when one compares the two episodes: Beatrice and the light of heaven on one hand, a waiting-room ceiling and a railway porter on the other. Production costs, even for spiritual experiences, have risen, and one has to make do with less. The satirical elements here and in similar passages indicate how Beckett alters the material he has borrowed. He alludes to many works in *Watt*, but none exerts an overwhelming influence, and the borrowed material is usually transformed. A similar point can be made about Schopenhauer's philosophy: Beckett admires it, makes use of it, but finally goes his own way. He agrees with Schopenhauer that the world is a place of unhappiness and illusion, but his response to this pessimistic vision differs from Schopenhauer's. Arsene points out that the spectacle of human misery can inspire either tears or ironic laughter; weeping, which too easily degenerates into self-pity, is often the less compassionate response. Beckett, like Arsene, chooses the "mirthless laugh" over "eyewater" (p. 48).

There is not much laughter in Schopenhauer's writing, but there is self-pity. One of Schopenhauer's recurring complaints is that other philosophers have treated him unfairly: they are so threatened by his ideas, he says, that they have conspired to ignore his works. In *The Fourfold Root* (where he attacks Descartes) he asks why one of his works has received little notice and then provides an answer: "Hush! Hush! lest the public notice anything!" This quotation ("zitto! zitto! dass nur das Publikum nichts merke!") appears in *Watt* in the original German.[47]

The passage Beckett has quoted indicates that he is aware of the shortcomings in Schopenhauer's philosophy. Describing man as an *animal metaphysicum*, Schopenhauer mocks those who cannot give up inquiries into the reasons for existence. But he himself is vulnerable to a similar charge. Reason and logic, he claims, can reveal only the world of appearances; yet this idea is presented in the form of a reasoned, logical argument. He argues persuasively that art is the best medium for approaching the deeper levels of reality; even so, he never abandons philosophy.[48]

In *Proust*, where Beckett refers to a number of Schopenhauer's most important ideas, his admiration for the philosopher seems unqualified. But in his fiction Beckett spends less time discussing Schopenhauer's ideas, and makes them—and those of other philosophers—subordinate to the aesthetic structure of the work. An example is the way divergent points of view are balanced in *Murphy*. Beckett has argued that poetic language is more direct and expressive than the language of metaphysics; it follows that in his fiction the poetic elements should be given the greater emphasis.[49] It is not that he is reluctant to use philosophical themes; rather, he is unwilling to permit them to undermine the aesthetic integrity of his works.

Abstract thought by itself is perhaps best expressed in an essay, but ideas within the context of a thinker's life can become a subject for art. Hence Beckett often includes details of philosophers' lives when he deals with their thought. In *Whoroscope* he alludes to Descartes' feelings, tastes, and habits. The quotation from Schopenhauer in *Watt* illuminates a human issue: momentarily abandoning his argument, the learned philosopher utters a cri de coeur. Beckett achieves a similar effect: Watt's thought touches on fascinating questions; Arsene's discourse is very sophisticated; yet it is the depiction of their emotional reactions that makes them memorable as characters.

Dante and Schopenhauer are among the authors Beckett most admires, but he never relies on their works to the extent that his own become derivative. The allusions in *Watt* often provide analogies which hint at the nature of events that are almost indescribable. Schopenhauer's arguments about the illusory nature of the world provide a way of understanding what occurs when the "screen" of outer reality breaks down. Watt's vision in the waiting room contains echoes of Dante's description of paradise. But for Beckett, inner events are finally personal and unique. Analogies can hint at the actuality, but the essentials remain indistinct.

In *Watt* the events that take place on the near side of the border between the ordinary world and the asylum are described, but those that occur in Watt's mansion are not. In *Proust* Beckett says that one way to apprehend what lies behind the world of appearances is to "escape into the spacious annexe of mental alienation."[50] The "annexe" may be an early form of the mansion metaphor in *Watt*, and what is experienced there is too profound

140

to be put into words. This is consistent with Arsene's comment on the futility of attempting to utter the unutterable (p. 62).

Beckett develops this idea by using different settings to define areas that are successively more and more remote from the realm of ordinary experience in the day-to-day world. Judgments there are often based on outward appearances, and Watt—lacking the accoutrements of middle-class life—is treated with contempt. Sam, though he retains a belief in conventional reality, recognizes that Watt's experiences are worth recording, but he is more interested in learning about what occurred at Mr. Knott's house. He seems to imagine that it represents the ultimate level of reality, just as Watt did when he first arrived there. But if the skepticism at Mr. Knott's house clears away the detritus left over from unworkable hypotheses, it offers no enduring answers; it, too, must be abandoned. Watt moves on to a higher stage of reality in the waiting room, where he gives up his rational methods and makes the transition to the other side of the "screen." Finally, inside his mansion, he is at the highest level of reality, the realm of the indescribable.[51]

When Watt leaves the asylum to converse with Sam, he is depicted walking backward and telling his story in inverted fashion. Yet it is more likely that Sam is the one who has things backward: he retains a belief in the values of the outer world and, even after hearing Watt's story, returns to it. He has not understood the significance of Watt's remarks any more than Watt had understood Arsene's. To those, like Sam, who believe in the primacy of conventional reality, a retreat from the world seems regressive.

The four parts of the novel are arranged in such a way that the scenes depicting the day-to-day world are at the beginning and end. But Sam admits that the narrative originally was organized in a different way: "Two, one, four, three, that was the order in which Watt told his story" (p. 215). In this version, the novel would begin after Watt had arrived at Mr. Knott's house, the tram-stop and railroad-station scenes would be somewhere in the middle, and the novel would end with Watt's return to the asylum. If the events are rearranged in this order, the episodes depicting outer reality are encapsulated by those dealing with inner experiences. In Watt's version, it is conventional reality that is dreamlike and insubstantial.[52]

Watt's reality is remote and intangible, and many readers will initially assume that Sam's point of view is the definitive one. His first name is the same as the author's. He thinks rationally, speaks normally, and is sane enough to win his release from the asylum. Such evidence may suggest that Sam's way of seeing the world is superior to Watt's. It is not.

Notes

1. Beckett has indicated that when it comes to philosophy he is a strict nonreader; see Gabriel d'Aubarède, "Waiting for Beckett," trans. Christopher Waters, *Trace*, no. 42 (Summer, 1961), p. 157. Among the critics who discuss the philosophical influences on Beckett's works are: Germaine Brée, "Beckett's Abstracters of Quintessence," *French Review*, 36 (May, 1963):567–76; Richard Coe, *Samuel Beckett* (New York: Grove Press, 1968); Ruby Cohn, *Samuel Beckett: The Comic Gamut* (New Brunswick, N.J.: Rutgers University Press, 1962) and *Back to Beckett* (Princeton, N.J.: Princeton University Press, 1973); Raymond Federman, *Journey to Chaos: Samuel Beckett's Early Fiction* (Berkeley: University of California Press, 1965); John Fletcher, *The Novels of Samuel Beckett* (London: Chatto and Windus, 1964); Lawrence Harvey, *Samuel Beckett, Poet and Critic* (Princeton, N.J.: Princeton University Press, 1970); David Hesla, *The Shape of Chaos* (Minneapolis: University of Minnesota Press, 1971); Jacqueline Hoefer, "Watt," *Perspective*, 11 (Autumn, 1959): 166–82; Frederick J. Hoffman, *Samuel Beckett: The Language of Self* (New York: Dutton, 1964); Hugh Kenner, *Samuel Beckett: A Critical Study* (Berkeley: University of California Press, 1968); Samuel Mintz, "Beckett's *Murphy:* A 'Cartesian' Novel," *Perspective*, 11 (Autumn, 1959):156–65; John Pilling, *Samuel Beckett* (London: Routledge and Kegan Paul, 1976); Steven Rosen, *Samuel Beckett and the Pessimistic Tradition* (New Brunswick, N.J.: Rutgers University Press, 1976); Nathan Scott, *Samuel Beckett* (London: Bowes and Bowes, 1963); W. Y. Tindall, *Samuel Beckett* (New York: Columbia University Press, 1964); Sidney Warhaft, "Threne and Theme in *Watt*," *Wisconsin Studies in Contemporary Literature*, 4 (Autumn, 1963):261–78.

2. *Proust* (1931; rpt., New York: Grove Press, 1957), pp. 8, 66, 70. In some passages in this work allusions to Schopenhauer's concepts are not identified, for example, Beckett's reference to "The Model, the Idea, the Thing in itself" (p. 69); cf. Arthur Schopenhauer, *The World as Will and Idea*, trans. R. B. Haldane and J. Kemp (1883; rpt., London: Routledge and Kegan Paul, 1957), 1:221.

3. *Watt* (1953; rpt., New York: Grove Press, 1959), pp. 249, 253; subsequent references to *Watt* are to this edition. On p. 249 "zitto! zitto! dass nur das Publikum nichts merke!" is from Schopenhauer's *Ueber die vier-*

fache Wurzel des Satzes vom zureichenden Grunde; see *Sämtliche Werke* (Wiesbaden: F. A. Brockhaus, 1958), 1:50. On p. 253 "parole non ci appulcro" is from the *Inferno* 7:60. The significance of these quotations will be discussed at greater length in the next chapter.

4. Harvey, p. 33 *et passim;* Deirdre Bair, *Samuel Beckett: A Biography* (New York: Harcourt Brace Jovanovich, 1978), p. 52; see also pp. 79, 90, 91. On Descartes' influence see Kenner, pp. 117–32; Harvey, pp. 3–66; and Hesla, pp. 78–79 *et passim.*

5. René Descartes, *Discourse on the Method of Rightly Conducting the Reason,* in *The Philosophical Works of Descartes,* trans. Elizabeth Haldane and G. R. T. Ross (Cambridge: Cambridge University Press, 1967), 1:87. Beckett mentions Descartes' "hot-cupboard" (the famous *poêle*) in *Whoroscope* and in *Proust;* see *Poems in English* (New York: Grove Press, 1961), p. 12; *Proust,* p. 51. Murphy's request for a warm stove at the M.M.M. may be based on a desire to emulate Descartes; see *Murphy* (1938; rpt., New York: Grove Press, 1957), p. 163; Mintz, p. 161.

6. Page 248. Watt is not mentioned in this passage, which appears among the addenda at the end of the novel. But since he is twice called "an experienced traveller" (pp. 20, 22), the passage probably refers to him.

7. Beckett mentions Gillot in the fourth line of *Whoroscope,* and in a footnote to the poem says, "Descartes passed on the easier problems in analytical geometry to his valet Gillot" (*Poems in English,* pp. 11, 16n).

8. Descartes, *Works,* 1:5. This is from Descartes' third rule, which in its entirety reads, "In the subjects we propose to investigate, our inquiries should be directed, not to what others have thought, nor to what we ourselves conjecture, but to what we can clearly and perspicuously behold and with certainty deduce; for knowledge is not won in any other way."

9. *Ibid.,* p. 28. The entire rule reads, "We ought to give the whole of our attention to the most insignificant and most easily mastered facts, and remain a long time in contemplation of them until we are accustomed to behold the truth clearly and distinctly." Watt contemplates mainly trivial facts because he never reaches the point where he can behold the truth clearly and distinctly.

10. *Ibid.,* p. 30. The entire rule reads, "In order that it may acquire sagacity the mind should be exercised in pursuing just those inquiries of which the solution has already been found by others; and it ought to traverse in a systematic way even the most trifling of men's inventions, though those ought to be preferred in which order is explained or implied."

11. *Ibid.,* p. 92. Beckett refers to a "Proustian *Discours de la Méthode*" in *Proust* (p. 25). *Watt* may be Beckett's version of the *Discours.*

12. The table on pp. 97–98 of *Watt* suggests that for any n solutions Watt proposes, there will be $\frac{n^2 + 3n}{2}$ objections.

13. In the *Meditations* Descartes begins by doubting the existence of

"the heavens, the earth, colours, figures, sound, and all other external things . . ." (*Works*, 1:148). After using the *cogito* to prove his own existence, he goes on to prove the existence of God and the world.

14. Descartes says that "those long chains of reasoning . . . of which geometricians make use" are the basis of his method (*Works*, 1:92). He then argues that God is the source of all physical laws and the creator of the world (*ibid.*, p. 144). God, then, is the first cause in any causal chain.

15. *Ibid.*, pp. 183–84.

16. Hoefer, for example, has argued that Arsene's comments on the limitations of language are based on Wittgenstein's philosophy; see Hoefer, pp. 180–81. According to Fletcher, however, Beckett read Wittgenstein only after completing *Watt*; see Fletcher, pp. 87–88. Bair said that Beckett told her he "abhors" the "many comparisons between his writings and the philosophy of Ludwig Wittgenstein"; see Bair, p. 655n. One of Hoefer's key points is that Arsene's ladder joke (p. 44) is based on Wittgenstein's comment that his argument is like a ladder which can be discarded after it has been used to reach a certain height (the remark is from the *Tractatus*, 6.54; and see Hoefer, p. 181). But Wittgenstein was influenced by two philosophers Beckett is known to have read before he wrote *Watt*: Schopenhauer and Fritz Mauthner. Schopenhauer criticizes language as a tool of the reason (*The World*, 1:47–48) and some of his other ideas anticipate Wittgenstein's; see Patrick Gardiner, *Schopenhauer* (Harmondsworth: Penguin Books, 1967), pp. 278–82, for a discussion of the issues. Beckett's joke and Wittgenstein's analogy could both have the following passage in Schopenhauer as a source: "But to him who studies in order to gain *insight* books and studies are only steps of the ladder by which he climbs to the summit of knowledge. As soon as a round of the ladder has raised him a step, he leaves it behind him" (*The World*, 2:256).

Mauthner's version of the argument that language cannot adequately represent reality also anticipates Wittgenstein's. Mauthner was influenced by Schopenhauer, wrote a book on Schopenhauer, and uses a ladder image very much like Schopenhauer's in his major work; see *Beitrage zu einer Kritik der Sprache* (Stuttgart: J. G. Gotta'sche Buchhandlung Nachfolger, 1906), 1:1–2. Wittgenstein may have borrowed the ladder image from Mauthner; see Max Black, *A Companion to Wittgenstein's Tractatus* (Cambridge: Cambridge University Press, 1970), p. 377n. For evidence that Beckett read Mauthner, see Richard Ellmann, *James Joyce* (New York: Oxford University Press, 1959), p. 661. Mauthner is mentioned in Beckett's play *Radio II*, which appears in his *Ends and Odds* (New York: Grove Press, 1976); see p. 118. Additional information on Mauthner's influence can be found in the following essays: Philip Howard Solomon, "A Ladder Image in *Watt*: Samuel Beckett and Fritz Mauthner," *Papers on Language and Literature*, 7 (1971):422–27; Jennie Skerl, "Fritz Mauthner's 'Critique of Language' in Samuel Beckett's *Watt*," *Contemporary Literature*, 15 (1974):474–87; Linda Ben-Zvi,

"Samuel Beckett, Fritz Mauthner, and the Limits of Language," *PMLA,*
95 (Mar., 1980):183–200.

Beckett has denied that Wittgenstein was the source of the ladder joke
(Fletcher, pp. 87–88) and had used similar jokes in works completed before *Watt.* There is a ladder joke in *Murphy* (p. 188), and in "Echo's
Bones" Beckett refers to "steps" that were set up "in every region of
Magna Graecia" and then drawn up by those who ascended on them (TS,
Dartmouth College Library, p. 14). This suggests a source that predates
all the others: Sextus Empiricus, the codifier of Greek skeptical philoso-
phy. In his *Against the Logicians* the ladder represents the arguments of
the skeptical philosophers; moreover, he uses the Greek word κλῖμαξ,
which can be translated as "ladder," "step-ladder," or "steps"; Sextus
Empiricus, *Against the Logicians,* trans. R. G. Bury (Cambridge, Mass.:
Harvard University Press, 1967), pp. 488–89.

17. Descartes, *Works,* 1:92.

18. *On the Fourfold Root of the Principle of Sufficient Reason,* trans.
Mme. K. Hillebrand (London: George Bell and Sons, 1897), p. 11; the attack on Descartes begins on p. 10; the discussion of the self-causing
cause is on pp. 41–42; the quotation about substituting a reason for a
cause is on p. 18. Beckett had read Kant and Schopenhauer by 1930; see
Pilling, p. 126. Beckett said of Schopenhauer, "Always knew that he was
one of the ones that mattered most to me"; see Bair, pp. 260–61.

19. *The World,* 2:382; on the thing-in-itself, 1:4–120, especially p. 39,
and 2:359–410. Some of these ideas are based on Kant's, and (as will be
discussed at greater length in the next chapter) Beckett includes a quotation from Kant in *Watt.* Since he alludes more often to Schopenhauer,
I have used Schopenhauer's version of the noumenon-phenomenon
concept.

20. Page 134. Brée (p. 573) considers "pre-established arbitrary" an allusion to Leibniz's "pre-established harmony." This seems very likely: in
the light of Schopenhauer's comments, Watt's and Leibniz's terms become weak props holding up a shaky proof of causality. Schopenhauer
attacks Leibniz on a similar point (*The Fourfold Root,* p. 20). In *The
World as Will and Idea* Schopenhauer praises Voltaire for mocking Leibniz in *Candide* and then mentions the Lisbon earthquake; Beckett, who
also alludes to the Lisbon earthquake, may have a similar idea in mind;
see *The World,* 3:394–96; *Watt,* p. 43.

21. *The World,* 2:404–6ff.; 1:228ff.

22. See *Proust:* "When the subject is exempt from will the object is
exempt from causality (Time and Space taken together). And this human
vegetation is purified in the transcendental aperception that can capture
the Model, the Idea, the Thing in itself" (p. 69).

23. In *Watt* the knowledge in Nackybal's mind is "dumbly flickering"
(p. 174); Arsene tells Watt he has said enough "to light that fire in your
mind that shall never be snuffed" (p. 62); the narrator, after explaining
that there was little likelihood of "shedding any light" on some ques-

tions, says, "But even there where there was no light for Watt, where there is none for his mouthpiece, there may be light for others" (p. 69). In an image that refers back to the one about the glowing ashes, Watt—four pages after he "ceased . . . to think"—sees "portions of a grate, heaped high with ashes, and cinders, of a beautiful grey colour" (p. 236). Descartes refers to intuitive understanding as an "inborn light" (*Works*, 1:41, and see also pp. 16 and 28); to "mental illumination" (*ibid.*, 2:75–76); and to knowledge as "the light of nature" (*ibid.*, 1:231). Beckett may also have had in mind Stephen Dedalus's comments on Shelley's image of the mind as a fading coal; see James Joyce, *Ulysses* (New York: Modern Library, 1946), p. 192.

24. *The Fourfold Root*, p. 166.

25. On the benefits of art and artistic contemplation, see *The World*, 1:226–59, especially pp. 253–54. In *Proust* Beckett refers to "Schopenhauer's definition of the artistic procedure as 'the contemplation of the world independently of the principle of reason' " (p. 66). This is Beckett's translation of a passage in *The World as Will and Idea* where Schopenhauer defines the artistic procedure as "*die Betrachtungsart der Dinge unabhängig vom Satze des Grundes*" (*Sämtliche Werke*, 2 [1961]:218; the italics are Schopenhauer's; for the Haldane-Kemp translation, see *The World*, 1:239).

26. *The World*, 1:254.

27. "On Man's Need of Metaphysics," *The World*, 2:359; the italics are Schopenhauer's.

28. *The World*, 2:361.

29. *Ibid.*, 1:404–5.

30. Page 44. The word "prog" is a slang term for food; see the *Oxford English Dictionary*, *s.v.* prog.

31. *The World*, 1:402. In *Proust* Beckett refers to this idea and uses Schopenhauer's image of the pendulum: "The pendulum oscillates between these two terms: Suffering . . . and Boredom . . ." (p. 16).

32. References to policemen, pp. 8, 238; to monetary transactions, pp. 17, 245; to periodicals, pp. 25, 237; to literary works, pp. 11, 228; to wives, pp. 30, 233; to mothers, pp. 13, 238. Other incidents help link the opening and closing sections, such as occasions when Watt is knocked down by a railway porter (pp. 24, 237); the appearances of Lady McCann (pp. 31, 242); and the scenes in which people ask questions about Watt's identity (pp. 18–23, 243–44). Recurring passages such as "there is not a moment to lose"—in each case a reaction to a train's imminent arrival at the station in Mr. Knott's town—are used for a similar effect (pp. 28, 239).

33. Page 246. This passage may contain an allusion to the second stanza of the hymn "For Ever with the Lord" (also known as "At Home in Heaven"), by James Montgomery (1771–1854): "Here in the body pent, / Absent from Him I roam, / Yet nightly pitch my moving tent / A day's march nearer home."

34. "On the Vanity and Suffering of Life," *The World*, 3:392; the italics are Schopenhauer's.

35. The limerick is by Maurice E. Hare; according to Harvey (p. 242), Beckett quoted it from memory. Like trams, human beings have limited freedom in space and time. A tram must stay on the tracks; most points in space-time are inaccessible to any one person because reaching them would involve journeys faster than the speed of light. For a human being, the maximum area that is even theoretically accessible is considerably less than a billionth of the universe (given that it is as yet impossible to achieve speeds at which relativistic time-slowing becomes appreciable). According to current estimates, the radius of the universe is some eighteen billion light years.

36. According to W. Y. Tindall, in Anglo-Saxon, *"Ic ne wāt* and *Ic nāt,* which suggest Watt and Knott, mean *I do not know.* Beckett studied Anglo-Saxon at Trinity." Tindall mentions, however, that Beckett denied he had these words in mind when he wrote *Watt;* see Tindall, p. 18. The usual way of interpreting the name is to assume that Watt stands for a question ("What?") and that Knott is a reply (either "Not," "Naught," or "Knot," in the sense of an enigma) indicating that the question is unanswerable. Arsene associates the name with Wat Tyler (c. 1381), a leader of the Peasants' Revolt (p. 48); this is probably a red herring. Beckett may be referring to another person named Watt: he is familiar with the work of Henry J. Watt, a Würzburg psychologist, the author of *The Sensory Basis and Structure of Knowledge* (London: Methuen, 1925) and of *Psychology* (1913; rpt., London: T. C. and E. C. Jack, n.d.); see *Murphy*, p. 81. In *Psychology* H. J. Watt discusses the mind-body question (p. 7), introspection (p. 9), and the role of the senses in conveying impressions of the outside world (pp. 16ff.). Though H. J. Watt dismisses idealistic views of the mind-body question, he is also opposed to the purely materialistic definition of the mind as an appendage of the body: "Every view which reduces mind to a mere inert series of phenomena, is belied by the experience and conviction of everyone and is useless and contrary to psychological knowledge" (p. 77). Beckett may also be using the name Watt to allude to James Watt (1736–1819), whose improvements on the steam engine helped to usher in the Industrial Revolution.

37. *Proust*, p. 52; *Waiting for Godot* (New York: Grove Press, 1954), p. 28.

38. Schopenhauer says that the outward behavior of those geniuses who can perceive the ultimate nature of reality is not far from what most people would label madness; see *The World*, 2:246ff. Watt has become like Mr. Endon in *Murphy*, a lunatic others look to for guidance. In *Proust* Beckett refers to "the rare dispensation of waking madness" in a discussion of madness as a way of escaping from the world of appearances (p. 19).

39. The apparition is related to a type of perception that Schopenhauer says begins when individuals begin to see themselves as creatures of pure

will. When one engages in artistic contemplation, the subject (the mind's image of itself engaged in contemplation) and the object (the mind's image of the self as pure will) begin to merge into a unified vision of a single thing-in-itself. One can perceive "the true world as idea" when "the subject and object reciprocally fill and penetrate each other completely," says Schopenhauer; "and in the same way the knowing and known individuals, as things in themselves, are not to be distinguished" (*The World*, 1:233).

40. According to Schopenhauer, even a momentary image of oneself as a creature in time and space can destroy the vision of the individual as thing-in-itself. "As soon as any single relation to our will, to our person . . . comes again into consciousness, the magic is at an end; we fall back into the knowledge which is governed by the principle of sufficient reason; we no longer know the Idea, but the particular thing, the link of a chain to which we also belong, and we are again abandoned to all our woe" (*The World*, 1:256). Watt's failure to understand the significance of the Tom-Dick-Harry series and his questions about the appearance of the apparition are related to this concept: as soon as he begins to inquire into their space-time characteristics or their causal connections, he reverts to the type of understanding governed by reason. Schopenhauer's idea, and his phrase "the magic is at an end," bring to mind a passage in Beckett's *Proust:* "when the object is perceived as particular and unique and not merely the member of a family, when it appears independent of any general notion and detached from the sanity of a cause, isolated and inexplicable in the light of ignorance, then and only then may it be a source of enchantment" (p. 11).

41. This reference can be linked with the tram metaphor discussed earlier. Discussions of train schedules in *Watt* (pp. 232, 239) suggest how the movements of trains are limited in time and space.

42. Harvey, p. 247.

43. *Ibid.* The idea of a confrontation with an alter ego is central in Beckett's poem "Arènes de Lutèce." The encounter described in the poem (which was written a few years before *Watt*) is somewhat like Watt's, but in the poem the speaker immediately realizes that he is seeing an aspect of himself. In *Molloy* both Moran and Molloy meet figures who similarly seem to be aspects of themselves. Beckett's reference to "a self that might have been but never got born" (Harvey, p. 247) resembles a phrase in *Watt*, "never been properly born" (p. 248). Beckett's comment about the unborn self may be related to Schopenhauer's distinction between a person's aspects as phenomenon and as thing-in-itself. He describes seeing one's body as "an object among objects"; this gives way to a perception of the individual as a thing-in-itself (*The World*, 1:228, 229–34; 2:404ff.). Artistic contemplation is another means of perceiving oneself as a thing-in-itself (*ibid.*, 1:238–39ff.). Some of Beckett's comments about the unborn self resemble Schopenhauer's description of a state of "pure contemplation . . . sinking oneself in per-

ception, losing oneself in the object, forgetting all individuality, surrendering that kind of knowledge which follows the principle of sufficient reason, and comprehends only relations; the state by means of which at once and inseparably the perceived particular thing is raised to the Idea of its whole species, and the knowing individual to the pure subject of will-less knowledge, and as such they are both taken out of the stream of time and all other relations" (*ibid.*, pp. 254–55).

44. This pertains to Schopenhauer's idea that the world we apprehend is actually a projection of the will (*The World*, 1:131 *et passim*). The title of Schopenhauer's major work, *The World as Will and Idea*, reflects this concept: he is arguing that the world we perceive is projected by the will and obscures the deeper reality of the Idea, or thing-in-itself. Beckett alludes to this concept, and mentions Schopenhauer as his source, in *Proust* (p. 8). In the same work Beckett introduces an idea similar to the "screen" mentioned in *Watt:* he refers to "the surface, the façade, behind which the Idea is prisoner" (*Watt*, p. 232; *Proust*, p. 59). Schopenhauer speaks of the similarities between "the Idea" (by which he means the Platonic Idea) and the thing-in-itself (*The World*, 1:221). Beckett, discussing how freedom from the will and causality leads to the perception of a deeper reality, mentions "the Idea, the Thing in itself" (*Proust*, p. 69). Schopenhauer sometimes describes the facade that obscures the deeper reality as the "veil of Mâyâ" (see, for example, *The World*, 1:9, 454). Beckett's concept of the "screen" also resembles Schopenhauer's image of the veil of Mâyâ.

45. Dante Alighieri, *Paradiso* 33:67–68, 44–45, 47–48. The English version is taken from *The Divine Comedy*, trans. John Sinclair (New York: Oxford University Press, 1969), 3:481. The significance of the passage in *Watt* (p. 253) that is taken from *The Divine Comedy* (*Inferno* 7:60) will be discussed in Chapter 11. Eugene Webb argues that *Watt* in its entirety is a parody of the *Paradiso*; see *Samuel Beckett: A Study of His Novels* (Seattle: University of Washington Press, 1973), p. 24.

46. Page 238. This passage is emphasized by a similar phrase on p. 233: "than he would have believed possible. . . ."

47. *Watt*, p. 249; Schopenhauer, *Ueber die vierfache Wurzel . . .*, *Sämtliche Werke*, 1:50.

48. See *The World*, 1:238–40, for example.

49. "Dante . . . Bruno. Vico . . Joyce," in *Our Exagmination Round his Factification for Incamination of Work in Progress* (1929; rpt., London: Faber and Faber, 1972), pp. 9–10. This issue was discussed in Chapter 4.

50. *Proust*, p. 19.

51. The word "mansion" has associations which suggest that Watt has found a kind of paradise in the asylum. Beckett may have in mind the biblical passage "In my Father's house are many mansions" (John 14:2); or he may be suggesting another link with Watt's name by alluding to the "mansions in the skies" in Isaac Watts's hymn "When I Can Read My Title Clear." It may also be that Beckett is referring to a passage in one of

Keats's letters in which he says that most human experiences are indescribable. Keats writes, "I compare human life to a large mansion of many apartments, two of which I can only describe, the doors of the rest being as yet shut upon me" (letter to John Hamilton Reynolds, Sept. 22, 1818). For Beckett's references to Watt's mansion, see *Watt*, pp. 151–54.

52. Estragon, in *Waiting for Godot*, indicates that in his view life is a dream (p. 11). Schopenhauer discusses a similar idea and connects it with the illusions of the world of phenomena (*The World*, 1:21).

11

The Addenda to *Watt*

At the end of *Watt* there is a section entitled "Addenda," consisting of thirty-seven items of various sorts: poems, quotations, bits of narrative, even a few lines of music. These addenda are introduced by a footnote that reads, "The following precious and illuminating material should be carefully studied. Only fatigue and disgust prevented its incorporation."[1] Some commentators have taken the footnote as Beckett's admission that the addenda are unimportant. But the footnote is written in the passive voice: the speaker's identity can only be guessed at, and the ironic tone cannot be trusted.

Some of the addenda seem peripheral, but others refer to themes in the main body of the novel. This is true of three poems included among the addenda. The poem beginning "who may tell the tale . . ." (p. 247) hints at the difficulty of locating a consistent narrative voice in the novel. It also touches on other important themes, the problems involved in depicting human suffering and in describing nothingness.

Another poem encourages readers to consider possible interpretations for the names Watt and Knott by juxtaposing them with the words "what" and "not":

> Watt will not
> abate one jot
> but of what
>
> of the coming to
> of the being at
> of the going from
> Knott's habitat
> (P. 249)

The remaining stanzas go on to present a synopsis of Watt's actions: his arrival at Mr. Knott's house, his disappointments there, his departure. The poem also clarifies a metaphor that is used in the main body of the novel. A reference to "the dim mind wayfaring / through barren lands" suggests that Watt's quest can be understood as a mental journey. In the fifth and sixth stanzas there is an image of a flame surrounded by dark winds, and a reference to a dark mind. The image refers to Watt's diminishing mental capacity and enforces the idea that Watt's game with the dying coals can be interpreted as a metaphor about epistemology.

The third poem contains a direct reference to the action in the earlier sections: it is introduced as the "descant heard by Watt on way to station (IV)" (p. 253). This indicates that the descant can be considered a fugitive bit of text: if it had been included in Part IV, it could have served as a symmetrical counterpart to the threne Watt heard after leaving the station in Part I. The fact that the descant is included among the addenda enforces an idea introduced at the beginning of Part IV: that Sam's ordering of the sections may not be the definitive one, and that a different sequence might be considered.

The descant, like the threne, has parts for soprano, alto, tenor, and bass; in both songs the bass cannot hold back an occasional expletive ("phew!" pp. 34, 253). If the soprano's part in the descant is written out in rhyming lines, its resemblance to the two poems just discussed becomes apparent:

> With all our heart
> breath head awhile
> darkly apart
> the air exile
> of ended smile
> of ending care
> darkly awhile
> the exile air

Again the word "dark" is emphasized, and references to the head and the heart hint at the intellectual and emotional difficulties that contribute to Watt's decision to go into exile.

No music is given for the descant. But one of the addenda is introduced by this statement: "Threne heard by Watt in ditch on way from station. The soprano sang . . . ," and then four lines of music are given (p. 254). The introductory statement answers a question raised many pages earlier in a footnote: "What, it may be enquired, was the music of this threne? What at least, it may be demanded, did the soprano sing?" (p. 33). The question makes it clear that the addendum is meant to be linked with the text.

The monotonous music of the threne is appropriate to its subject matter: strings of numbers proliferating endlessly together with descriptions of the proliferation of humanity as it marches toward oblivion. The numbers in each stanza are surds in which a series of six digits is repeated ad infinitum: 52.285714285714 . . . and 52.142857142857 . . . ; they can be derived by dividing 366 and 365 by 7.[2] The recurring digits (based on the cyclic number 142857, which has long fascinated mathematicians) have many intriguing properties. In both of them the fractional values are numbers made up of related groups of digits, 285714 and 142857. The digits in the two groups are the same, they follow one another in the same order, and 142857 is exactly half of 285714. The attempt to settle a trivial question, the exact number of weeks in a year and in a leap year, produces mysterious numbers that stretch toward infinity. For Beckett, the surds become metaphors for the generations of humanity stretching through time. They raise a question that Arsene touches on when he enumerates his ancestors: what is the purpose of the generations that keep popping into the world with such regularity? As Arsene and Watt both learn, teleological questions are more easily raised than answered.

Another addendum conveys a sense of the briefness of life. It begins with the idea of creation: "dead calm, then a murmur, a name, a murmured name . . ." (p. 248). This is followed by an image of a wave that crests and subsides: "cold calm sea whitening whispering to the shore, stealing, hastening, swelling, passing, dying, from naught come, to naught gone." The fragment suggests that a life is like an unnoticed wave, an insignificant event that interrupts the expansive emptiness between "from naught come" and "to naught gone."

Some of the addenda are leftover bits from earlier drafts of *Watt*, and one of these again touches on the theme of the briefness of life.[3] The addendum begins with the description of a meeting between Arthur and a beggar (pp. 251–52). The beggar claims to remember Arthur as a boy—he seems to think he is addressing Mr. Knott. Arthur then tells Watt about the encounter, and mentions that the beggar was once employed by the Knott family. Watt reacts to this news in an interesting way:

> This was the first time Watt had heard the words Knott family.
> There had been a time when they would have pleased him, and the thought they tendered, that Mr Knott too was serial, in a vermicular series. But not now. For Watt was an old rose now, and indifferent to the gardener. (P. 253)

Watt no longer wants to know about Mr. Knott's origins. A reason for this change of attitude is based on Diderot's fable of the roses —Beckett is again referring to a theme he touched on in *More Pricks than Kicks.* In *D'Alembert's Dream* Diderot describes roses who are certain that the gardener who tends them is immortal.[4] But Watt, an old rose, no longer cares about whether Mr. Knott is "serial." This indicates that Watt has begun to give up his role as an *animal metaphysicum:* he is content to let questions about Mr. Knott's origins go unanswered. Watt's transition runs parallel to the way the novel developed through successive drafts. In the earlier version details about Mr. Knott's family were supplied (there were descriptions of his parents, for example). In the published version Mr. Knott—who represents paradox—becomes more paradoxical, and such details are omitted.

Some of the very short addenda also help to create an aura of mystery. If one knows that drawsheets are used to cover hospital beds, the meaning of the addendum which reads, "her married life one long drawsheet," seems clear (p. 247). But it cannot be determined if the passage is about Tetty Nixon, or one of the Lynch women, or someone else entirely. The function of the fragment is not to describe the life of a particular woman but to provide a thematic connection with the addenda that deal with the proliferation of life and its apparent pointlessness.

One addendum consists of two words, "Watt snites" (p. 248). This perhaps refers to the hero's contemplative nose-picking when he arrives at Mr. Knott's house, and it may be when he leaves Mr. Knott's that Watt looks "as though nearing end of course of injections of sterile pus" (p. 253). Passages like these are tantalizing, and one of their functions is to encourage readers to speculate about how they can fit into the novel.

Another short addendum reads, "like a thicket flower unre-corded" (p. 251). This may refer to a flower Watt crushes under-foot when he is distracted by the waxen lilies, or to one of the daisies—mentioned in the story about Arthur and the beggar—which is not crushed (pp. 135–36, 252). What is clear, however, is the paradoxical nature of the statement: once Beckett has de-scribed the flower, it can no longer be thought of as "unrecorded."

In some instances an entire episode is suggested by a short de-scriptive addendum. A fragment that tells about how Watt marks the position of Mr. Knott's bowl at mealtimes conjures up a vi-sion of the hero as indefatigable researcher, still convinced that empirical investigations will yield significant information about his employer (p. 248). In another addendum there is a description of a round wooden table (p. 249). The table is perhaps the place where the positions of Mr. Knott's bowl were marked. Another addendum consists of this passage: "One night Watt goes on roof" (p. 248). Has Watt decided that an increase in elevation will lead him to new heights of understanding about Mr. Knott's es-tablishment? Like Watt, the reader discovers new paradoxes with every elucidatory detail. The cultivation of uncertainty in these fragments is related to Beckett's view that enigma enhances art.

In one of the longer addenda Watt is described standing on a dark waste under a dark sky (p. 249). The passage is called a "soul-landscape," which indicates that it is a metaphor: Beckett is us-ing a description of the outer world to create an image of inner reality. The style and content of the addendum are very much like those in Beckett's later works—*Lessness* in particular—where similar metaphors are used. Obscurity is an important feature in the soul-landscape in *Watt:* the word "dark" is repeated twelve times.

The word "dark" occurs again in the addendum which reads, "the sheet of dark water, the widening fret of ripples, the deaden-ing banks, the stillness" (p. 248). The images here resemble those in the addendum where life is compared to a cresting wave. But questions about how the passage fits in with the other addenda, or even what it depicts, give way to admiration for its poetic qualities.

This process is related to Beckett's idea that aesthetic apprecia-tion flourishes best when rational needs subside. His approach is not entirely anti-intellectual: he sees rationality as a means of moving beyond the need for rationality.[5] Arsene speaks of a ladder which can be taken away while one is still standing on it (p. 44). Such an idea may seem irrational, but it suggests that it is on the uppermost rung of the ladder of reason that one begins to transcend rationality.

A related issue emerges in discussions of the two paintings in Erskine's room. Watt sees the first one, a picture of a broken circle with a dot outside it, while he is at Mr. Knott's house (p. 128). The second picture, a portrait of a naked pianist, is described in an addendum. Though the pianist is unnamed in the published version of the novel, in an earlier draft he is identified as Mr. Knott's father.[6] The introduction to the addendum, "Second picture in Erskine's room . . . ," suggests that the two pictures should be compared.

The portrait of the pianist is the work of a Mr. O'Connery, whose meticulous concern for detail is compared to that of Jan de Heem, the seventeenth-century Dutch still-life painter (p. 250). Mr. O'Connery is probably the person mentioned in an earlier addendum, "Art Conn O'Connery, called Black Velvet O'Connery, product of the great Chinnery-Slattery tradition" (p. 247). In this passage O'Connery is linked with two realistic painters who were active in Ireland, George Chinnery and John Joseph Slattery. Chinnery resided for a number of years in Dublin during the late eighteenth century; his works consist mainly of portraits and landscapes. Slattery was a portraitist who lived in Dublin between 1846 and 1858. O'Connery is associated with still another realist, Jan Brueghel. As Dougald McMillan points out, "The fictitious painter is referred to as 'Black Velvet' O'Connery, recalling Jan 'Velvet' Brueghel, who attempted to render all five senses visually in a series of allegorical paintings called *The Senses*."[7] The surname "Velvet" also introduces a satirical note: in Ireland a "black velvet" is a drink made by mixing stout and champagne.[8]

The man in O'Connery's portrait, says the narrator, uses his right hand to play "a chord which Watt has no difficulty in identifying as that of C major in its second inversion. . . ." With his left hand "he prolongs pavilion of left ear" as he tries to hear the music (p. 250). Like Jan Brueghel, O'Connery has attempted to depict an auditory experience in a visual medium, but even the musician in his picture seems to have trouble hearing any sounds. The painting raises expectations it cannot fulfill; in this way it demonstrates the limitations of realistic art. The painting is a failure in both practical and artistic terms: the piano cannot be played, and a photographic rendering of a commonplace event is worth little aesthetically. O'Connery's trompe l'oeil effects misleadingly suggest that objects in a painting exist in the same plane of reality as their three-dimensional counterparts. As the painter's name suggests, his kind of art is a trick, an art con.

The unnamed artist who painted the picture of the dot and broken circle has made no attempt to depict material objects. Yet the painting has a mysterious ability to evoke a sense of space and movement: "How the effect of perspective was obtained Watt did not know. But it was obtained. By what means the illusion of movement in space, and it almost seemed in time, was given, Watt could not say. But it was given" (pp. 128–29). Even in terms of dealing with time-space reality the abstract painting triumphs over its realistic counterpart. Moreover, the abstract is also arresting aesthetically: the dot, says the narrator, "was blue, but blue!" (p. 128). But the intensity of color does not interest Watt: he is busy speculating about "what the artist had intended to represent" (p. 129). As the narrator helpfully explains, "Watt knew nothing about painting." A moment later Watt begins to wonder whether the dot is the misplaced center of the circle and then—as so often occurs when he asks the wrong questions—he loses himself in a morass of pointless reasoning. Reverting to his old Cartesian method, he focuses on the geometry of the picture instead of seeing it as an aesthetic object.

One of Watt's reactions to the portrait is also mentioned: the narrator says that the chord the pianist is playing is one "which Watt has no difficulty in identifying . . ." (p. 250). This suggests that Watt, who saw the picture, later described it to Sam, who earlier had identified himself as the narrator of the novel (pp. 125–28, 153). Sam claims never to have participated in the action directly: "all that I know on the subject of Mr Knott," he says, "and of all that touched Mr Knott, and on the subject of Watt, and of all that touched Watt, came from Watt, and from Watt alone" (p. 125). But this disclaimer raises a problem. Could the knowledgeable description of the portrait ("Beads of sweat, realized with a finish that would have done credit to Heem . . .") have originated with Watt, who knows nothing about art? The allusions to artists in the other addenda bring this inconsistency into sharper focus.

One can try to wriggle out of the dilemma: Sam may have embellished his description of the picture; or Watt, after leaving Mr. Knott's house, may have developed an interest in painting; or the addendum may have been written by a different narrator, who was familiar with the picture. Even so, still another inconsistency must be resolved. Sam mentions that there was a bell in Erskine's room. He then insists that the picture of the broken circle was the "only other object of note in Erskine's room . . ." (p. 128). The opening of the addendum ("Second picture in Erskine's room . . .") refutes this statement. It may be that the narrator does not consider the portrait an object of note; nevertheless, he does note it.

The best alternative is to assume that the narrative in *Watt*, as in Beckett's other novels, is at times unreliable. This would suggest a way out of another difficulty: how the narrator can give detailed descriptions of events that occurred in Watt's absence, like those depicted in the opening pages of the novel. Here again similar concepts are embodied both in the content and in the form. A comparison of the two paintings indicates that Watt's rational approach to art is faulty, and it reveals an inconsistency which suggests that the narrative itself is not strictly governed by rational principles.

Beckett's approach, which departs from the conventional way of depicting reality, is similar to one often encountered among modern painters. The need to represent events as they occur in time and space has disappeared, and with it the rational principles derived from the observation of time-space phenomena. This leaves artists free to shape and arrange their materials in accordance with the internal requirements of their works. Such works may seem enigmatic because their subjects cannot be identified in terms of commonplace experiences, but they often can offer new insights into the nature of reality.

A related idea is introduced in the addendum which reads, "Watt's Davus complex (morbid dread of sphinxes)" (p. 251). Davus, as was mentioned in an earlier chapter, is a character in Terence's *Andria* who is remembered for the line "I am Davus, not Oedipus."[9] The Davus complex is Beckett's term for a condition involving a horror of the paradoxical. Davus and Oedipus are polar opposites: Davus dreads sphinxes; Oedipus found the answer to the sphinx's riddle—an event which so mortified her that she threw herself from a rock. Sphinxes, then, presumably have a reason to dread Oedipus.

Beckett mentions Davus in a review that appeared a few years before he began *Watt*. Attacking those who insist that everything in art must be immediately comprehensible, Beckett complains about "the go-getters, the gerrymandlers, Davus and the morbid dread of sphinxes, solution clapped on problem like a snuffer on a candle, the great crossword public on all its planes. . . ." Art, Beckett insists, has always been "pure interrogation, rhetorical question less the rhetoric—whatever else it may have been obliged by the 'social reality' to appear. . . ." Few people have recognized that great art incorporates a "need to need"; hence, much that is significant in modern music, painting, and literature has been dismissed as obscure.[10]

Watt's hunger for explanations, his need to know what a painting represents, and his inability to deal with symbols can all be considered symptoms of his Davus complex. He dreads things or persons (Mr. Knott, for example) of an inscrutable nature. He does not understand that it is not the similarity but the difference between a material object and its artistic representation that is important, for it is here that the idea of its transcendental reality resides.[11] This reality is mysterious, difficult to apprehend; hence, to deal with it the artist must go beyond the depiction of what is immediately discernible. As Watt learns to his dismay, even the most mundane objects possess strange and unfamiliar qualities. At Mr. Knott's house he focuses his attention on a pot until he finds that it has become so transformed that he can no longer call it by its old name. Watt finally is forced to admit that the pot "was not a pot, any more" (p. 82).

The structure of the novel follows a similar pattern. If Beckett initially seems to be dealing with reality in a conventional way, it is only to provide a contrast with what follows. The satirical distortions and unreliable narrative soon give way to a general breakdown of verisimilitude. Episodes like the one about the pot invest ordinary objects with enigmatic qualities. Then, in the portions of the novel that may have seemed the least meaningful, one begins to see glimmers of an underlying reality. In order to apprehend this view of reality the reader—like Watt—must be willing to make the transition from a rational to a more aesthetic approach.

Questions about art, rationality, and paradox occur again in the addendum which reads, "the Master of the Leopardstown Half-lengths" (p. 247). Leopardstown is a racecourse between Dublin and Foxrock, the town where Beckett spent his childhood. Mr. Knott's house resembles the Beckett family home in Foxrock; Watt, on his way to Mr. Knott's, sees a racecourse (p. 29). But the Master of the Halflengths is not, as one might suppose, a minor racing official. The phrase refers to the Master of the Female Half-Lengths, an unknown sixteenth-century painter whose name is based on the way he typically portrayed his subjects.[12] The reference to the halflengths of the racecourse suggests another allusion, to a paradox of Zeno of Elea called "The Race Course." Zeno describes a runner who is attempting to complete a given course. He traverses half the distance to the finish line, then half the remaining distance, then half of each new remainder, ad infinitum. The runner, who must pass through an infinite number of spaces in a finite span of time, can never complete the course.[13] Zeno's version of the paradox did not survive from antiquity; it is known because it was paraphrased in Aristotle's *Physics.*[14] This introduces still another allusion suggested by the reference to the Master of the Halflengths: an old epithet for Aristotle is "the master of those who know."[15]

In the *Physics* Aristotle provides a way of refuting Zeno's paradox. He argues that if the runner must traverse an infinite number of half-units of length, he also has an infinite number of half-units of time in which to accomplish the task.[16] But Aristotle's solution never laid the matter to rest, and a number of modern philosophers have attempted to find new ways of refuting the paradox. One argument, put forward by Henri Bergson, denies that time and space can be divided into discrete units.[17] Bertrand Russell and other thinkers who favor an empirical or positivistic point of view have introduced refutations that utilize recent mathematical innovations, notably Georg Cantor's theory of the varying orders of infinity.[18] The most radical alternative of all is based on the raison d'etre of Zeno's paradoxes: a demonstration of the illusory nature of time-space reality. It seems likely that this approach is the one Beckett favors.

The stylistic attributes of the addendum about the halflengths are no less important than its content: in a passage as concise and suggestive as a line of poetry, Beckett deals with issues as far-ranging as Greek philosophy, art history, and Irish horse racing, and then connects them with themes in his novel. This abundance of significance characterizes many of the addenda, especially those that initially seem inconsequential or digressive.

Some of the addenda are elucidatory, some are puzzling, and some of the elucidations add new puzzles. One addendum reads, "Note that Arsene's declaration gradually came back to Watt" (p. 248). This supposedly explains how, if Watt forgot Arsene's declaration, he later was able to repeat it to Sam. But Arsene's "short statement" is more than twenty pages long, and it was not forgotten—Watt had never really listened to it in the first place (p. 39). The following passage makes this clear: "He wondered also what Arsene had meant, nay, he wondered what Arsene had said, on the evening of his departure. For his declaration had entered Watt's ear only by fits, and his understanding, like all that enters the ears only by fits, hardly at all. He had realised, to be sure, that Arsene was speaking, and in a sense to him, but something had prevented him, perhaps his fatigue, from paying attention to what was being said and from enquiring into what was being meant" (pp. 80–81). If this is true, the addendum which specifies that "Arsene's declaration gradually came back to Watt" can be taken as another of the novel's unreliable passages.

Beckett's technique is to depict a world which seems clean and tidy only so long as one fails to notice that the incongruities have been swept under the rug. This approach is illustrated in the addendum which reads, "limits to part's equality with whole" (p. 247). At first glance the passage seems to be a qualification of a mathematical principle: either one of Euclid's axioms ("The whole is greater than the part") or one derived by a commentator on Euclid, Christopher Clavius ("The whole is equal to the sum of its parts").[19] But the third word in the addendum is not "parts'" but "part's." Beckett is suggesting that the part can sometimes, but not always, be equated with the whole; a similar concept is expressed in the French version of the novel.[20] The addendum underlines a difference between logical and aesthetic modes of thought: in Euclidean geometry the part can never be equal to the whole; in literature the idea of synecdoche is commonplace. Beckett may also be alluding to Zeno's arguments against plurality, which deal with the illogicality of the part-whole distinction.[21] Beckett uses the addendum to demonstrate how much can ride on the transposition of a single punctuation mark, and how easily such details can slip by.

Another easily misunderstood addendum is the last one, which reads, "no symbols where none intended" (p. 254). At first glance this dictum (which resembles the saying "no offense taken where none intended") seems to suggest that there are not too many symbols in *Watt*. But the addendum is not really about the number of symbols in the novel; rather, it indicates that the symbolism is not unintentional. A related issue is introduced when the narrator describes Watt's need to provide every event he observes with a meaning: "The most meagre, the least plausible [meaning], would have satisfied Watt, who had not seen a symbol, nor executed an interpretation, since the age of fourteen, or fifteen, and who had lived, miserably it is true, among face values all his adult life, face values at least for him. . . . And he had experienced literally nothing, since the age of fourteen, or fifteen, of which in retrospect he was not content to say, That is what happened then" (p. 73). The repeated phrase in this passage ("since the age of fourteen, or fifteen") underlines the idea that Watt has rejected imaginative activity as a reversion to the illogicality of childhood thinking. But living with face values exclusively is, as the narrator says, a miserable sort of existence. Beckett uses "no symbols where none intended" to mock those readers who may have taken it as an endorsement of their own unwillingness to deal with the symbolism in the novel.

Beckett at times deliberately encourages readers to jump to misleading conclusions; this personalizes their subsequent discoveries about the deceptive nature of face values. After a cursory reading of the novel it is easy to assume that Watt has lost touch with reality when he arrives at the asylum. By hinting that Watt may be confused or deranged, Beckett misleadingly suggests that he is supporting a conventional view of reality. He uses a similar approach in the following addendum, where the narrator seems to be trying to fill in one of the gaps in the story: "*Watt learned to accept* etc. Use to explain poverty of Part III. Watt cannot speak of what happened on first floor, because for the greater part of the time nothing happened, without his protesting" (p. 248). The poverty of Part III, then, is presumably based on the fact that nothing worth describing occurred during the latter half of Watt's stay at Mr. Knott's house. But this proposition is misleading in two ways. The most extensive descriptions of Watt's encounters with Mr. Knott are in Part III—although these are transcribed in an inverted language that may have led some readers to skip over them. Moreover, as Beckett skillfully demonstrates, the fact that nothing happens hardly implies that one cannot speak about it. In Part II Watt experiences "a thing that was nothing" that takes ten pages to describe (pp. 70–80). The quotation at the beginning of this addendum ("*Watt learned to accept* etc.") covertly suggests this idea by referring back to the conclusion of the ten-page description of the "thing that was nothing": "Watt learned towards the end of this stay in Mr Knott's house to accept that nothing had happened, that a nothing had happened, learned to bear it and even, in a shy way, to like it. But then it was too late" (p. 80). Watt eventually learns to accept the idea of nothingness, but by then he is about to leave Mr. Knott's house; hence the knowledge comes too late to help him deal with the nothingness he encounters there. The reader, however, can return to the descriptions of Mr. Knott's house and try to understand the "thing that was nothing." The addendum obscures this idea if it is taken in its superficial sense, as an admission that it is impossible to speak about nothing. But if one realizes that it refers back to the earlier passage, it becomes clear that the addendum has to do with Watt's growing ability to accept the concept of nothingness.

Watt undergoes another change—this time just after leaving Mr. Knott's house—that is at first similarly difficult to understand. When he is knocked down at the railroad station, he thinks of a few phrases from a German poem, "Hyperions Schicksalslied," by Hölderlin.[22] A moment later he recalls some fragments from an English work, Farquhar's comedy *The Beaux' Stratagem*.[23] Watt, ignoring the stimuli of the outer world, preoccupied with lines from a poem and a play, is making a transition from rational thought to aesthetic contemplation.

His ability to quote from these authors suggests that Watt (as the narrator says) is "a very fair linguist," and that (as Mrs. Nixon assumes) he may well be "a university man" (pp. 208, 23). A related point arises when Mr. Nixon says, twice, that Watt is at times "a little strange" (pp. 20, 22). The addendum which reads, "the maddened prizeman," suggests that Watt's strangeness may be an effect of intense intellectual activity (p. 248). The passage contains a punning reference to the Madden Prize, a scholarly award at Trinity College, Dublin. Beckett, a graduate of Trinity College, mentions a "Madden prizeman" in "Echo's Bones."[24]

Another reference to the debilitative effects of the intellectual life comes in the addendum which reads, "judicious Hooker's heat-pimples" (p. 247). Richard Hooker (1554?–1600) was a noted English theologian; the epithet "Judicious" is a tribute to his thoughtful reasoning. Beckett's addendum is based on a passage in *The Life of Mr. Richard Hooker*, by Izaak Walton. According to Walton, when Hooker's works made him famous, his parsonage near Canterbury became a shrine for visitors:

> many turn'd out of the Road, and others (Scholars especially) went purposely to see the man, whose life and learning were so much admired; and alas, as our Saviour said of *St. John Baptist, What went they out to see? a man cloathed in purple and fine linnen?* no indeed, but an *obscure, harmless man, a man in poor Cloaths, his Loyns usually girt in a course Gown, or Canonical Coat; of a mean stature, and stooping, and yet more lowly in the thoughts of his Soul; his Body worn out, not with Age, but Study, and Holy Mortifications; his Face full of Heat-pimples, begot by his unactivity and sedentary life.*[25]

The idea that knowledge alone does not bring happiness recurs in an addendum that consists of a Latin quotation: "faede hunc mundum intravi, anxius vixi, perturbatus egredior, causa causarum miserere mei" ("I entered this world in filth; I lived in it uneasily; in confusion I leave it; cause of causes have mercy on me"). These once were thought to be the last words of Aristotle.[26] The prayer is addressed to the cause of causes, Aristotle's prime mover, and not to the Lamb of God (it is based on "Agnus Dei . . . miserere nobis," from the Latin Mass). Even "the master of those who know" did not leave the battlefield unscarred: the unknown

author of these lines sees Aristotle, for all his wisdom, as someone who led a joyless life. The passage also recalls a source of
Watt's intellectual despair; some of his difficulties with the Cartesian concept of causality stem from his failure to recognize
that, for Descartes, God is the cause of causes.

A sense of despair is again conveyed in the addendum consisting of a four-line stanza that begins, "Bid us sigh on from day to
day . . ." (p. 248). The stanza is the second verse of James Thomson's poem "To Fortune." Beckett uses the quoted material in an
ingenious way. When the stanza is removed from the poem, the
speaker seems to be an old man, weary of life and the world. Actually, however, the lines are taken from a lover's complaint:

To Fortune

> For ever, Fortuné, wilt thou prove
> An unrelenting foe to love,
> And, when we meet a mutual heart,
> Come in between and bid us part;
>
> Bid us sigh on from day to day,
> And wish, and wish the soul away;
> Till youth and genial years are flown,
> And all the life of life is gone?
>
> . . . .
>
> All other blessings I resign;
> Make but the dear Amanda mine![27]

By isolating the second stanza and deleting a question mark Beckett transforms, and improves on, the original.

It is equally difficult to guess what some of the other excerpts
signified in their original contexts. An addendum in German
reads, "zitto! zitto! dass nur das Publikum nichts merke!"
("hush! hush! lest the public notice anything!"; p. 249). By itself
this may seem like a challenge to readers who are unwilling to
delve into the mysteries of a complicated text. But the passage, it
will be recalled, is taken from Schopenhauer's charge that his
contemporaries were conspiring against him.[28]

Another addendum consists of a quotation from a German philosopher who felt he was being dealt with unfairly; again, its
meaning is unclear because it has been removed from its original
context. The addendum reads, "das fruchtbare Bathos der Erfah-

rung" ("the fruitful *bathos* of experience"). It is from Kant's *Prolegomena to Any Future Metaphysics*, a work written shortly after the completion of the *Critique of Pure Reason*.[29] The *Prolegomena* was intended to serve as a guide to the *Critique*, which was not well received when it first appeared; in an appendix to the *Prolegomena* Kant attacks a reviewer who, he feels, had misunderstood the earlier work. The reviewer referred to Kant's philosophy as an example of the higher idealism. Kant rejects this designation in a colorful footnote: "Not on your life the *higher*. High towers, and metaphysically tall men like them, round both of which there is commonly a lot of wind, are not for me. My place is the fruitful *bathos* of experience. . . ."[30] By *bathos* Kant means a deep place: he has in mind not the English but the Greek word. He is justifiably annoyed that his philosophy has been taken for high-flown, airy speculation; even so, his disclaimer is hard to accept. Kant, a leading exponent of transcendental idealism, can hardly be considered a down-to-earth empiricist.

In the original the quoted passage poses another problem: *bathos* is used in its original sense, which can easily lead those who know its English meaning to misunderstand Kant's argument.[31] This seems to be what Beckett has planned for his readers, since his excerpt still makes sense when "bathos" is misinterpreted. It is a commonplace in Greek tragedy that suffering (*pathos*) brings wisdom. Beckett does not agree: bathos is what follows pathos; the fruits of bitter experience are self-pity and maudlin complaints. Even great philosophers cannot maintain a dignified silence when they feel they have been wronged.

In another addendum—itself a quotation—Beckett wittily comments on his own use of quoted material: "pereant qui ante nos nostra dixerunt" ("let those who used our words before us perish"; p. 250). Ironically, the source of the quotation is uncertain; thus one cannot determine precisely whom to condemn for having originated it. The quotation is sometimes attributed to St. Jerome, but he indicates that he took it from Aelius Donatus, who in turn seems to have based it on a line in one of Terence's comedies. Some authorities throw up their hands and call the quotation anonymous.[32] Beckett's use of the quotation is ironic in still another way: since he so often alters the material he borrows, he has little reason to feel apologetic about his literary debts.

In most instances Beckett provides a new context that alters the meaning of the material he quotes, but he sometimes introduces other changes. One addendum is based on a line from Goethe's *Faust*, "die Erde hat mich wieder!"[33] Faust, about to take his life, hears bells and a chorus: it is Easter. His faith in life renewed, he changes his mind about committing suicide and joyously proclaims, "the Earth has me once again!" Beckett adds a letter to "Erde" and the result is a witty macaronic: "die Merde hat mich wieder" (p. 250). When Beckett's characters give up the idea of suicide, it is with a grim understanding that they are returning to the muck of existence.

There is a similar revision in the addendum which reads, "sempiternal penumbra." Near the end of the *Paradiso* Dante sees a brilliant circle of celestial light, the "rosa sempiterna" ("eternal rose").[34] In Beckett's rendering the light is considerably diminished. The addendum recalls his mock-heroic comparison of the whiteness of the waiting-room ceiling and the light in paradise. Beckett's shadowy vision of eternity is as appropriate to his way of seeing the world as a luminous rose is to Dante's.

There is another allusion to *The Divine Comedy* among the addenda, this time from the *Inferno*: "parole non ci appulcro" ("I will add no more words to embellish it").[35] Virgil utters this line to indicate that he will not waste his breath describing the corruption of the popes and cardinals who were guilty of avarice. But though he has promised to remain silent, Virgil cannot refrain from speaking: he lectures Dante on the vanity of a life wasted in the pursuit of worldly goods. Virgil's remark fits in well with the mockery of bourgeois life in *Watt*, as well as with its critique of philosophical materialism. On one level the remark calls attention to the purposeful silences in the novel. But Beckett also hints at an ironic aspect of the passage: the addendum comes near the end of the novel—but not at the very end. Like Virgil, Beckett adds a few words after indicating that he intends to remain silent.

To understand this and the other quoted passages, it helps to know where they originated; but such information is seldom given. Beckett says little about the sources of Watt's ideas, but when a minor character like Mr. Spiro holds forth on esoteric theological issues (such as the excommunication of vermin), a list of the authorities he invokes is included (p. 29). Beckett's operative principle seems to be that the sources are identified only when they are of little use to the reader.

The same principle governs the addendum which reads, "the foetal soul is full grown (Cangiamila's *Sacred Embriology* and Pope Benedict XIV's *De Synodo Diocesana,* Bk. 7, Chap. 4, Sect. 6)."[36] Cangiamila's work deals with religious questions pertaining to abortion; Pope Benedict, in the specified section, is concerned with determining who may receive the sacrament. Readers with the inclination to delve into these works will be rewarded with a great deal of information about eighteenth-century medico-theology, but with little that pertains to *Watt.*

The allusions to Cangiamila and Pope Benedict encourage readers to go outside the novel for information about the development of the fetal soul. This may distract them from an adjacent addendum that deals with a related subject; it reads, "never been properly born" (p. 248). Beckett used a similar description of an unborn self in a conversation with Lawrence Harvey; he spoke of "a presence, embryonic, undeveloped, of a self that might have been but never got born, an *être manqué.*"[37] Beckett's quest for the unborn self is part of an introspective process that involves searching beneath the self of appearances to discover the underlying authentic self. This theme becomes more important in Beckett's later works.[38]

Some of the seemingly peripheral addenda (like those with quotations from other authors) turn out to have links with themes in the novel. At times this process is reversed, and allusions are concealed in passages that seemingly pertain only to the subject-matter of the novel. The addendum which reads, "for all the good that frequent departures out of Ireland had done him, he might just as well have stayed there," is apparently about Watt, but it may also refer to Descartes.[39] Another addendum of this type reads, "change all the names" (p. 253). This seems like a memorandum about an idea Beckett considered; although in *Watt* the characters' names are not changed, they are in some of his other works.[40] The addendum, however, also recalls a passage in Horace's *Satires:* "Why do you smile? Change but the name and it is of yourself that the tale is told."[41] Beckett mentions Horace's works a number of times in his earlier fiction, and there is another allusion to Horace in *Watt*.[42]

Horace's suggestion that readers might find themselves mirrored in his satirical portraits introduces a type of personal involvement with the work which is important in *Watt*. Beckett's protagonist poses difficult questions and is frustrated when he finds he cannot answer them. The addenda encourage readers to engage in a similar process: to formulate problems, track down clues, and, finally, to endure frustration when the answers are not forthcoming. Moreover, at times, readers are even given an authorial role. The fragmentary addenda and omissions in the narrative make it tempting to fill in the gaps and compose the literary equivalent of a cadenza. This prepares the way for a more complicated process involving speculation about entities that are suggested but not defined, such as the nature of the reality within Watt's mansion. For Beckett, the ultimate arena of literature is the mind, not the page, and his novels can be thought of as scripts for mental performances. The scripts are left incomplete so that readers' improvisations become a part of the creative activity; this makes their experience of the work more immediate. As readers become more familiar with *Watt*, their understanding of it changes; hence the novel can sustain many readings. These are among the reasons why Beckett feels that incomplete descriptions and enigmatic passages are often more effective than explicit statements.

When readers begin to give up the purely rational way of seeing the world, as Watt finally does, irritation about the novel's obscure meanings gives way to aesthetic pleasure. Inconsistencies are described with brilliant precision; enigmas are incorporated into a profound view of reality. The rational approach cannot be given up at the outset, however; in order to share in Watt's discoveries, one must be willing to repeat his mistakes. Watt is motivated by an urgent need to know; its counterpart is the intellectual curiosity Beckett uses to lure readers toward the hidden recesses of the novel. The addenda play a central role in the process: as the introductory footnote indicates, they are in fact precious, illuminating, and deserving of careful study.

Notes

1. *Watt* (1953; rpt., New York: Grove Press, 1959), p. 247; the addenda are on pp. 247–54. Page numbers in the text refer to this edition.

2. Pages 34–35. Both the threne and the music have been omitted in the French version of *Watt*. It should be noted that there is an error in the Grove edition of *Watt:* on p. 35 the first line of the second verse of the threne reads, *"Fifty-one point one"*; in the manuscript of the novel the lines read, *"Fifty-two point one."* The number in the manuscript, unlike the one in the Grove edition, is the result of dividing 365 by 7. My thanks to Samuel Beckett, the officers of the Humanities Research Center of the University of Texas at Austin, and Mrs. Sally Leach, assistant librarian at the Center, for permission to consult the manuscript of *Watt*. Some interesting properties of the cyclic number 142857 are described in Martin Gardner's *Mathematical Circus* (New York: Knopf, 1979), pp. 111ff.

3. As was explained in Chapter 5, n. 26, although the story of the gardener and the roses came originally from Fontenelle, Beckett probably took it from Diderot's *D'Alembert's Dream;* see Denis Diderot, *Rameau's Nephew and D'Alembert's Dream,* trans. L. W. Tancock (Harmondsworth: Penguin Books, 1966), p. 177. Beckett also refers to the story in *Dream of Fair to Middling Women* (TS, Dartmouth College Library), p. 156; *More Pricks than Kicks* (1934; rpt., New York: Grove Press, 1970), p. 191; and "Echo's Bones" (TS, Dartmouth College Library), p. 19.

4. For descriptions of the earlier version of *Watt*, see J. M. Coetzee, "The Manuscript Revisions of Beckett's *Watt*," *Journal of Modern Literature,* 2 (1972):472–80; Sighle Kennedy, " 'The Simple Games That Time Plays with Space—' An Introduction to Samuel Beckett's Manuscripts of *Watt*," *Centerpoint,* 2(1977):55–61.

5. A similar idea is expressed in a later work, *Molloy:* "For to know nothing is nothing, not to want to know anything likewise, but to be beyond knowing anything, to know you are beyond knowing anything, that is when peace enters in, to the soul of the incurious seeker"; *Molloy* (New York: Grove Press, 1955), p. 86.

6. See Coetzee, p. 475; the addendum is on pp. 250–51.

7. Dougald McMillan, "Samuel Beckett and the Visual Arts: The Embarrassment of Allegory," in Ruby Cohn, ed., *Samuel Beckett: A Collection of Criticism* (New York: McGraw-Hill, 1975), p. 129.

8. In "Echo's Bones" Lord Gall mixes himself "a stiff black velvet" (p. 11).

9. "Davos sum, non Oedipus"; Terence, *Andria,* l. 194. In Latin the name is spelled "Davos," but translators often render it "Davus" in English (e.g., John Sargeaunt, the translator of the Loeb edition). The remark is famous enough to be listed in *Bartlett's Familiar Quotations* (14th ed.).

10. Samuel Beckett, "Denis Devlin," *Transition*, no. 27 (Apr.-May, 1938), pp. 289–90.

11. This is very much like Schopenhauer's idea that rational methods cannot be used to investigate metaphysical reality; see Arthur Schopenhauer, *The World as Will and Idea*, trans. R. B. Haldane and J. Kemp (1883; rpt., London: Routledge and Kegan Paul, 1964), 2:382. Beckett makes a similar point in another novel: when Molloy describes the laws of his mind, it becomes apparent that they are parodies of physical laws; *Molloy*, p. 16.

12. A description of the Master of the Female Half-Lengths can be found in *Encyclopedia of the Arts*, ed. Herbert Read (New York: Meredith Press, 1966), pp. 608. In an earlier version of *Watt* a portrait of Mr. Knott's mother is attributed to the Master of the Leopardstown Halflengths; see Coetzee, p. 474. Beckett parodies this convention for referring to unknown artists when he speaks of "the Master of Tired Eyes" in *More Pricks than Kicks* (p. 44). Beckett himself followed in the tradition of the Master of the Female Half-Lengths when in *Happy Days* he depicted Winnie partly immersed in a mound.

13. My summary of the paradox is based on an article by Gregory Vlastos on Zeno in *The Encyclopedia of Philosophy*, ed. Paul Edwards (New York: Crowell Collier and Macmillan, 1967), 8:372–74.

14. Aristotle, *Physics*, 233a, 22; 239b, 10; 263a, 4.

15. For example, Dante refers to Aristotle by this title: "vidi 'l maestro di color che sanno"; *Inferno* 4:131.

16. *Physics*, 263a, 12.

17. See Sir William Dampier, *A History of Science* (Cambridge: Cambridge University Press, 1966), p. 463.

18. This argument is too technical to be summarized here; see Vlastos, pp. 372ff. For Russell's views, see his *A History of Western Philosophy* (New York: Clarion Books, 1967), pp. 828–30.

19. "The whole is greater than the parts" is the fifth of the "Common Notions" in Book I of Euclid's *Elements*. Christopher Clavius (1537–1612) was a German mathematician who derived his axiom from Euclid's. See Sir Thomas Heath, ed., *The Thirteen Books of Euclid's Elements* (New York: Dover Publications, 1956), 1:232.

20. In French the addendum reads, "des limites à l'égalité de la partie avec le tout"; *Watt* (Paris: 10:18, Editions de Minuit, 1972), p. 299. *Watt* was translated by Ludovic and Agnès Janvier "in collaboration with the author"; see Raymond Federman and John Fletcher, *Samuel Beckett, His Works and His Critics* (Berkeley: University of California Press, 1970), p. 46.

21. According to ancient authorities, Zeno had forty arguments against plurality; of these, three have survived; see Vlastos, pp. 369–72. Sir William Dampier summarizes one of these arguments in this way: "A manifold must be divisible to infinity and therefore must itself be infinite,

but, in trying to build it up again, no number of infinitely small parts can make a finite whole" (pp. 19–20).

22. Page 239. The lines are quoted imperfectly: there are omissions and the first word in the second line of the excerpt, "Endlos," should be "Jahrlang." In the original the last three lines of the poem read, "Wie Wasser von Klippe / Zu Klippe geworfen, / Jahrlang ins Ungewisse hinab" ("hurled like water from precipice to precipice down through the years into uncertainty"). The original and translation are taken from Leonard Forster, ed., *The Penguin Book of German Verse* (Baltimore: Penguin Books, 1961), p. 290. In *Watt* this passage is quoted after Mr. Gorman suggests that he and Mr. Nolan throw some water on *Watt* (p. 239). His comment is perhaps what causes Watt to think of the lines from Hölderlin. This possibility becomes apparent when one realizes that "Wasser" ("water") is the word that is missing in the fragment quoted in the novel.

23. The complete passage reads, "O, sister, sister, if ever you marry, beware of a sullen, silent sot, one that's always musing but never thinks"; George Farquhar, *The Beaux' Stratagem*, II, i, 57–58. The passage is from a speech in which Mrs. Sullen complains to her sister-in-law, Dorinda, about her husband. I am grateful to my colleague Professor Reginald Saner for identifying the source of this allusion. The passage is quoted when it becomes clear that Mr. Gorman, instead of using a water bucket, intends to douse Watt with the contents of a slop bucket. Mr. Gorman is probably the son of Mrs. Gorman, the fishwoman with whom Watt attempts a "perfunctory coalescence" (p. 141). This is suggested in a passage that comes a page before the quotation: "Mr Nolan found Mr Gorman on his doorstep, taking leave of his mother" (p. 238). Here, as in the passage where the Hölderlin poem is used, an omitted phrase may explain why Watt thinks of the quotation. In *Watt* "if ever you marry" is deleted; it may be that Watt realizes that if he were to marry Mrs. Gorman, his oppressor, the sullen Mr. Gorman, would become his stepson. Another possibility is that "never thinks" refers to Watt, who by this time has given up rational thought.

24. "Echo's Bones," p. 1. The Madden Prize is named for Samuel Madden (1696–1765), who left the bequest used to establish it; see Sidney Lee in *DNB*, s.v. Madden, Samuel; Constantia Maxwell, *A History of Trinity College Dublin, 1591–1892* (Dublin: The University Press, Trinity College, 1946), pp. 154–56. Beckett's poem "Gnome" deals with the emotional price of a life devoted to learning, and Lucky, in *Waiting for Godot*, is another of Beckett's deranged scholars. The idea of Watt's journey as an intellectual quest is strengthened by Arsene's comment, "Erskine will go by your side, to be your guide . . ." (p. 63). This is based on lines spoken by Knowledge in the medieval play *Everyman*: "Everyman, I will go with thee, and be thy guide, / In thy most need to go by thy side" (*Everyman*, ll. 522–23).

25. Izaak Walton, *The Lives of John Donne, Sir Henry Wotton, Richard*

Hooker, et al., ed. George Saintsbury (London: Oxford University Press, 1927), p. 216. The italics are Walton's. Walton's biography of Hooker was first published in 1655; an explanation of how Hooker came to be called "Judicious" is given on p. 213.

26. See John Lemprière, *Classical Dictionary* (London: George Routledge and Sons, n.d.), p. 79. The source of this passage was identified by John Pilling in his *Samuel Beckett* (London: Routledge and Kegan Paul, 1976), p. 125. On the same page Pilling notes another connection between *Watt* and Aristotle: Beckett originally planned to have portions of the novel follow the ten categories in Aristotle's *Categoriae*. In *More Pricks than Kicks* the narrator speaks ironically of "the benevolence of the First Cause" (p. 32). The addendum appears on p. 253; the translation (like others where no source is given) is my own.

27. I have quoted the first two stanzas and the last two lines of the poem, which has four stanzas. The poem can be found in *The Complete Poetical Works of James Thomson*, ed. J. L. Robertson (London: Oxford University Press, 1908), pp. 427–28. Lawrence Harvey was the first to note that the addendum is from Thomson's poem; see *Samuel Beckett, Poet and Critic* (Princeton, N.J.: Princeton University Press, 1970), p. 391.

28. The addendum appears on p. 249. The quotation (discussed in the last chapter) is from Schopenhauer's *Ueber die vierfache Wurzel des Satzes vom zureichenden Grunde*; see *Sämtliche Werke* (Wiesbaden: F. A. Brockhaus, 1958), 1:50.

29. The addendum appears on p. 253. The original can be found in *Prolegomena zu einer jeden künftigen Metaphysik die als Wissenschaft wird auftreten können*, in *Immanuel Kants Werke*, ed. Ernst Cassirer (Berlin: Bruno Cassirer, 1913), 4:129n.

30. Immanuel Kant, *Prolegomena to Any Future Metaphysics That Will Be Able to Present Itself as a Science*, trans. P. G. Lucas (Manchester: Manchester University Press, 1966), p. 144n.

31. According to the *OED*, bathos, in the sense of a "ludicrous descent from the elevated to the commonplace," was introduced into English by Alexander Pope's satire, "Bathos, the art of sinking in Poetry" (1727). Kant's *Prolegomena* appeared in 1783, and the footnote was written a year or two before that, but it is unlikely that Kant knew the English meaning of bathos. A reader unfamiliar with German Gothic script might misconstrue Kant's passage for another reason. *Bathos* is not a German word, but *Pathos* is; in Gothic script the letter "B" looks very much like the letter "P"; hence one could easily misread the passage, or assume that there was a typographical error in the original.

32. Among the authorities who attribute the passage to St. Jerome are Norbert Guterman, in *A Book of Latin Quotations* (Garden City, N.Y.: Anchor Books, 1966), pp. 362–63. H. P. Jones, in *Dictionary of Foreign Phrases and Classical Quotations* (Edinburgh: John Grant, 1963), p. 92, gives Donatus as the source. In *Bartlett's* the passage is attributed to an

anonymous author; see John Bartlett, *Bartlett's Familiar Quotations*, 14th ed., ed. E. M. Beck (Boston: Little, Brown, 1968), p. 151. The confusion arose because St. Jerome, in the first chapter of his *Commentary on Ecclesiastes*, attributes the saying to his teacher, Aelius Donatus. This reference comes in an explication of the passage "there is no new thing under the sun" (Ecclesiastes 1:9). Jerome points out a similar line in the preface to Terence's play *The Eunuch:* "nothing is said that has not been said before" ("nullumst iam dictum quod non sit dictum prius": "Prologus," *Eunuchus*, 1. 41). See S. Eusebii Hieronymi, *Commentarius in Ecclesiasten*, in *Patrologiae Cursus Completus* (Paris, 1845), Tomus XXIII, p. 1019. Beckett may have found the "pereant qui . . ." saying in Schopenhauer's *Parerga und Paralipomena*; see Schopenhauer, *Sämtliche Werke*, 5:143.

33. The addendum is on p. 250; for the original see *Faust*, 1. 784. The choral songs Watt hears in the novel—the threne and the descant—may be parodies of the songs in *Faust*, ll. 737ff. I am grateful to Matthew and Uta Winston for pointing out that *Faust* is the source of the original quotation.

34. The addendum is on p. 248. Dante describes the "rosa sempiterna" in *Paradiso* 30:124; he also refers to it in *Paradiso* 12:19.

35. The addendum is on p. 253; and see *Inferno* 7:60. The source of this quotation was first noted by Susan Senneff in "Song and Music in Samuel Beckett's *Watt*," *Modern Fiction Studies*, 11 (Summer, 1964):143.

36. The addendum is on p. 248. Benedict XIV (1675–1758) was elected pope in 1740; his *De Synodo Diocesana* was published in Rome in 1748. Francesco Emanuello Cangiamila (1702–63) was a Sicilian theologian whose *Embriologia Sacra* was published in Palermo in 1745.

37. Harvey, p. 247.

38. As Richard Coe has pointed out, "never been properly born" is similar to a description of a little girl mentioned by Mrs. Rooney in *All That Fall* ("she had never been really born!"); see Richard Coe, *Samuel Beckett* (New York: Grove Press, 1968), p. 59; *All That Fall* in *Krapp's Last Tape and Other Dramatic Pieces* (New York: Grove Press, 1960), p. 84. According to Deirdre Bair, Beckett's source for the description in *All That Fall* was a lecture given by C. G. Jung in 1935; see *Samuel Beckett: A Biography* (New York: Harcourt Brace Jovanovich, 1978), pp. 209–10. In the earlier version of *Watt* it was Mr. Knott who had never been properly born; see Coetzee, p. 473. In the final version, however, it is no longer possible to determine to whom the passage refers.

39. The addendum is on p. 248. As was mentioned in Chapter 10, the addendum probably is based on a similar passage at the end of Part I of Descartes' *Discourse on the Method*; see *The Philosophical Works of Descartes*, trans. Elizabeth Haldane and G. R. T. Ross (Cambridge: Cambridge University Press, 1967), 1:87.

40. Beckett did drop Watt's first name in the final version of the novel: the hero was originally named Johnny Watt. There is a good example of a

name being changed in *Malone Dies* when Sapo is renamed Macmann;
see *Malone Dies* (1956; rpt., New York: Grove Press, 1970), p. 55.

41. Horace, *Satirae*, I, i, 69: "Quid rides? Mutato nomine, de te fabula narratur." The English translation is by Gutérman (p. 145).

42. In *Watt* "Bandusia" (p. 142) is an allusion to Horace's "O fons Bandusiae" (*Odes*, III, 13). Horace is mentioned in *Dream of Fair to Middling Women* (p. 123); "atra cura" (from Horace's *Odes*, III, 1) is used in *More Pricks than Kicks* (p. 151) and in the poem "Sanies I." Horace's "limae labor" (from *Ars Poetica*, l. 292) is used twice in *More Pricks than Kicks* (pp. 50, 143) and in the poem "Serena I."

12

Conclusion:
The Deterioration of Outer
Reality in Beckett's Fiction

As Beckett's career developed, he began to abandon the dense, learned style that characterized his early works. In his first novels and poems he sometimes imitated, and more often parodied, writers like Joyce and T. S. Eliot. Beckett's vocabulary in these works is a lexicographer's paradise; the allusions, a scholar's purgatory; the syntax, a grammarian's inferno ("I see main verb at last," he announces in "Sanies I," a poem of this period). Beckett was ultimately to deplore this kind of cultured display, and he began to use simpler words, fewer allusions, and shorter sentences. But his later works incorporate a different kind of complexity: the visible world—a Dublin salon, a London rooming house—begins to fade, and the furniture of mundane reality disappears.

Beckett's early fiction, with its allusions and conventional settings, displays an interest in outer reality that runs counter to his protagonists' announced desire to withdraw into themselves. In the later novels chronology is vague, geographical locations are unspecified, settings are spare and strange, and requirements for maintaining verisimilitude are replaced by a need to depict inner reality. *More Pricks than Kicks* still gives the appearance of dealing with chronology and settings in a conventional way. But in *Murphy* Beckett uses hyperbole to mock conventional descriptions of locale: the narrator's compulsive notation of time and place for the most trivial events is undercut by his use of misleading information. In other passages the reiteration of details about the locale underline their ultimate uselessness. When Celia describes how she first met Murphy, her comments about the setting lead Mr. Kelly to urge her to be "less beastly circumstantial. The junction for example of Edith Grove, Cremorne Road and Stadium Street, is indifferent to me. Get up to your man."[1] For the narrator of *Murphy*, elaborate descriptions of time and place finally serve to define the prison from which the hero hopes to escape.

In the novels completed after *Murphy* the chronology becomes somewhat indistinct. There is a vagueness about seasons in *Watt*: the hero assumes it is summer "because the air was not quite cold."[2] With exquisite linguistic precision, Watt asks a passerby for the time: "Could you tell me what time it was." The narrator omits the response—there is no real need for the reader to know the time—but Watt's reaction to it is given: "It was as he feared, earlier than he hoped" (p. 228). Normal chronological sequence is violated in word order (the reversals in Watt's comments to Sam), sentence order (the second half of a paragraph appears some seventy pages before the first), and in the ordering of the parts of the novel (Sam indicates that he has rearranged them).[3] Moreover, the hypnotic and stagnant qualities of the novel's repetitious sections suggest an internal sense of chronology that is independent of conventional ideas about the passage of time.

In *Watt*, unlike works meant to be read only once, the meaning of a given passage does not always emerge at the moment it is before the reader. The significance of an entire section of the novel—Arsene's speech is an example—can be heightened or altered by successive readings as connections with other passages are established. In this respect Beckett's writing resembles music: the cumulative effect of repeated exposures to the work often overshadows one's response to what is apprehended at a given moment. As the linear quality of the work becomes less important, one recalls earlier passages and anticipates those yet to come, just as when a series of notes heard sequentially is apprehended as a melody. In Beckett's works the parts are interwoven with a thematic whole, and the sense of the action being fixed in time is reduced.

A lack of specificity about settings in *Watt* runs parallel to the vagueness about chronology.[4] A minor character is introduced in a way that makes it clear that such omissions are not oversights: "I come from —, said Mr Micks, and he described the place whence he came. I was born at —, he said, and the site and circumstances of his ejection were unfolded" (p. 216). Readers are similarly kept in the dark about other locales. Mr. Spiro, who meets Watt on a train, asks about his destination:

> Where do you get down, sir?
> Watt named the place.
> I beg your pardon? said Mr Spiro.
> Watt named the place again.
> Then there is not a moment to lose, said Mr Spiro. (P. 28)

Mr. Spiro may learn where Watt is going, but the reader will not. A number of critics have concluded that the journey began in Dublin and that Watt's destination is Foxrock, but the repetition in this passage makes it clear that such information is pointedly being withheld.[5]

When the descriptions of time and place are eliminated, Beckett's style becomes simpler and more lucid: as the field of vision grows narrower, the images become sharper. Early in his career Beckett often indulged in stylistic flourishes, but later on he tried to overcome the effects of an elaborate style by using it in an inappropriate manner. The following passage is an example: "For Watt, in order to save himself the washing, and no doubt also for the pleasure of killing two birds with one stone, never blew his nose, except when the circumstances permitted of a direct digital emunction, in anything but toilet-paper, each separate slip, when thoroughly imbibed, being crumpled up into a ball, and thrown away, and the hands passed through the hair, to its great embellishment, or rubbed the one against the other, until they shone" (pp. 234–35). Like cosmetics, an ornate style can heighten beauty—or it can transform homely plainness into the comically grotesque. This latter alternative is what Beckett is striving for, and his style is often more appropriate than it seems at first to be.

Eventually Beckett began to eliminate stylistic ornamentation entirely, and this is a reason he decided to compose his works in French. In *Dream of Fair to Middling Women* Belacqua, musing about how one produces a literary pearl ("the little sparkle hid in ashen, the precious margaret"), explains this: "The uniform, horizontal writing, flowing without accidence, of the man with a style, never gives you the margarita. But the writing of, say, Racine or Malherbe, perpendicular, diamanté, is pitted, is it not, and sprigged with sparkles, the flints and pebbles are there, no end of humble tags and commonplaces. They have no style, they write without style, do they not, they give you the phrase, the sparkle, the precious margaret. Perhaps only the French can do it. Perhaps only the French language can give you the thing you want."[6] Even at the time he was working on his first novel, then, Beckett had begun thinking about the advantages of writing in French.

Along with his effort to eliminate stylistic excesses, Beckett tried to curtail emotional effusiveness in his later works. In "Assumption" the hero's suffering is described, and some of the reasons for it are given. But if one learns about Dr. Nye's pain in "A Case in a Thousand," its cause is not specified. In *More Pricks than Kicks* Beckett uses comic hyperbole to depict outbursts of emotion in an ironic light: the Smeraldina's tears are quickly followed by a geyser of passion, a sequence which makes it difficult to believe that her unhappiness is genuine. In the later works pathos is implied, sentimentality is suppressed, and references to suffering are almost entirely eliminated. Reversing the idea that an objective correlative is necessary for expressing emotion in art, Beckett supplies the ingredients for a particular response and then stops short of eliciting it.[7]

An example occurs in a passage at the beginning of *Watt:* "the lady held the gentleman by the ears, and the gentleman's hand was on the lady's thigh, and the lady's tongue was in the gentleman's mouth. . . . Taking a pace forward, to satisfy himself that the gentleman's other hand was not going to waste, Mr Hackett was shocked to find it limply dangling over the back of the seat, with between its fingers the spent three quarters of a cigarette" (p. 8). Mr. Hackett is not shocked—though readers may have expected him to be—by an open display of what Beckett elsewhere calls oyster kisses. This reversal, like the narrator's clinical tone, contributes to the comic effect.

Other love scenes, like the one involving Watt and Mrs. Gorman, are written in a similarly detached style. The function of the anaphrodesia in such passages is not to mollify puritanical readers, or even puritanical nonreaders. After a frank, if clinical, description of love-making in *Murphy* ("Miss Counihan had never enjoyed anything quite so much as this slow-motion osmosis of love's spittle") the narrator says, "The above passage is carefully calculated to deprave the cultivated reader."[8] As for uncultivated nonreaders, in the same novel Beckett inveighs against "the filthy censors" and "their filthy synecdoche."[9] The austere descriptions of love-making can be contrasted with the stylistic elegance of the passage about Watt's nose-blowing. The contemporary reading public, jaded by sexual frankness, is perhaps ready for graphic descriptions of more private pleasures.

In a sense, Beckett is parodying the feverish style commonly encountered in romantic and pornographic fiction. His tone in dealing with potentially arousing material can be linked to the idea that the satisfaction of desire leads to unhappiness. In *Watt* Arsene mentions a starving glutton and a celibate lecher as examples of human felicity. Later, as if to illustrate this point, he tells the story of Mary, whose life is devoted to satisfying an unremitting desire for food.[10] In using a detached tone to describe love-making and Mary's constant eating, Beckett emphasizes his refusal to glorify what he sees as frustrating experiences. Satisfaction of desire is momentary; it is replaced by a new, intensified hunger. Again it becomes clear that Beckett's tone in these passages is only seemingly inappropriate.

The problems traditionally encountered by lovers rarely trouble Beckett's characters: their complaints are more fundamental. Sam, the Casanova of the Lynch clan, is a paralytic. Watt is involved with two women, Mrs. Watson and Mrs. Gorman; the first one has had a leg amputated and the second, a breast. Watt and Mrs. Gorman never go beyond kissing because "Watt had not the strength, and Mrs Gorman had not the time . . ." (p. 141). The narrator comments on the ironic circumstance that "a trifling and in all probability tractable obstruction of some endocrinal Bandusia, that a mere matter of forty-five or fifty minutes by the clock, should as effectively as death itself, or as the Hellespont, separate lovers" (p. 142). The old romantic tradition—Leander, love-inspired, swimming the Hellespont; Byron, inspired by Leander, emulating him—seems puerile. A sentimental view of love makes the reality seem insufficient; love ends not in an operatic crescendo but in a humiliating diminuendo. Poetic exaggeration, which seemingly presents an enhanced view of life, finally heightens the potential for disappointment.

A similar point can be made about the romantic view of nature. The narrator of *Watt* says that the moon's appearance "would be that compared, by some writers, to a sickle, or a crescent" (p. 222). But when he gives his own description of the moon, he says that it "was of an unpleasant yellow colour" (p. 30). Many of the flowers that adorn the landscape in *Watt*, "the foxgloves, the hyssop, the pretty nettles, the high pouting hemlock," are bothersome or poisonous (p. 33).

A view of nature which specifies that only certain creatures should be esteemed is naively anthropomorphic. Sam says that he and Watt killed birds "of every kind," and enjoyed the companionship of their "particular friends," a family of rats. Parodying biblical prose, Sam tells how they "would sit down in the midst of them, and give them to eat, out of our hands, of a nice fat frog, or a baby thrush." Sometimes they would feed a young rat to one of its relatives. "It was on these occasions," says Sam, "that we came nearest to God" (pp. 155–56).

In Beckett's view, the harshness of existence makes even tragic gestures futile. His decaying heroes never shake their fists defiantly: nature cannot be rebuked. Existence inflicts suffering in an impersonal way, and this is reflected in Beckett's fictional style. The deaths of Belacqua and Murphy, the tears of Kelly and Watt, the diseases of members of the Lynch clan—all are described in a detached tone. On occasions when sympathy might too easily be evoked, the relevant passages are deleted. The scene where Murphy knocks himself unconscious is omitted. At the railroad station Watt is hit by a door and soon afterward a slop bucket is dropped on his head. The narrator says as little as possible about these events, and distracts readers with intrusive parentheses— "(Hiatus in MS)" and "(MS illegible)"—that shift the focus of the narrative away from Watt's suffering (pp. 238, 239, 241).

At times Beckett uses similar methods to demonstrate how appearances can veil an underlying level of reality. When Arsene speaks about what he has learned at Mr. Knott's house, he keeps digressing into distracting parenthetical comments: "Why even I myself, strolling all alone in some hard earned suspension of labour in this charming garden, have tried and tried to formulate

this delicious haw! and may I add quite useless wisdom so dearly
won, and with which I am so to speak from the crown of my head
to the soles of my feet imbued, so that I neither eat nor drink nor
breath in and out nor do my doodles but more sagaciously than
before, like Theseus kissing Ariadne, or Ariadne Theseus, towards the end, on the seashore, and tried in vain. . . ."[11] If the
parenthetical statements are deleted, the central idea soon
emerges: "Why even I myself . . . have tried . . . to formulate
this . . . wisdom . . . with which I am . . . imbued . . . and tried in
vain. . . ." But expressing the idea this way would contradict the
point Arsene is making about the difficulty of formulating what
he has understood. The distracting parentheses are necessary:
they lead to a union of form and content.

Beckett often uses an obscure style or misleading ideas to create a screen that conceals the underlying levels of his novels. The
mishandled narrative in *Dream of Fair to Middling Women*; the
moral insensitivity in *More Pricks than Kicks*; the erroneous information in *Murphy*; the suggestions in *Watt* that the hero is
mentally incompetent: all are used to replicate the misleading
outer reality one encounters in the world. Beckett, like Murphy,
loathes "the complacent scientific conceptualism that made contact with outer reality the index of mental well-being." As the
narrator of *Murphy* observes, the "nature of outer reality remained obscure. . . . The definition of outer reality, or of reality
short and simple, varied according to the sensibility of the
definer."[12]

This comment explains why the outer world so often seems
distorted in Beckett's fiction. Initially, the distortions appear to
be misrepresentations of reality. But as the outer world deterio-
rates, one gains a clearer view of inner reality, and it is the inner
reality that shapes and colors one's perception of the outer world.
The illusory outer reality is not Beckett's invention: he is only
reporting on what already exists. It is ironic that many readers
should consider his writing absurd or unrealistic; in fact, *Comment c'est* could have served as the title for any of his works.

Notes

1. *Murphy* (1938; rpt., New York: Grove Press, 1957), p. 13. Two repeated passages call attention to this point: "Edith Grove, Cremorne

Road and Stadium Street" (pp. 12, 13, 18), and "Get up to your man" (twice, p. 13).

2. *Watt* (1953; rpt., New York: Grove Press, 1959), p. 215. Subsequent references to *Watt* in the text are to this edition.

3. For examples of Watt's inverted speech, see pp. 164ff. The passage on p. 164 that begins, "So to every man . . . ," is the concluding sentence of the paragraph on pp. 236–37, which begins, "The flies, of skeleton thinness. . . ." (This paragraph ends with the phrase "the long summer's day," which links it with this sentence near the end of the novel: "The long summer's day had made an excellent start"; see p. 245. Reading these passages in conjunction makes it clear that the second one is ironic.) The events in Part IV occurred before those in Part III; Sam discusses the ordering of the parts at the very beginning of Part IV (p. 215).

4. Ludovic Janvier gives a useful discussion of Beckett's use of settings in his essay "Place of Narration / Narration of Place," trans. Ruby Cohn, in *Samuel Beckett: A Collection of Criticism*, ed. Ruby Cohn (New York: McGraw-Hill, 1975), pp. 96–110. Raymond Federman has commented on the loss of realistic features in Beckett's later fiction; see *Journey to Chaos* (Berkeley: University of California Press, 1965), pp. 13 *et passim*.

5. Vivian Mercier is one of the critics who discusses the connections between Beckett's home in Foxrock and Mr. Knott's house; see *Beckett / Beckett* (New York: Oxford University Press, 1977), pp. 20–21.

6. *Dream of Fair to Middling Women* (TS, Dartmouth College Library), p. 42. Lawrence Harvey says Beckett told him that "English because of its very richness holds out the temptation to rhetoric and virtuosity, which are merely words mirroring themselves complacently, Narcissus-like. The relative asceticism of French seemed more appropriate to the expression of being . . ."; see *Samuel Beckett, Poet and Critic* (Princeton, N.J.: Princeton University Press, 1970), p. 196. Beckett made a similar comment to Niklaus Gessner; see his *Die Unzulänglichkeit der Sprache* (Zurich: Juris-Verlag, 1957), p. 32n. Melvin J. Friedman makes the interesting point that Beckett's "literary personality" changes as he changes language; see "The Creative Writer as Polyglot: Valery Larbaud and Samuel Beckett," *Transactions of the Wisconsin Academy of Sciences, Arts, and Letters*, 49 (1960):234–35.

7. In his essay "Hamlet and His Problems," T. S. Eliot writes, "The only way of expressing emotion in the form of art is by finding an 'objective correlative'; in other words, a set of objects, a situation, a chain of events which shall be the formula of that *particular* emotion; such that when the external facts, which must terminate in sensory experience, are given, the emotion is immediately evoked"; see T. S. Eliot, *The Sacred Wood* (London: Methuen, 1934), p. 100.

8. *Murphy*, pp. 117–18.

9. *Ibid.*, p. 76.

10. See *Watt*, p. 44: "The glutton castaway, the drunkard in the desert, the lecher in prison, they are the happy ones." The story of Mary begins on p. 50.

11. Pages 62–63. In *Waiting for Godot* Lucky's speech provides another example of how Beckett uses distracting parentheses to obscure a central statement; again, the parentheses finally serve to enhance the meaning of the core idea.

12. *Murphy*, pp. 176–77.

Appendix I

Repeated Sentences, Phrases, and Rare Words in *Murphy*

Entries are arranged alphabetically according to the first repeated word in the passage, or the second repeated word if the first word is *a, an, the,* or *and.* Only examples of repetition that seem significant are included in this list. For example, the two appearances of "in the meantime" on p. 34 are included as "34 (2)," but the appearances of the phrase on pp. 36, 55, and 128 are not. Page references are to *Murphy* (1938; rpt., New York: Grove Press, 1957).

Abbreviations:

cf.	Compare the entry listed to another one that is thematically related.
v	The passage on the page listed varies from the form in the heading for the entry.
etc.	Only part of a recurring passage has been quoted in the heading for the entry.
r	The passage on the page listed does not repeat the language in the heading, but is thematically related to it.
II	In Appendix II.

Account, expurgated, accelerated, improved and reduced, of how . . . came to . . . gives the following, 12, 48, 87r, 119.

Act[s] of love, 112, 221, 222, 222v.

Adored . . . many things, 95, 95v.

Advantage of this view . . . is that while one may not look forward to things getting any better, etc., The, 58, 200–201. Cf. "They will always be the same," "Closed system," "Syndrome."

Aeruginous, 71 (2).

Ah well . . . we all have our troubles, 144, 148.

Alive and well . . . in Calcutta, 61, 125. Cf. "Deserted his wife," "Cox, Ariadne" (II), "Dublin" (II).

185

All out, 153, 281 (5), 282. Cf. "Coupled abreast," "Hyde Park, Round Pond" (II).
All over again, 56, 65, 149.
Amourously disposed, 11, 151.
Any more than . . . for an animal, 118, 191.
Any other available means, 184 (3), 185.
Apmonia [*harmonia*], 3 (2), 4. Cf. "Called the," "Isonomy," "Pythagorean philosophy" (II).
Approach my child, 23, 24, 24r.
Arrived and, 135 (2), 135–36.
As described in section six, 2, 7, 9. Cf. "Murphy, mind and body compared" (II).
As happy as a . . . could desire, 48 (2). Cf. "Despairing of recommending," "Flight-Lieutenant Elliman, women" (II), "Miss Dwyer, men" (II).
As it seemed to Murphy, 35, 184. Cf. "It seemed to Murphy."
As she supposed, 28, 82.
As was sometimes bound to happen even in the M.M.M., 159, 160. Cf. entries under "M.M.M." (II).
At regular intervals of not more than twenty minutes, 185, 237, 247v. Cf. "Visited at regular intervals," entries under "M.M.M." (II).
At that time, 3 (2).
At the usual, 8 (2).
Avoid exhaustion by speech, 32, 37, 138v. Cf. "Murphy, quarrels" (II).
Away and back, 265 (2).
Away on business, 143, 226.

B— [used in place of an epithet], 174, 277.
Based on the . . . system outside . . . in which he . . . the least confidence, 22–23, 75–76, 183–84r. Cf. "In which . . . confidence," "Murphy, canons" (II).
Been good jokes, 65 (2). Cf. "Had never been," "Murphy, jokes, types" (II).
Belonged to the same great group, 204, 210. Cf. "If the worst."
Best he could do, 188 (2). Cf. "Murphy, both ways" (II).
Best of his knowledge, the, 214, 216. Cf. "To the best of his ability."
Better-class mentally deranged, the, 87, 89. Cf. entries under "M.M.M." (II).
Biddable, 160, 240.
Big blooming . . . confusion, 4, 29, 245. Cf. "Figure . . . ground," "Psychology, Gestalt" (II).
Bim and Ticklepenny . . . the sheet, 261 (2).
Body, mind and soul, 269, 271, 275. Cf. "You, my body . . . my mind."
Body . . . with its fatigue, 175 (2), 189.
Break[ing] . . . bed, 212, 212–13.
Browbeat Cooper . . . into reporting to her [him] at the end of every day before he did so to, etc., 196, 197. Cf. "Directed by Cooper."

Bull of incommunication, 31, 93. Cf. "Murphy, horoscope, euphemisms" (II).

But in the night of Skinner's, 236, 240. Cf. entries under "M.M.M., Skinner's" (II).

But only . . . himself improved out of all knowledge, 79, 105. Cf. "Murphy, trances" (II).

But that did not trouble her, who knew how addicted he was to, 26, 27.

But whether, 264 (2). Cf. "Coroner, verbal repetition" (II).

"By all means," said the coroner, 262, 266. Cf. "Coroner, verbal repetition" (II).

Called . . . the, 3 (2), 3–4, 4, 5v. Cf. "Apmonia."

Came to be turned off, 119, 174. Cf. "I do be turned off."

Candle . . . its own tallow . . . at the head of the bed, 162, 175.

Celia, s'il y a, 115 (2).

Celia said . . . work . . . back to hers, 22, 76.

Chessy eye, the, 242 (2).

Child . . . had . . . her good night, the, 153, 281. Cf. "Hyde Park, Round Pond" (II).

Clapped to . . . head, 4, 7. Cf. "Gestures, similar" (II).

Clean up . . . messes, 158 (2).

Clinch it, 179 (2), 179v.

Closed system, a, 57, 102, 109, 117, 182–83v, 200. Cf. "Advantage," "Syndrome," "Horse leech's."

"Come in," said Celia, 68, 132. Cf. "Nice . . . cup," "Drink it," "Miss Carridge, tea" (II).

Come . . . when . . . Murphy, not before, 199 (2). Cf. "You shall find me," "I can never forget," "It is too," "Keep . . . on your hands," "Letters, Neary's" (II).

Coming [come] alive in . . . mind, 2, 111, 189. Cf. "As described," "Tried to come out," "Murphy, mind and body compared" (II).

Considerable receptacle for refuse, 274 (2).

Considered himself better off than, 254 (2). Cf. "Neary and Wylie," "Staggered reverently."

Corpus of deterrents, 22r, 34, 93. Cf. "Murphy, horoscope, euphemisms" (II).

Could not disguise, 67, 150v.

Could you find . . . ? 123 (2). Cf. "Did you know . . . ?"

Coupled abreast, 15, 152, 281v. Cf. "Kites, tandem" (II).

Course was clear, the, 14, 150. Cf. "Temptation to," "There would be time."

Cropping . . . ruminating, 99, 106v.

Cruel . . . kind, 55 (2).

Cupidity . . . imagination, 144, 148. Cf. "Miss Carridge . . . alms," "Miss Carridge, tea," (II).

Curious feeling . . . over, 224 (2).

Danger of . . . fits, 32, 75, 140r. Cf. "Pains in the neck."

"Darling," said Bim. . . . "That is entirely up to you," 157, 270.

Days and places and things and people, 149 (2).

Dayspring, 78, 275. Cf. "Dante" (II).

Dead . . . to the voices of the street, 229, 230.

Defence . . . of . . . by . . . against, 120, 121.

Defrauded a vested interest, 81, 84. Cf. "Murphy, lunch, tea" (II).

Deserted his wife, 61v, 123, 125. Cf. "Alive and well," "Cox, Ariadne, abandoned" (II), "Cox, Ariadne, sought" (II).

Despairing of recommending, 48 (2). Cf. "As happy as a," "Flight-Lieutenant Elliman, women" (II), "Miss Dwyer, men" (II).

"Did you know . . . ?" "I did," said Cooper, 123 (2). Cf. "Could you find?"

Dimly. . . . Dimly, very dimly, 2, 252.

Directed by Cooper . . . went to Neary . . . behind . . . back . . . and made a clean breast of the whole situation, 196, 197. Cf. "Bribed and browbeat," "New Testament, employers" (II).

Do not leave me, 223, 271. Cf. "Have [had]," "You are all I have."

Dog's life, 77, 111.

Door . . . opened and closed . . . neither loudly nor softly, 155, 270. Cf. "Stopped listening."

Doubt, a, 227 (2). Cf. "Miss Carridge, verbal repetition" (II), "Wylie as mimic" (II).

Dr. . . . Killiecrankie, the Outer Hebridean R.M.S., 185, 257.

Drink [drank] a little more, 46, 47.

Drink it before it, 68, 133. Cf. "Nice . . . cup of tea," "Come in," "Miss Carridge, tea" (II).

Dublin, where Wynn's Hotel would always find her [him], 54, 55, 55–56r, 117r, 122r. Cf. "Hotels, Dublin" (II).

'E ain't, 77 (4).

Eaten, drunk, slept, and put his clothes on and off, 1, 1v.

Edith Grove, Cremorne Road and Stadium Street, 12v, 13, 18, 150v.

Envelope . . . grasped it to tear it across, 93, 269. Cf. "Solitude," "Envelope" (II).

—Er— [usually used before a euphemism], 52 (2), 54 (2), 55, 60, 126, 129, 219, 227, 272 (2). Cf. "Miss Counihan, verbal repetition" (II), "Wylie as mimic" (II).

Etc. Other times, 235 (2). Cf. "Sometimes he sang."

Etymology of gas? the, 175 (2). Cf. "Gas . . . chaos."

Eye? Say rather . . . eye, 241, 242. Cf. "Eye upon him," "Chessy eye."

Eye upon him and made his preparations accordingly, 241, 242. Cf. "Eye? Say rather," "Chessy eye," "Great magical ability."

Eyes, cold and unwavering as a gull's, 2, 39. Cf. "Eye upon him," "Great magical ability."

Face . . . turned to the window, 254 (2). Cf. "Window, leaning out of" (II).

Fancy . . . not far short of love, 156, 157. Cf. "Homosexuals" (II).

Faster and faster, 9 (2), 252, 253, 276. Cf. entries under "Rock got faster," "Chairs, rocking and wheel" (II).
Fawn under the table, 92, 94v.
Felo-de-se, 145 (2), 145v. Cf. "My rump," "Deaths, accidents or suicides?" (II).
Few minds are [were] better concocted than this native's, 32, 34.
Figure . . . ground, 4, 5v, 48v, 245v. Cf. "Big blooming confusion," "Psychology, Gestalt" (II), "Neary, complaints" (II).
Fool and a brute, a, 34 (2). Cf. "She said."
For every symptom that is eased another is made worse, 57, 200. Cf. "Syndrome," "Horse leech's."
For good and all, 141, 142. Cf. "For just a little while."
For just a little while, 141 (2). Cf. "For good and all."
For that same reason . . . whatever it may be, 6 (2). Cf. "For whatever reason."
For whatever reason you cannot love, 6 (2). Cf. "For that same reason."
Forecourt of lawn, 165, 259. Cf. "M.M.M., mortuary, climbing plants" (II).
Fragment[s] of Job, 70 (2). Cf. "Old Testament, Job, allusions."
From a . . . experience to a person of, 66 (2).
From the moment . . . that, 212, 213.
Funnel vailed to . . . Bridge, 15, 150v. Cf. "Tug and barge, coupled" (II).
Funny old chap, 8, 9, 24, 26r.

Game between . . . and his stars, 85 (2). Cf. "Shakespeare, stars" (II).
Garret that . . . was . . . not an attic, nor . . . a mansarde, 162, 164. Cf. "Than an attic," "Garrets" (II).
Garret . . . the fug . . . these, The, 188, 189–90.
Gas . . . chaos, 175, 175v, 253. Cf. "Etymology."
Gave him pleasure, 2 (2). Cf. "Pleasure."
Gem[s] . . . to ensure success, 33, 75.
Gentle passion, the [of love], 27, 38.
Get up to your man, 13 (2). Cf. "Edith Grove."
Glens, the, 272 (2). Note: Miss Counihan repeats the words "the glens" to avoid completing a passage from Milton's *Paradise Lost*, "lakes, fens, bogs, dens, and shades of death" (Book II, line 621). See also "—Er—."
Grave of Father Prout (F. S. Mahony), 50, 124. Cf. "Dublin" (II), "Pseudonyms" (II).
Great magical ability, 32, 39, 80, 157v, 183, 242r, 249r. Cf. "Moon in the Serpent," "Sudden," "Eye upon him," "Eyes, cold."
Gripping . . . then sliding a little, 155 (2). Cf. "Hands."

Had never been . . . good joke[s], 65 (2). Cf. "Been good jokes," "Murphy, jokes, types" (II).
Half as . . . twice as, 148, 162v.

Hand on the banister, 154 (2), 155. Cf. "Gripping . . . then sliding."

Hands . . . their point of departure, 4–5, 24. Cf. "Clapped to . . . head," "Gestures, similar" (II).

"Hark" . . . said . . . pointing upward, 69, 228. Cf. "Soft . . . to and fro," "Never still," "Celia, actions like the old boy's" (II).

Hark to the wind, 20, 25.

Have [had] no one [nobody], 11r, 18r, 25, 35, 102v, 115 (2). Cf. "Do not leave me," "You are all I have," "Possibly Murphy," "Mr. Kelly, flat" (II).

He begged her to believe, 21 (2).

He could love himself, 7, 107r [in Latin: "se ipsum amat"], 179.

He did not hear her, he was, 143, 153.

He found it hard to think, 115 (2). Cf. "Mr. Kelly, thinking" (II).

He had . . . been able to imagine, 181 (2). Cf. entries under "M.M.M." (II).

He hurried back to . . . only pausing on the way to wire the, etc., 122 (2). Cf. "Telegrams" (II).

He let her go, 25, 41. Cf. "Let me go," "Made to rise."

He let himself in, therefore he lived there, 120, 153v. Cf. "Made a mental note," "Cooper tracks Murphy and Celia" (II).

He took off his . . . and threw them away, 251 (2).

He was sorry . . . when eight o'clock came and, 170, 188. Cf. entries under "M.M.M., Skinner's" (II).

He worked up the chair. . . . Slowly, 6, 9. Cf. "Slowly he felt better."

He would never lose sight of the fact he was, 158, 159. Cf. "He would never on any account."

He would never on any account, 158 (2), 159. Cf. "He would never lose."

Heads in the pillories of their shoulders, 131, 142v. Cf. "Window, leaning out of" (II).

Hears the . . . fidget and, 110 (2).

Hell roast this . . . I shall never, etc., 15 (2).

Her quantum of wantum cannot vary, 57, 200. Cf. "Horse leech's," "For every symptom," "Syndrome."

Her solitude . . . without, 232, 269. Cf. "Envelope."

Here the pleasure was, 111 (2). Cf. "Pleasure."

Herschel in Aquarius stops the Water, 33, 252. Cf. "Square of Moon," "Planets, discoverers of" (II), "Planets, Uranus and Neptune" (II).

Herself a last chance, 27 (2). Cf. "Celia, omens" (II).

Hexagon of crimson . . . its asterisk of sticks, 115, 277. Cf. "Mr. Kelly, kite repair" (II).

Highest attribute . . . silence, 32, 39, 164v.

Himself improved out of all knowledge, 79, 105.

Hips, etc., 10, 11. Cf. "Celia, list of measurements" (II).

His body . . . set him free . . . in his mind, 2, 113. Cf. "Murphy, mind and body compared" (II).

His landlady . . . or . . . some other lodger, 7 (2). Cf. "Landladies" (II).

His own dark, 91 (2).

His success with the patients, 180, 181, 183 (2).

His "tab," 184 (2), 185v.

Hope[d] . . . better things, 170, 176.

Horse leech's daughter . . . a closed system, The, 57, 117, 200. Cf. "For every symptom," "Her quantum," "Closed system."

Human eyelid is not teartight, The, 51, 115. Cf. "Whinge."

Hyleg, 33, 75, 252. Cf. "Square of Moon."

I can never forget your loyalty, 130r, 199 (2). Cf. "Keep . . . on your hands," "Come . . . when," "Tell Cooper," "It is too," "You shall find me," "Letters, Neary's" (II).

I do be turned off, 118, 119 (2). Cf. "Came to be turned off."

I do not even, 215 (2).

I don't believe, 266 (3). Cf. "Deaths, accidents or suicides?" (II).

"I greatly fear," said Wylie, "that . . . ," 57, 61. Cf. "Syndrome."

I have it, 8, 23. Cf. "Murphy, horoscope, euphemisms" (II).

"*I* thank you," said Neary, 211, 225. Cf. "Thanks" (II).

If the worst comes to the worst, thought . . . cannot be found . . . there is always, 130 (2). Cf. "Belonged to the same great group."

If things were . . . the round took . . . minutes than it should, etc., 237 (2).

If you have, 119 (2).

I'll be back, 140, 141 (2).

I'll have it with me, 8, 9.

In a short time you will be sitting down and taking off your hat and doing, etc., 123–24, 198. Cf. "Cooper never sits" (II), "Cooper never takes off his hat" (II).

In a somewhat similar way, 208, 257. Cf. "Bed, sitting and lying" (II), "Neary, loves" (II).

In such . . . that it seemed on the point of, 3 (2).

In the bed, which . . . his eyes, 12, 17.

In the meantime, 34 (2), 36.

In the mouth of Stadium Street, 12–13, 15, 16. Cf. "Edith Grove."

In the south of, 166 (2).

In the universe . . . it, 107 (2).

In vain, 24, 26, 51, 56, 105, 141, 162, 185, 251 (4).

In which . . . the least confidence, 22–23, 75–76, 76. Cf. "Based on the," "Murphy, canons" (II).

Insmell, 132, 134.

Into a . . . , 34 (2). Cf. "This . . . ," "Corpus of deterrents."

Is all rather irregular, 271 (2).

Isonomy, 4 (2). Cf. "Apmonia," "Pythagorean philosophy" (II).

It had taken him . . . hour to, 171 (3).

It is too, 199 (2). Cf. "I can never forget," "Letters, Neary's" (II).

It seemed to Murphy . . . Mr. Endon, 184 (3). Cf. "As it seemed."

It was at this moment that they all . . . simultaneously . . . and with common good breeding refrained, etc., 213, 227.

It was largely thanks to, 156 (2). Cf. entries under "M.M.M." (II).

It was not, 193 (2).

It was pleasant to, 112 (2). Cf. "Gave him pleasure," "Here the pleasure," "Pleasure."

It was September [August] . . . and, 17, 53. Cf. "Murphy, love and success" (II).

Job, 137 (6), 138. Cf. "Murphy, quarrels" (II).

Jossy, 27, 31, 37.

"Just so," said Neary, 6 (3). Cf. "For whatever reason," "For that same reason."

Keep . . . on your hands, 199 (2). Cf. "I can never forget," "Letters, Neary's" (II).

Kept [keep, keeps, keeping] nothing, 11, 13r, 20, 30, 46. Cf. "Might give . . . pain," "While she was with him."

Keyword[s] here, the, 83, 86, 212v.

Kick . . . caress, 108, 109, 240. Cf. "Kicks" (II), "Murphy, mind and body compared" (II).

Knock[ed] into, 53, 60 (3). Cf. "What folly is this?"

Known to the wittier . . . as the, 166, 167. Cf. entries under "M.M.M." (II).

Large profits and a quick turnover, 33, 82v.

Latter matter, the, 261 (2). Cf. "Coroner, verbal repetition" (II), "Coroner, functions" (II).

Lead us to him, 211, 257. Cf. "Celia will lead to Murphy" (II).

Leaned . . . against the railings, 78, 79. Cf. "Railings" (II).

Led to Murphy, 66 (2). Cf. "From a . . . experience."

"Let me go," said Celia, 25 (2), 40 (2). See "Pinioned," "Made to rise," "He let her go," "Celia's wrists pinioned" (II).

Lie, a, 144 (2), 145v (2), 154, 173. Cf. "Miss Carridge, verbal repetition" (II).

Life-warrant, 31, 93. Cf. "My. . . . Thank you," "Murphy, horoscope, euphemisms" (II).

Lit, indicated, extinguished [repeated in permutations], 247. Cf. "Permutations" (II).

Little apartment, 228 (2).

Little doggy, 97 (2).

Little luxuries to which she was [I am] accustomed, the, 53, 226. Cf. "Murphy, love and success" (II).

Little short of scandalous, 181–82, 182. Cf. "His success."

Lost all his yellow, 31r, 33–34r, 38, 164.

Lost in the shadows, 64 (2).

Love requited, 5, 16. Cf. "Short circuit."

Made a mental note of the number, 120, 153. Cf. "Cooper tracks" (II).

Made to rise . . . pinioned her wrists, 24, 40. Cf. "Pinioned," "Let me go," "Celia, wrists pinioned" (II).

Make his . . . move . . . go away, 187 (2). Cf. entries under "Chess game" (II).

Many sizes too, 276 (2). Cf. "Heads, large" (II).

Margin of the pond, the, 152, 282. Cf. "Hyde Park, Round Pond" (II).

Matter of the manner of death, the, 263 (2). Cf. *"Modus morendi,"* "Deaths, accidents or suicides?" (II), "Coroner, verbal repetition" (II).

Medium-sized cage[s] of . . . aspect, 1 (2). Cf. "Soon he would have to."

Merciful coincidence, a, 121, 223.

Might give . . . pain, 11, 12, 30r. Cf. "Kept . . . nothing."

"Million thanks, A," said Murphy, 168, 174. Cf. "Thanks" (II).

Miss . . . a brunette, a, 206 (2). Cf. "With Miss . . . ," "Cooper, women" (II).

Miss Carridge . . . alms, 143, 154. Cf. "Cupidity," "Miss Carridge, tea" (II).

Miss Counihan did not know when she was beaten, 209 (2).

Miss Counihan followed slowly, 272, 272v, 273.

Modus morendi, the, 262 (2). Cf. "Deaths, accidents or suicides?" (II), "Coroner, verbal repetition" (II).

Moon by a striking coincidence full and at perigee, The, 26, 121. Cf. "Cooper passes Celia" (II), "Astronomy-astrology" (II).

Moon . . . in the Serpent, the, 32v, 93, 182, 183. Cf. "Great magical ability," "Astronomy-astrology" (II).

More . . . and . . . less [in various combinations], 113.

"Most happy," said Miss Carridge, 143, 149.

Most things under the moon . . . and then stopped, 9, 253. Cf. "Slowly he felt better," "Rock got faster," "Soon his body."

Mote in . . . absolute freedom, a, 112, 113.

Mr. Clinch, please, 261, 263. Cf. " 'Mr. Clinch,' said."

"Mr. Clinch," said Dr. Killiecrankie, 266, 267. Cf. "Mr. Clinch, please."

Mr. Kelly fell back, 12, 18. Cf. "Mr. Kelly, bed, eyes" (II).

Murphy, a strict non-reader, 162, 234.

Murphy did not come back to, 149 (2). Cf. "I'll be back."

Murphy, his quarry, 116, 121.

Murphy never wore a, 72, 73. Cf. "Cooper never takes off his hat" (II).

Murphy . . . or Mr. Murphy? 267, 268.

Murphy . . . was inclined to think, 64, 92 (2).

Music, MUSIC, MUSIC, 236, 252.

My county, 260 (2). Cf. "Counties, English" (II), "Coroner, verbal repetition" (II).

"My poor friend," said Wylie, 51, 56. Cf. "Hands held" (II).

My rump, 12, 20, 145, 277. Cf. *"Felo-de-se."*

My. . . . Thank you, 31 (2). Cf. "Thanks" (II).

Pace [pacing] to and fro, 12, 18. Cf. "Soft padding."
Pain[s] in the neck . . . feet, 33, 36 75r.
Passed . . . on . . . who having endorsed it, 184–85, 185. Cf. entries under "M.M.M." (II).
Pictured itself as a . . . sphere, 107, 107r, 110.
Pine of smoke, 276, 278.
Pinioned, 24, 40. Cf. "Made to rise," "Let me go," "Celia's wrists pinioned" (II).
Pity . . . and a touch of, 230–31, 248.
Pleasure that pleasure was the word, 2, 112–13v. Cf. "Gave him pleasure," "Here the pleasure," "It was pleasant."
Poem that he alone, etc., the, 93, 183 (2). Cf. "Murphy, horoscope, euphemisms" (II).
Position of the highest trust, a, 84, 157.
Possibly Murphy, and, 11, 18, 25v. Cf. "Have [had]."
Principle of the thing, the, 147 (2). Cf. "Miss Carridge, verbal repetition" (II), "Wylie as mimic" (II).

Quid pro quo, 2 (2), 6.
Quite a new technique, 83, 101. Cf. "Lettuce, heads of" (II).
Quite exceptionally anthropoid, 118, 118r, 202.

Ravaged face, 115, 282.
Rest, A, 234 (3), 234v, 250 (2), 250v. Cf. "No matter what I did," "Rest, a" (II).
Resumed . . . no . . . slowly than before, but perhaps . . . less surely, 155, 234.
Return[ing] to the dear land of his [our] birth, 122, 272.
Rich[er] in acoustic properties, 155, 233.
Right word, 62 (3).
Rock got faster and faster and then stopped, a, 9, 253. Cf. "Rock got faster and faster, shorter," "Slowly he felt better," "Soon his body," "Faster and faster."
Rock got faster and faster, shorter and shorter, 9, 252–53. Cf. "Rock got faster and faster and then," "Faster and faster."

Sad truth was that, the, 86, 188, 242.
Sat [seated] . . . on the edge of the bed, 23, 37, 207v, 212, 231, 231v. Cf. "Sit on the bed," "Bed, sitting and lying" (II).
Seedy solipsist, 82 (2).
Serenade, nocturne . . . albada, 74 (2), 252.
Set him free . . . in his mind, 2, 113. Cf. "Murphy, mind and body compared" (II).
Sharp little, 45 (2).
She could not, 20 (2).

Supposing that to be permitted, 58, 202.
Surd [used to describe Murphy], 77, 112.
Surgical quality, 62, 80.
Syndrome known as life is too diffuse to admit of palliation, the, 57, 200. Cf. "For every symptom," "Horse leech's daughter," "Her quantum," "Advantage," "I greatly fear."

Tell Cooper, 199 (2). Cf. "I can never forget," "Letters, Neary's" (II).
Tell me what to do, 23, 24.
Temptation to . . . was strong . . . but she set it aside, The, 14, 150. Cf. "Course was clear," "There would be time."
Than an attic. An attic! 162 (2). Cf. "Garret that . . . was," "Garrets" (II).
"That is not possible," said Murphy, 8 (2).
—That was the position, 4, 24. Cf. "Their point of departure," "Gesture, ways to conclude" (II).
That'll [that will] be all right, 207 (2). Cf. "You know what women are," "Cooper, women" (II).
Their point of departure. See "Hands . . . their point of departure."
Then there would be no, 190 (2). Cf. "Murphy, both ways" (II).
There has not [hasn't] been a . . . stir out of him, 133 (2). Cf. "Hark."
There, there, 46, 266 (3), 267.
There would be time for that, 14, 150. Cf. "Course was clear," "Temptation to."
They could be extended? 163 (2). Cf. "Tubes and wires."
They gazed at one another [each other] in silence, 23, 25.
They went a little . . . in silence, 62 (2).
They will always be the same as they always were, 58, 201. Cf. "Advantage of this view," "Syndrome."
Thinking of Miss Counihan, 56 (2).
This . . . , 34 (2). Cf. "Into a . . . ," "Murphy, horoscope, euphemisms" (II).
Those of the cozeners [cozened], 79 (2).
Those that slept . . . and those that did not, 239 (2). Cf. "M.M.M., Skinner's, groups" (II).
Throughout the day, 187 (2).
Thus this [the] sixpence worth of sky . . . changed . . . the poem that he alone of . . . the living could write, 93, 183. Cf. "Poem that he alone," "Murphy, horoscope, euphemisms" (II).
Ticklepenny nudged Murphy, 168, 169, 169r.
Times what it cost to, 83 (2). Cf. "Murphy, lunch, tea" (II).
To begin with, 195 (2).
To climb the stairs in the dark, 26, 153.
To go back no further than the vagitus, 71 (2). Cf. "Vagitus."
To sit . . . we are now met, 221, 222.
To the best of his ability, 214, 216. Cf. "Best of his knowledge."
To throw up . . . job, 91 (2). Cf. "Job."

When the boots . . . a . . . telegram, 56–57, 57. Cf. "Telegrams" (II).

While she was with him. He now, 30 (2). Cf. "Might give pain," "Kept . . . nothing."

Whinge, 37, 122. Cf. "Human eyelid."

Who loved a, 5 (3). Cf. "Flight-Lieutenant Elliman, women" (II), "Miss Dwyer, men" (II), "Neary, deserted wives" (II), "Neary, loves" (II).

With and from himself, 221, 221v.

With Miss . . . before . . . Miss, 206 (2). Cf. "Miss . . . a brunette," "Cooper, women" (II).

With the light turned . . . to begin with he had, 247 (2). Cf. "Lit, indicated," "Permutations" (II).

Without Cooper . . . never find Murphy, 125, 127.

Work . . . end of them both, 22, 27. Cf. "Job," "Work . . . she."

Work . . . she . . . back to hers, 22, 76. Cf. "Work . . . end."

Worse for her outing, the, 103, 153. Cf. entries under "Hyde Park" (II).

Would be explained to him, 159 (2). Cf. entries under "M.M.M." (II).

"Wretched girl!" said Mr. Kelly, 15, 16.

Wylie supported Miss Counihan, 260, 268.

Yes, June to October . . . the blockade, 65, 74.

You are all I have in the world, 11, 18. Cf. "Possibly Murphy," "Have [had]," "Do not leave me."

You are quite sure, 227 (2). Cf. "Wylie as mimic" (II).

You can't love, 36 (3). Cf. "For whatever reason," "Murphy, love and success" (II).

"You cur," said Miss Counihan, 210 (2). Cf. "Belonged to the same great group."

You know what women are, 205, 206. Cf. "Cooper, women" (II).

You, my body . . . my mind . . . one . . . go, 40, 190. Cf. "One . . . or two or all," "Body, mind and soul."

You shall find me . . . not ungrateful, 62, 199, 221v. Cf. "Not . . . find . . . ungrateful," "I can never forget," "Letters, Neary's" (II).

You take [took] the tone out of my mouth, 210, 214.

You want to, 194 (3). Cf. "Well that beats."

Appendix II

Repeated Episodes, Objects, and Allusions in *Murphy*

Included in this appendix are recurring scenes, incidents, locales, objects, and allusions; characters with similar traits or professions; and dual entities. Objects and dual entities are listed alphabetically according to the object duplicated ("Telegrams") or the word modified by "two" ("Sinners"). When different locales are compared, entries are according to the name of the category ("Counties, Irish"; recurring place names are listed according to the name ("Battersea Park"). When recurring entities are associated with a particular character, they are listed under that character's name ("Celia, bags"). Characters' names are listed alphabetically according to the form most commonly used in the novel ("Celia," "Mr. Kelly"). Allusions are listed under the author's name ("Berkeley"); anonymous works are listed by title ("Old Testament"). When two works are compared, entries are according to the category ("Elizabethan songs"). Characters with similar professions are listed according to the profession ("Landladies"). Repeated characteristics are listed by category ("Heads, large"). Cross-references are given to sets that are linked to the one listed either by proximity or by theme. Where no Roman numeral is given after a cross-reference, the heading is listed in Appendix II. Page references are to *Murphy* (1938; rpt., New York: Grove Press, 1957).

Abbreviations:
    cf.   Compare the entry listed to another one.
    I   In Appendix I.

Academic fellows. There are two references to academic fellows, both times in connection with death (58, 224).
Alcoholics. Two alcoholics appear in the novel, Ticklepenny (86–88) and Cooper (54).

Astronomy-astrology. Celestial objects are considered sometimes from the point of view of astronomy and sometimes from the point of view of astrology. See, for example, references to the moon on pp. 26 and 32; these passages are both repeated. Cf. "Moon by a striking" (I), "Moon . . . in the Serpent" (I).

Asylums. Two insane asylums are mentioned in the novel, John o' God's, in Stillorgan, on the outskirts of Dublin; and the Magdalen Mental Mercyseat, "a little way out of" London (43, 156). Both names have religious connotations. Cf. "Asylums, John o' God's" and the entries under "M.M.M."

Asylums, John o' God's. John o' God's is mentioned twice (43). Cf. "Asylums," "M.M.M., chapters."

Balzac chairs. There are two references to the two "Balzac chairs" in the room Murphy and Celia rent from Miss Carridge (63, 228).

Battersea Bridge. Battersea Bridge is mentioned twice (14, 15). Cf. "Battersea Park."

Battersea Park. Battersea Park is mentioned twice (16, 106). Cf. "Battersea Bridge," "Parks," and entries under "Hyde Park."

Bed, sitting and lying. Many important exchanges in the novel take place with one person lying on a bed and another (or others) sitting nearby. The person lying down is usually more powerful than the person sitting; typically, the sitting person wants to have or to continue a relationship with the reclining person, but is rejected. In the following examples the first-named person is the one sitting: Celia and Mr. Kelly (23); Celia and Murphy (29, 39); Murphy and Ticklepenny (191); Miss Counihan and Neary (207); Neary and Celia (232); Mr. Endon and Murphy (242); Murphy and Mr. Endon (248). Many of these scenes are accompanied by verbal repetition: see "In a somewhat similar" (I), "Started up in the bed" (I), "Made to rise" (I), "Sat . . . on the edge of the bed" (I), "Sit on the bed" (I). See also "Celia's wrists pinioned."

Bell. Neary's chambermaid does not come when he rings the bell but waits "for the bell to ring a second time" (210).

Berkeley. There are three allusions to Berkeley and his philosophy: he is mentioned together with a reference to his philosophy of immaterialism (58); a reference to "idealist tar" alludes to Berkeley's *A Chain of Reflexions and Inquiries Concerning the Virtues of Tar-Water* (108); and a reference to *percipere* and *percipi* alludes to a passage in Berkeley's *Philosophical Commentaries* (246); see *Philosophical Commentaries*, ed. A. A. Luce (London: Thomas Nelson and Sons, 1944), p. 139.

Buckets. Wylie says, "Humanity is a well with two buckets" (58).

Celia, actions like the old boy's. After the old boy dies, Celia wants to see his room (137) and then arranges things so that she moves into it

(146). The description of how she paces the floor in the old boy's room resembles an earlier description of the old boy pacing (69, 228). Moreover, the language in these descriptions is similar: see " 'Hark' . . . said" (I), "Soft padding" (I), "Never still" (I).

Celia, bags. Celia, moving into the old boy's room (the second room she occupies at Miss Carridge's), takes two bags with her (148). Cf. "Celia, actions like the old boy's," "Celia, rooms," "Flats."

Celia, Irish sky. Twice Celia is reminded of Ireland when she looks at the sky (41, 280).

Celia, list of measurements. Two items on the list of Celia's measurements, her neck and knee, have a circumference of 13¾ inches; two, her age and her instep, are "Unimportant" (10). Cf. "Hips, etc." (I).

Celia, omens. Celia, wondering whether to remain with Murphy, flips a coin, but she ignores "the omen of the coin," which indicates that she should leave Murphy (28). Soon afterward a second omen suggests that she should leave: she breaks a mirror. But she also disregards this omen (30). Cf. "Herself a last chance" (I).

Celia, reasons. The narrator says, "Celia was conscious of two equally important reasons for insisting" that Murphy find a job (65).

Celia, rooms. Celia occupies two rooms in Miss Carridge's rooming house (147–48). Cf. "Celia, bags," "Flats," "Half as . . . twice as" (I).

Celia will lead to Murphy. The idea that Celia will lead to Murphy is mentioned a number of times. It is first suggested by Cooper (203), then by Miss Carridge (208), and then by Wylie (211). Later, when this turns out to be the method they used to find Murphy, Wylie says, "Didn't I tell you she would lead us to him?"—without giving credit to Cooper as the person who originated the idea (257).

Celia's wrists pinioned. In two scenes Celia's wrists are "pinioned" by men who are trying to persuade her to do what they ask (24, 40). In the first of these scenes Mr. Kelly advises Celia to leave Murphy; in the second Murphy asks her to remain with him. Cf. "Made to rise" (I), "Pinioned" (I), " 'Let me go' " (I), "He let her go" (I). In both scenes the man is in bed and Celia is sitting on the bed. Cf. "Bed, sitting and lying."

Chairs, rocking and wheel. Murphy's rocking chair is compared to Mr. Kelly's wheel chair (277). The chairs are also linked by the word "rocking" (227) and by the recurring phrase "Faster and faster" (I).

Chapter openings and closings. The last two chapters open with references to the time of day, the date, and the weather (254–76). Chapter 1 and Chapter 11 end with the longest recurring passage in the novel. See "Slowly he felt better" (I) and related entries. Cf. "M.M.M., chapters," "Epigraphs."

Chess game, repeated moves. In the chess game Murphy plays with Mr. Endon, fifteen of Murphy's moves (numbers 2, 3, 4, 6, 7, 9, 11, 13, 14, 15, 16, 17, 19, 22, and 24) are the same as moves that Mr. Endon had made one or two turns previously (243–44). Cf. "Make his move" (I).

Chess game, salons. In the comments about the chess game there are references to two chess salons, the Café de la Régence and Simpson's Divan (244).

Chess game, *Zweispringerspott*. The chess game is called a *"Zwei-springerspott* ("two-knight mockery"). This is the second name that the game is given (243).

Cities, continental Europe. Murphy makes extended visits to two cities in continental Europe, Hanover and Paris (73, 162). Cf. "Countries."

Cities, Holland. Murphy's uncle, Mr. Quigley, lives in two cities in Holland, Amsterdam and Scheveningen (53).

Cities, Ireland. The scenes in the novel that take place in Ireland are set in two cities, Cork and Dublin. Cf. "Cork," "Dublin."

Cooper never sits. There are numerous references to the fact that Cooper cannot sit, which prepare the way for the narrator's astonishment when he does sit. See pp. 54, 118, 119, 123–24, 198, 254, 260, 273. Cf. "Cooper never takes off his hat," "In a short time" (I).

Cooper never takes off his hat. There are numerous references to the fact that Cooper never takes off his hat, which prepare the way for Neary's astonishment when he removes his hat. See pp. 54, 118, 123–24, 198, 260, 273. Cf. "Cooper never sits," "In a short time" (I).

Cooper, no cause for embarrassment. Wylie, kissing Miss Counihan, is not embarrassed when Cooper arrives: "Wylie would not have broken off his love game for Cooper, any more than for an animal . . ." (118). Similarly, Miss Counihan undresses in front of Cooper without reflecting "that Cooper for all his shortcomings was a man like other men . . ." (204).

Cooper passes Celia. The scene where Cooper passes Celia in the hallway of the West Brompton rooming house is described twice, first from Celia's point of view and then from Cooper's (26, 121). The scenes are linked by a cross-reference, "the appalling position described in section three" (121), and by a recurring passage: see "Moon by a striking coincidence" (I).

Cooper, pub openings. The narrator twice gives an enthusiastic and detailed description of a pub that opens as Cooper watches (120, 274). In each case Cooper, succumbing to temptation, gives up his mission and enters the pub.

Cooper's reports. Cooper gives similar reports to Miss Counihan and to Wylie (196, 197). Cf. "Browbeat Cooper" (I), "New Testament, employers."

Cooper tracks Murphy and Celia. Cooper discovers Murphy's residence in West Brompton by following him home after spotting him in the Cockpit at Hyde Park; he discovers Murphy's Brewer Street residence after spotting Celia near the Cockpit in Hyde Park and following her there (120, 151–53). Cf. "Hyde Park, Cockpit," "He let himself in" (I), "Made a mental note" (I).

Cooper, women. The only two women Cooper ever loved, his "two good

angels," he loved simultaneously (206). Cf. "Miss . . . a brunette" (I),
"With Miss . . ." (I), "You know what women are" (I).

Cork. Two scenes are set in Cork, both are flashbacks, and both contain
descriptions of Neary's love for a woman (3ff., 48ff.). Cf. "Cities,
Ireland."

Coroner, functions. The second coroner's functions are to determine,
"one, who is dead, and, two, how" (261). Cf. "Latter matter" (I),
"Coroners."

Coroner, matches. The second coroner, describing how he thinks Murphy died, mentions two kinds of matches that might have set off the
explosion, a "Brymay safety" and a "wax vesta" (263). Cf. "Very
feature" (I), "Coroners."

Coroner, verbal repetition. The second coroner often repeats himself
when he gives an opinion about whether Murphy's death was accidental. Cf. "Deaths, accidents or suicides?" "Coroners," "But
whether" (I), " 'By all means' " (I), "Latter matter" (I), "My county"
(I), "Matter of the manner" (I), "*Modus morendi*" (I), "Very feature of
the" (I).

Coroners. Two coroners are mentioned in the novel; both hold inquests
in which they must decide on similar questions (145, 259). Cf.
"Deaths, accidents or suicides?"

Counties, English. The M.M.M. is located "on the boundary of two
counties" (156). Cf. entries under "M.M.M.," "My county" (I).

Counties, Irish. There are references to two Irish counties, Cork County
and Dublin County (6, 84). Cf. "Counties, English," "Cities, Ireland."

Countries. Murphy lives in two countries in the British Isles, Ireland and
England, and makes extended visits to two countries in continental
Europe, France and Germany. Cf. "Cities, continental Europe,"
"Countries, British Isles."

Countries, British Isles. The action of the novel is set in two countries in
the British Isles, Ireland and England. Cf. "Countries."

Cox, Ariadne, abandoned. Ariadne Cox, Neary's second deserted wife, is
abandoned a second time, by Sacha Few (61, 272). Cf. "Neary, deserted wives," "Alive and well" (I), "Deserted his wife" (I).

Cox, Ariadne, sought. Miss Counihan tells Cooper to stop looking for
Murphy; instead he is to search for Neary's deserted wife Ariadne,
whom she hopes to use in blackmailing Neary (204). Wylie, with a
similar motive in mind, gives Cooper similar instructions (204). Cf.
"Belonged to the same great group" (I), "Deserted his wife" (I), "Cox,
Ariadne, abandoned."

Dante, Belacqua. There are two allusions to Dante's Belacqua (see *Purgatorio* 4:97ff.). In each passage there are references to watching the
dawn break, and Belacqua is mentioned twice in each passage (78,
112). The repetition of the word "dayspring," which occurs in one of

the Belacqua passages and in a passage about the disposal of Murphy's remains, suggests that Murphy has joined Belacqua in Purgatory (78, 275). Cf. "Dayspring" (I).

Deaths, accidents or suicides? In two scenes there is disagreement with a coroner's verdict about whether a death was accidental or a suicide (145, 262). Cf. "Coroners," *"Felo-de-se"* (I), "Matter of the manner" (I), *"Modus morendi"* (I), "I don't believe" (I), "Shock following burns" (I), "Very feature of the" (I).

Democritus. There are two allusions to Democritus: "guffaw of the Abderite" (246) and "the famous ant on the sky of an airless world" (248; and see Aristotle, *De Anima*, 419a).

Descartes. There are two allusions to Descartes: "conarium" (6) and "dream of Descartes" (140).

Distress, in. Neary says, "Two in distress . . . make sorrow less" (52).

Doctors, named and unnamed. Four doctors appear in the novel. Two of them have names, Dr. Fist (88) and Dr. Killiecrankie (88). Both names contain puns based on German words. The unnamed doctors are the obstetrician who delivers Murphy (71) and the physician who is summoned when the old boy takes his life (135).

Dublin. Two scenes are set in Dublin; Wylie, Miss Counihan, and Cooper appear in both of them (42ff., 117ff.). Cf. "Cities, Ireland," "Alive and well" (I), "Grave of Father Prout" (I).

Elizabethan songs. Excerpts from two Elizabethan songs are quoted on the same page (235). Both excerpts are couplets; the first is from "Sephestia's Song to her Child" by Robert Greene; the second is from "What Thing is Love?" by George Peele.

Envelopes. Two envelopes are mentioned in the novel, the "black envelope" that contains Murphy's horoscope (30, 31, 93), and the "singed envelope" that contains his will (258). Cf. "Envelope . . . grasped" (I).

Epigraphs. Two chapters (Chapters 6 and 9) have epigraphs; both refer to an aspect of Murphy's retreat into his mind, and both are in foreign languages (107, 156). Cf. "Chapter openings."

Evils. Miss Counihan considers Wylie "the lesser of two evils that had befallen her" (257).

Experiences. The narrator refers to physical activity and mental activity as "the two experiences" (109). Cf. "Murphy, mind and body compared."

Eyes, deeply imbedded. Two characters have deeply imbedded eyes: Mr. Kelly, whose eyes "could not very well protrude, so deeply were they imbedded" (11), and Mr. Endon, whose eyes are "both deep-set and protuberant, one of Nature's jokes" (248). Cf. "Heads, large."

Famous. The word "famous" is twice used to call attention to allusions, and each of these allusions figures in another dual set. Cooper, says the narrator, "experienced none of the famous difficulty in serving two employers" (197); later the narrator refers to "the famous ant on the sky of an airless world" (248). The first passage is an allusion to the New Testament; see "New Testament, employers." For the source of the second passage, which is an allusion to Democritus, see "Democritus."

Flats. Murphy rents two flats in London, in West Brompton and on Brewer Street (7, 68); Celia occupies two rooms in the second boarding house: see "Celia, rooms." The landladies in the two boarding houses have similar characteristics: see "Landladies."

Flight-Lieutenant Elliman, women. Flight-Lieutenant Elliman is involved with two women, Miss Farren and Miss Dwyer (48). Cf. "Miss Dwyer, men," "Despairing of recommending" (I), "As happy as a," (I).

Fortunetellers. Two fortunetellers appear in the novel, Suk and Rosie Dew. See "Rosie Dew," "Murphy, horoscope."

Friendships. Murphy loses interest in Celia (189) at a time when he is eager to become friends with Mr. Endon (184), but his feelings of friendship are not reciprocated (241). Neary loses interest in Miss Counihan at the time he feels a need to become friends with Murphy (199–201), but Murphy dies before this need can be satisifed. Cf. "Neary, deserted wives," "Murphy, women."

Furies. There are two allusions to the Furies: "a Fury coming to carry him off" (27) and "Sleep, half-brother to the Furies" (175). Cf. "Sleep, mythological figure."

Garrets. Murphy occupies two garrets, in Hanover and at the M.M.M. The garret at the M.M.M. is "not half, but twice as good as the one in Hanover, because half as large" (162). Cf. "Garret . . . the fug" (I), "Garret that" (I), "Than an attic" (I), "Half as . . . twice as" (I).

Gesture, ways to conclude. Murphy feels that there are "two equally legitimate ways" in which Neary's gesture "might be concluded" (4). Cf. "Gestures, similar," "—That was the position" (I), "Hands . . . their point of departure" (I).

Gestures, similar. Celia's gesture of despair is compared to Neary's; though Neary does not conclude his gesture in one of the two "legitimate ways" defined by Murphy (4), Celia, in Murphy's opinion, resolves her gesture "quite legitimately" (35). Cf. "Gesture, ways to conclude," "Clapped to . . . head" (I), "Hands . . . their point of departure" (I).

Geulincx. There are two allusions to the philosophy of Arnold Geulincx. The first is a quotation from his *Metaphysica* (178); see Geulincx, *Opera Philosophica* (1891–93; facsim. rpt., Stuttgart: Friedrich Fromann Verlag, 1965–68), 2:155. The second is a reference to "Reason and Philautia" (216), an allusion to Geulincx's *Ethica*; see *Opera Philosophica*, 3:9–15 *et passim*.

Handfuls. When Miss Counihan leans out of a window, she almost falls; Wylie, "making two skilful handfuls of her breasts," saves her (131). Cf. "Window, leaning out of."

Hands held. Mr. Kelly holds Celia's hands when she cries (23); Wylie holds Neary's hands when he cries (51). Cf. "My poor friend" (I).

Heads, large. Two characters, Mr. Kelly and Mr. Endon, have unusually large heads (186, 276). Cf. "Eyes, deeply imbedded," "Many sizes too" (I).

Heads, tiny. Two characters, Cooper and Wylie, have "tiny heads" (131). Cf. "Heads in the pillories" (I), "Heads, large."

Hindus. Two Hindus appear in the novel: Suk, a swami (23, 32), and a "Hindu polyhistor" (196).

Homer, heroines. Celia is mentioned in conjunction with two famous women who figure in Homer's works, Penelope and Helen (149, 175). Cf. "Miss Counihan, queens."

Homosexuals. Two homosexuals appear in the novel, Ticklepenny and Bim (156). Cf. "Fancy . . . not far short of love" (I), "Ticklepenny, men."

Hotels, Dublin. After arriving in Dublin from Cork, Miss Counihan stays first at Wynn's Hotel and then moves to another, unnamed hotel; then she goes to London (117, 122). Neary similarly begins his stay in Dublin after arriving from Cork in Wynn's Hotel, moves to an unnamed hotel (but not the same one as Miss Counihan's), and departs for London (55). Cf. "Dublin, where Wynn's Hotel" (I).

Hyde Park, Cockpit. In two scenes Murphy is near the Cockpit in Hyde Park (96, 120), and in two scenes Cooper tracks his quarry from the Cockpit in Hyde Park. See "Cooper tracks Murphy and Celia." Cf. other entries under "Hyde Park," "Battersea Park," "Parks."

Hyde Park, Long Water. In two scenes Rosie Dew appears near the Long Water in Hyde Park (99, 278). Cf. other entries under "Hyde Park," "Was waiting . . . from Lord Gall" (I).

Hyde Park, Round Pond. In two scenes Celia appears near the Round Pond in Hyde Park. In both she watches kite flyers and sees a boy with two kites yoked in tandem (152, 280); in both she is approached by a potential client (151, 278–79). Cf. "Kites, tandem," "All out" (I), "Coupled abreast" (I), "Margin of the pond" (I), "Child . . . had" (I), and other entries under "Hyde Park."

Hyde Park, Victoria Gate. Both Rosie Dew and Celia, on their visits to Hyde Park, pass by the dahlias near Victoria Gate (103, 150–51). In the first of these scenes the narrator mentions a dogs' cemetery; in the second he mentions an animal hospital. Cf. other entries under "Hyde Park."

Impeded views. When Neary feasts his eyes on Miss Counihan, Wylie gets between the two of them and Neary asks him to move (220).

Later, in a parallel scene, Miss Counihan impedes Wylie's view of Celia, and he takes her by the wrists to try to move her (272).

Kicks. The narrator contrasts the "kick *in intellectu*" and the "kick *in re*" (109). Cf. "Experiences," "Murphy, mind and body compared," "Kick . . . caress" (I).

Kites, tandem. A boy with a pair of kites flown in tandem from a double winch figures in two scenes (152–53, 280—81). Cf. "Hyde Park, Round Pond," "Coupled abreast" (I), "All out" (I).

Landladies. Murphy has two landladies in London; both "cook" his bill (19, 146–47), and he has problems keeping both of them out of his room (7, 68). Cf. "Flats," "His landlady" (I).

Latin style. There are two comments in the novel about the style of a Latin author who wrote in relatively recent times. The narrator criticizes the "goatish Latin" of Bishop Bouvier, but praises the "beautiful Belgo-Latin of Arnold Geulincx" (72, 178). Cf. "Geulincx."

Letters, Murphy's. Murphy writes two letters to Celia (22). Cf. "Telephone conversations," "Letters, Neary's."

Letters, Neary's. Neary writes two letters with similar texts to Wylie and Miss Counihan (199). Cf. "Telegrams," "Letters, Murphy's," "I can never forget" (I), "Tell Cooper" (I), "Come . . . when" (I), "It is too" (I), "You shall find me" (I), "Keep . . . on your hands" (I).

Lettuce, heads of. Rosie Dew twice (using different techniques) unsuccessfully tries to feed two heads of lettuce to sheep in Hyde Park; the two heads of lettuce are mentioned twice (99, 101). Cf. "Lettuce vs. cabbage," "Quite a new technique" (I), "Stood . . . in an attitude of" (I).

Lettuce vs. cabbage. Rosie Dew's two heads of lettuce are twice mistakenly described as cabbage, first by Murphy (101) and then by the narrator (106). Cf. "Lettuce, heads of."

Met. Murphy, commenting on the nature of his first encounter with Celia, feels that the word "met" hardly describes the beginning of their relationship (36). Miss Counihan similarly rejects the word "met" in a description of her relationship with Wylie and Neary (221). Cf. "Met, allusions."

Met, allusions. There are allusions in two of Miss Counihan's comments related to the word "met" (221). "Do you really mean to . . . tell me . . . that you consider we are now met?" refers to "Mercy and truth are now met" (Psalms 85:10). "Who ever met . . . that met not at first sight?" is from Christopher Marlowe's "Hero and Leander" (First Sestiad, line 176). This allusion was first noted by Robert Harrison in *Samuel Beckett's Murphy: A Critical Excursion* (Athens: University of Georgia Press, 1968), p. 85.

Miss Carridge, striking grammar. The narrator twice uses the word "striking" when describing Miss Carridge's unusual grammatical forms. He speaks of her "striking nominative" and her "striking use of the passive voice" (133, 144).

Miss Carridge, tea. When Miss Carridge feels that her recent economic transactions have been particularly profitable, she brings Celia a cup of tea (6–7, 132, 143). Cf. "Nice . . . cup of tea" (I), "Drink it" (I), "None of those things" (I), " 'Come in' " (I), "Cupidity . . . imagination" (I), "Miss Carridge . . . alms" (I).

Miss Carridge, verbal repetition. Miss Carridge at times repeats phrases, a sign that she is lying. Cf. "Doubt" (I), "Principle of the thing" (I). Wylie seems to understand this and mimic her: see "Wylie as mimic."

Miss Counihan, queens. Miss Counihan is compared to two famous queens in antiquity: Dido and Jezebel (195, 199). Cf. "Virgil, *Aeneid*," "Homer, heroines."

Miss Counihan, verbal repetition. Miss Counihan often says "—er—" before a euphemism. Cf. "—Er—" (I), "Miss Carridge, verbal repetition." Wylie notices her mannerism and mimics her: see "Wylie as mimic."

Miss Counihan, vulnerable points. The narrator says that Miss Counihan has only two vulnerable points, "her erogenous zones and her need for Murphy" (126–27).

Miss Dwyer, men. Miss Dwyer is involved with two men, Flight-Lieutenant Elliman and Neary (5, 48). Cf. "Neary, deserted wives," "Flight-Lieutenant Elliman, women," "Despairing of recommending" (I), "As happy as a" (I).

Mistresses, famous. There are references, in similar contexts, to two ambitious women who became famous as the mistresses of rulers who lost their power because of the liaisons. Neary feels that his need for Murphy to provide "a mind to pillow his beside" is "a sorer lack than any wife or even mistress, were she Yang Kuei-fei herself" (117). Yang Kuei-fei (719–756) was the concubine of the emperor Hsüan Tsung; after being forced to execute her, he abdicated. When Murphy refuses to share a room with Ticklepenny, the narrator explains that there was no reason for Ticklepenny to feel slighted: he would have been refused "had he been Cleopatra herself" (161). Cf. "Neary, Chinese attractions," "Were she . . . herself" (I).

M.M.M., buildings for staff. "Two large buildings, one for males, the other for females," says the narrator, housed the staff at the M.M.M. (161).

M.M.M., chapters. Two chapters (9 and 11) are set at the Magdalen Mental Mercyseat; both deal with similar matters and both end with Murphy in his garret (156–94, 236–53). Cf. "Asylums," "Asylums, John o' God's," and other entries under M.M.M."

M.M.M., convalescent houses. There are "two convalescent houses" at the M.M.M. (165).

M.M.M., mortuary, climbing plants. The mortuary at the M.M.M. is covered with two types of climbing plants, traveller's joy and ampelopsis; these are mentioned twice (165, 258). The lawn of the building is twice referred to as a "forecourt"; see "Forecourt of lawn" (I), "Traveller's joy" (I).

M.M.M., mortuary, couples. Two couples go into the mortuary together: Dr. Killiecrankie and the coroner, who are "twined together"; and Bim and Ticklepenny, who are "wreathed together" (259). Cf. "M.M.M., mortuary, duel."

M.M.M., mortuary, duel. Dr. Killiecrankie and the coroner participate in a "little duel" to decide which of them "would pass second" into the mortuary. Cf. "M.M.M., mortuary, couples."

M.M.M., mortuary, refrigerators. Murphy's corpse is stored in one of the M.M.M.'s "double-decker refrigerators"; there are two rows of these refrigerators (259).

M.M.M., Skinner's, corridors. The wards in Skinner's House "consisted of two long corridors" (166). Cf. "Known to the wittier" (I).

M.M.M., Skinner's, groups. Murphy, comparing "two groups" at the M.M.M. ("those that slept" and "those that did not"), is reminded of a pair of matching statues, "Puget's caryatids of Strength and Weariness" (239). Cf. "Sculptors," "Sleep and Insomnia," "Those that slept" (I).

M.M.M., Skinner's, males and females. Skinner's House is divided into two sections: male patients are housed in the eastern half, and female patients in the western half (165). Cf. "M.M.M., buildings for staff."

M.M.M., Skinner's, obelisk. Skinner's House is "dilated at both ends like a double obelisk" (165).

M.M.M., Skinner's, stories. Skinner's House is a "two-storied building" (165).

Monographs. Two characters in the novel write monographs, and both titles are given: Neary's *The Doctine of the Limit* and the Hindu polyhistor's *The Pathetic Fallacy from Avercamp to Kampendonck* (50, 196). Two lines of dialogue are spoken by the polyhistor (196). Neary and the polyhistor both live in London but are not natives of that city, are both involved with Miss Counihan, and both contemplate suicide (55, 196).

Mr. Kelly, bed, eyes. Whenever Mr. Kelly sits up in bed his eyes open, and when he lies down his eyes close, "as though he were a doll" (12). This occurs five times (12, 17, 18, 279, 280). Cf. "Mr. Kelly fell back" (I).

Mr. Kelly, flat. Two scenes are set in Mr. Kelly's flat (11ff., 114–15). Cf. "Have . . . no one" (I), "Mr. Kelly, kite repair."

Mr. Kelly, kite. In an early scene Mr. Kelly imagines flying his kite out of sight (25); in a later scene he does this (280). Cf. "Out of sight" (I), "Out, back" (I).

Mr. Kelly, kite repair. Mr. Kelly is twice seen repairing his kite; this occurs in each of the scenes that are set in his flat (25, 114). Cf. "Hexagon of crimson" (I).

Mr. Kelly, thinking. Mr. Kelly twice finds it difficult to think because of a feeling that his attention is dispersed among various parts of his body (19, 115). Cf. "He found it hard to think" (I).

Murphy, birthmark. In the first scene in which Celia and Murphy appear together, she sees a birthmark on one of his buttocks (28–29); the last time she sees him, at the inquest, she once again sees the birthmark and uses it to identify the corpse. The coroner is charmed: "birthmark deathmark, I mean, rounding off the life somehow . . . ," he says (267).

Murphy, both ways. The narrator says that Murphy felt happy among the lunatics "and sorry when the time came to leave them. He could not have it both ways" (189). Murphy's horoscope specifies that he resembles the type of person who wants "to be in two places at a time" (32). Both comments hint that Murphy wants to withdraw into the little world without being ready to give up the pleasures of the big world. Cf. "Murphy, horoscope, places," "Vicarious autology" (I), "Nor did he" (I), "Best he could do" (I), "Then there would be no" (I).

Murphy, canons. Murphy, says the narrator, has confidence in "only two canons"; they are astrology and his own internal system (76). Cf. "Based on the . . . system" (I), "In which" (I).

Murphy, coat, childhood. Murphy's coat is in its "second childhood" (141).

Murphy, horoscope, euphemisms. Murphy's horoscope is always referred to euphemistically; the word "horoscope" does not appear in the novel. Many of the euphemisms are used twice. The references are as follows: "it" (8); "what you told me—" (8); "what you mean" (8); "corpus of incentives" (22); "it" (23); "What he told me to get" (23); "Are you afraid to call it by its name?" (23); "sixpenny writ" (27); "life-warrant" (31, 93); "bull of incommunication" (31, 93); "Corpus of deterrents" (34); "Separation order" (34); "celestial prescriptions of Professor Suk" (38); "Suk's theme of Murphy's heaven" (74); "diagram" (75); "sixpence worth of sky" (93, 183); "ludicrous broadsheet" (93); "corpus of deterrents" (93); "the poem that he alone of the living could write" (93); "the poem that he alone of all the living could write" (183); "the poem that he alone of all the born could have written" (183). See also the following entries in Appendix I: "Corpus of deterrents," "What . . . told me," "I have it," "Life-warrant," "Bull of incommunication," "Thus this sixpence," "This . . . ," "My. . . . Thank you," "Into a. . . ."

Murphy, horoscope, motifs. Murphy notes "a clash," and later "a syzygy," in "two hitherto distinct motifs" in the horoscope (87, 93, 87). Cf. "Sudden clash" (I).

Murphy, horoscope, places. According to the horoscope, people like

Murphy have been known to express "a wish to be in two places at a time" (32). Cf. "Murphy, both ways."

Murphy, jokes, favorite. Murphy has two favorite jokes; both involve stout (139). Cf. "Murphy, jokes, types."

Murphy, jokes, types. Murphy distinguishes between two types of jokes: those "that had once been good jokes" and those "that had never been good jokes" (65). Cf. "Murphy, jokes, favorite," "Had never been" (I).

Murphy, love and success. Murphy explains to Miss Counihan that to make love and to succeed in business are more than he can manage at the same time (51). He gives Celia a similar excuse (36ff.). Cf. "You can't love" (I), "Little luxuries" (I). Miss Counihan and Celia both complain when Murphy goes off to look for work: see "It was September" (I).

Murphy, lunch, bills. The waitress Vera makes out a second bill for Murphy's lunch (94).

Murphy, lunch, sits. Murphy, sitting down for his lunch, enjoys the experience so much that he gets up and sits again. But the "second sit," says the narrator, "was a great disappointment" (80).

Murphy, lunch, tea. Murphy, who has little money to spend on his lunch, uses two stratagems to get more tea than he paid for. First he pretends that the waitress brought him the wrong kind of tea, and then, that he was given too much milk. The second trick, says the narrator, involves two "keywords" (83). Cf. "Defrauded a vested interest" (I), "Times what it cost" (I), "Keyword[s]" (I).

Murphy, lunch, twopence. The two items Murphy buys for his lunch each cost twopence. "Twopence the tea, twopence the biscuits," says the narrator, "a perfectly balanced meal" (80).

Murphy, mind and body compared. Murphy often reveals his dualistic philosophical views by comparing his mind and his body (see pp. 2, 109, 110, 111, 113, 190). This can be contrasted with the language in what is purportedly Murphy's will: see "Body, mind and soul" (I). A cross-reference emphasizes the passages that deal with Murphy's views on the mind-body connection: see "As described in section six" (I). Cf. "Kicks," "Murphy, mind and body, convictions," "Coming . . . alive" (I), "His body" (I), "Kick . . . caress" (I), "Set him free" (I), "Tried to come out" (I).

Murphy, mind and body, convictions. The narrator says that Murphy's belief that he is not of the big world but of the little world is "a conviction, two convictions" (178). Cf. other entries under "Murphy, mind and body."

Murphy, mind and body, split. The narrator repeatedly refers to Murphy's mind and body as "split" (109, 110, 188).

Murphy, mind and body, two worlds. Murphy feels that there are two worlds, the "little world" of mind and the "big world" of body (6-7,

178, 180, 181, 184). Cf. other entries under "Murphy, mind and body."

Murphy, M.M.M., rounds. Murphy's last round at the M.M.M. is called "round two" (240).

Murphy, M.M.M., shift. Murphy's first shift at the M.M.M. begins at two o'clock (170).

Murphy, M.M.M., week of duty. Murphy's last round at the M.M.M. comes at the beginning of his "second week" of duty there (159).

Murphy, points. Mr. Kelly says of two parallel arguments Murphy makes, "Points one and two" (22). Cf. "New Testament, Murphy's points," "Was that a point?" (I).

Murphy, quarrels. Celia and Murphy quarrel twice about whether he should look for a job. Cf. "Avoid exhaustion" (I), "Job" (I). Miss Counihan similarly urged Murphy to find a job: see "Murphy, love and success."

Murphy, questions about. The coroner's questions about Murphy are similar to those Mr. Kelly had asked in an earlier scene (267, 17). Both of them interject comments when they hear that Murphy is from Dublin.

Murphy, questions from. After interviewing Murphy, Bim asks if he has any questions; Bom, his twin, does the same (159, 168).

Murphy, religious figures. Murphy is compared to two religious figures, Christ and Muhammed. Celia calls Murphy's change of flats "the hegira" (64; the hegira is Muhammed's flight from Mecca to Medina). Miss Counihan calls London Murphy's "Mecca" (52–53). For links between Murphy and Christ, see "New Testament, Christ."

Murphy, theological student's clothing. The narrator calls Murphy's suit "a relic of those sanguine days" when he had been "a theological student" (71–72). Later the narrator refers to Murphy's "one time amateur theological student's shirt" (139).

Murphy, trances. Murphy's trances are similar, and they are described with recurring phrases which suggest that they should be compared. The trance in Hyde Park is linked to one at the M.M.M. by a phrase of this sort: see "When he came to" (I). The first and last trances both occur in the rocking chair and are described with many recurring phrases: see "Slowly he felt better" (I), "Rock got faster and faster" (I), and related passages. Murphy's need for a trance is emphasized by a phrase that is repeated when he enters a trance: see "But only . . . himself" (I).

Murphy, women. Murphy is involved with two women, Miss Counihan and Celia. Neary and Wylie are both attracted to the same two women. Cf. "Friendship," "Wylie, women."

Museums. There are two references to the Harpy Tomb in the British Museum (84, 95). There are also allusions to two other London museums; both are referred to only by their locations. The Tate

Gallery is called "Millbank" (225) and the National Gallery is called "Trafalger Square" (228).

Narcissus. There are two references to Narcissus in the novel (186, 228).

Neary, Chinese attractions. Neary asks Wylie to help him become interested in "some Chinese attractions other than Miss Counihan" (59). Later, when he wants to become friends with Murphy, Neary feels "a sorer lack than any wife or even mistress, were she Yang Kuei-fei herself" (117). Cf. "Mistresses, famous," "Were she . . . herself" (I).

Neary, complaints. Neary complains to Murphy about his unrequited love for Miss Dwyer; later he similarly complains to Wylie about his unrequited love for Miss Counihan (4–6, 48–59). These scenes are linked by allusions to Gestalt psychology and to the Dives-Lazarus story. Cf. "Psychology, Gestalt," "Figure . . . ground" (I), "New Testament, Dives and Lazarus."

Neary, deserted wives. Neary has deserted two wives, one in London and one in Calcutta (61). Cf. "Cox, Ariadne, abandoned," "Cox, Ariadne, sought," "Alive and well . . . in Calcutta" (I), "Who loved a" (I), "Friendships," "Miss Dwyer, men."

Neary, former students of. Two characters in the novel are former students of Neary's: Murphy and Wylie (3, 45). Cf. "Neary, complaints."

Neary, kept waiting. Both Miss Counihan and Wylie are very late for their appointments with Neary (50, 224).

Neary, keys. Before Neary leaves for Dublin, he "closed the Gymnasium, put a padlock on the Grove, sunk both keys in the Lee" (54). Cf. "Rivers."

Neary, loves. Neary is in love with Miss Dwyer, but she rejects him because she is in love with Flight-Lieutenant Elliman (5). Neary then falls in love with Miss Counihan, who rejects him because she is in love with Murphy (52). He then is attracted to Celia, but she is in love with Murphy (257). Cf. "Neary, deserted wives," "Friendships," "Who loved a" (I), "In a somewhat similar way" (I).

Neary, salts of lemon. Neary twice thinks about committing suicide by taking salts of lemon (55, 229).

Neary, touts. Neary employs Cooper, a "tout," to find Murphy; this is part of his plan to win Miss Counihan (54). Later he discovers that his ex-wife's "touts" are looking for him (116). Cf. "Neary, deserted wives."

New life. Celia tells Murphy that the move to Brewer Street will mark the beginning of a new life for them (64). Wylie promises Miss Counihan that their move to Dublin will be the beginning of a new life for them (130). Later there is a description of dead leaves; each one "as it fell had an access of new life" (150). Cf. "New life" (I).

New Testament, Christ. There are repeated allusions to Christ in the novel; many of them link Murphy and Christ. Murphy turns his "other cheek" and assumes a "crucified position" (28; cf. Luke 6:29). Murphy says of Celia, "Father forgive her" (39; cf. Luke 23:34). Murphy ponders "Christ's parthian shaft: *It is finished*" (72; cf. John 19:30). Bom hears "Pilate's hands rustling in his mind" (170; cf. Matthew 27:24). Murphy walks "round and round at the foot of the cross" (236). Murphy is "stigmatised" in Mr. Endon's eyes (249). On the first page of the French version of *Murphy* (but not in the English version), Murphy lives "dans l'impasse de l'Enfant-Jésus, West-Brompton, Londres."

New Testament, Dives and Lazarus. There are two allusions to the story of Dives and Lazarus (see Luke 16:19ff.): "little finger . . . to cool its tongue" (5) and a reference to Dives, Lazarus, and Father Abraham (48–49). Cf. "New Testament, Lazarus," "Neary, complaints."

New Testament, employers. The narrator says that Cooper "experienced none of the famous difficulty in serving two employers" (197). This is an allusion to "No man can serve two masters . . ." (Matthew 6:24) and to "No servant can serve two masters . . ." (Luke 16:13). Cf. "Famous," "Browbeat Cooper" (I), "Directed by Cooper" (I), "Belonged to the same great group" (I).

New Testament, Lazarus. There are two figures named Lazarus in the New Testament: the beggar associated with Dives (Luke 16:19ff.) and the brother of Martha and Mary of Bethany who was raised from the dead (John 11:1ff.). There is a reference to the first of these figures on p. 48 and to the second on p. 180. Cf. "New Testament, Dives and Lazarus," where a second reference to Lazarus the beggar is given, and the reference to the "toil from St. Lazare up Rue d'Amsterdam" in Paris (73).

New Testament, Murphy's points. Celia gives Mr. Kelly two examples of Murphy's points in an argument; both are based on passages from the New Testament. "The hireling fleeth because he is an hireling" (22) is based on John 10:13, and "What shall a man give in exchange for Celia?" (22) is based on Matthew 16:26 and Mark 8:37. Cf. "Murphy, points," "Was that a point?" (I).

New Testament, thieves. Neary, addressing Miss Counihan and Wylie as "the two of you," says, "do not despair. . . . Remember also one thief was saved" (213). This is an allusion to the story of the two thieves who were crucified next to Christ (see Matthew 27:38).

Newton. There are two references to Newton in the novel (112–13, 201).

Nudges. Ticklepenny nudges Murphy; he then gives Murphy a "second nudge" (169).

Old boy, meals. Miss Carridge leaves a meal for the old boy "twice daily" (69).

Old boy, seizures. Miss Carridge says that the old boy "might have a seizure any minute, he had two this year already . . ." (145).

Old Testament, Ecclesiastes. There are two allusions in the novel to Ecclesiastes; both are modified. "The sun shone . . . on the nothing new" (1) is based on Ecclesiastes 1:9; cf. "Advantage of this view" (I), "They will always be the same" (I), "New life." "Miss Carridge found her bread, it came bobbing back to her . . ." (132) is based on Ecclesiastes 11:1; cf. "Miss Carridge, tea."

Old Testament, Job, allusions. There are four allusions to the book of Job in the novel; two of them are parallel (see the next entry). The remaining two are: a reference to Job and to two of his comforters (70–71), and Neary's reference to "eyes of flesh" (222), based on Job 10:4. Cf. "Fragment[s] of Job" (I).

Old Testament, Job, allusions, parallel. In describing his suffering to Wylie, Neary refers to parallel passages from the third chapter of Job (46). "Neary . . . cursed, first the day in which he was born, then—in a bold flash-back—the night in which he was conceived" is based on Job 3:3. "Why the—, . . . is light given to a man whose way is hid" is based on Job 3:23. Cf. "Old Testament, Job, allusions."

Old Testament, twins. There is a reference in the novel to the twins Jacob and Esau (23). Cf. "Twins," "Vagitus" (I).

Parks. Two London parks figure in the action of the novel: Hyde Park (96ff., 151–53, 276ff.) and Battersea Park (16, 106). Cf. entries under "Hyde Park" and "Battersea."

Permutations. Murphy thinks about the permutations related to the order in which he eats his biscuits (96–97); Mr. Endon works out the permutations related to the ways an indicator and light can be turned on and off (247). Cf. "Lit, indicated, extinguished" (I), "With the light" (I).

Planets, discoverers of. There are allusions in the novel to two discoverers of planets, Sir William Herschel (33) and John Couch Adams (280). In the first of these allusions Uranus is called by an old name, Herschel; originally, the planet was named for its discoverer. Cf. "Planets, Uranus and Neptune," "Herschel in Aquarius" (I).

Planets, Uranus and Neptune. The narrator speaks of "Mr. Adams" and "his beautiful deduction of Neptune from Uranus" (280; Adams, measuring irregularities in the orbit of Uranus, deduced the existence of Neptune). In the horoscope Uranus (called by an old name, Herschel) and Neptune are also mentioned in close proximity (33). Cf. "Planets, discoverers of," "Herschel in Aquarius" (I), "Astronomy-astrology."

Points of contrast. The narrator says that Neary and Ticklepenny have two "points of contrast with Murphy in common." The first is a fear of going mad; the second, an "inability to look on, no matter what the spectacle" (89). Cf. "Vision."

Prostitutes. Two prostitutes appear in the novel: the woman who occupied Murphy's room before he moved into it, and Celia, who occupies his room in the second boarding house after he leaves it (7, 154).

Pseudonyms. The pseudonyms of two Irish writers are given together with their real names. In one instance the real name is given in parentheses: "Father Prout (F.S. Mahony)" (50, 124). In the second instance the pseudonym is given in parentheses: "George Russell (A.E.)" (155). Cf. "Grave of Father Prout" (I).

Psychology, Gestalt. The novel contains references to the work of two Gestalt psychologists, Kurt Koffka (48) and Wolfgang Köhler (5; "Teneriffe and the apes" is an allusion to Köhler's work with apes on the island of Teneriffe). See also references to an important idea in Gestalt psychology, the figure-ground concept, under "Figure . . . ground" (I); "Neary, complaints."

Psychology, Külpe school. The Külpe school of psychology (also known as the Würzburg school) is mentioned twice in the novel, and there are references to four of its members (80–81). Cf. "Psychology, schools of, German."

Psychology, schools of, German. There are allusions to the work and members of two German schools of psychology, the Gestalt movement and its predecessor, the Külpe school. Cf. "Psychology, Gestalt," and "Psychology, Külpe school."

Psychology vs. lunacy. Insanity is sometimes described from the point of view of the psychologists, sometimes from the point of view of the lunatics; see, for example, pp. 176–78. The narrator describes this as "the battle . . . between the psychotic and psychiatric points of view" and the "psychiatric-psychotic issue" (165, 176). Cf. "Psychology vs. philosophy."

Psychology vs. philosophy. Withdrawal from the world is seen sometimes as a psychological issue, as in the description of Mr. Endon's schizophrenia (186), and sometimes as a philosophical issue, as in descriptions of Murphy's solipsism (82) and his mind (107ff.).

Pythagorean geometry. Neary refers to two secrets of the Pythagoreans revealed by Hippasos: "the incommensurability of side and diagonal" and "the construction of the regular . . . dodecahedron" (47, 47–48). Cf. "Pythagorean philosophy."

Pythagorean philosophy. There are a number of allusions to Pythagorean philosophy in the novel. Neary is called a Pythagorean (3), and he repeats a number of Greek words (or variations on Greek words) that refer to the idea of perfection in Pythagorean philosophy: Apmonia, Isonomy, and tetrakt (3–5; Apmonia is based on the Greek *harmonia*). Passages about the drowning of Hippasos (47), Neary's "great master's figure of the three lives" (90), the title of Neary's monograph, *The Doctrine of the Limit* (50), and Neary's "unction of an *Ipse dixit*" (102), are all based on Pythagorean lore; a fuller explanation of these ideas is given in the text. Cf. "Pythagorean geometry," "Apmonia" (I), "Isonomy" (I).

Railings. Murphy, feeling weak after being insulted by the chandlers, twice leans against the "railings of the Royal Free Hospital" (78, 79); cf."Leaned . . . against the railings" (I). When he leaves Celia, he again leans against the railings of a building, an image which Celia "continued to see, at the most unexpected times, whether she would or no . . ." (142–43).

Reader addressed directly. The reader is directly addressed twice in the novel: as "gentle skimmer" (84) and as "monster of humanity and enlightenment" (170).

Rest, a. The narrator, describing how Celia pauses when she goes over the reasons that Murphy will not return to her, uses the phrases, "A rest. . . . A rest. . . . A long rest" (234). Later, describing how Murphy pauses when he goes over the reasons that Mr. Endon will not become his friend, the narrator uses the same phrases (250). See "Rest, a" (I).

Rivers. Two rivers figure in the action of the novel, and each one is linked to another dual entity. Neary drops two keys into the river Lee, in Cork (54); cf. "Neary, keys." Celia sees a coupled tug and barge on the Thames (15) when she is at "a point about half-way between the Battersea and Albert Bridges" (14); cf. "Battersea Bridge," "Tug and barge, coupled." Though the Thames is not mentioned by name, the reference to the two bridges makes it clear that the river is in fact the Thames.

Rosie Dew. Rosie Dew appears twice in the novel; she is one of the two professional fortunetellers in the book (Suk is the other one). In both of the scenes in which Rosie Dew appears there are references to her dog, to the Long Water, and to Lord Gall (98–99, 278). Cf. "Was waiting . . . from Lord Gall" (I), "Hyde Park, Long Water."

Sculptors. The narrator mentions two classical sculptors, Phidias and Scopas; then on the next page he refers to two other sculptors, Barlach and Puget, and to a matched pair of caryatids by Puget (238, 239). Cf. "M.M.M., Skinner's, groups."

Shakespeare, sleep. Two quotations in the novel are from Shakespeare plays and deal with sleep; they are on the same page (239). The passage about "nature's soft nurse" is taken from "O sleep, O gentle sleep / Nature's soft nurse . . ." (2 Henry IV, III, i, 5–6). The passage "knit up the sleave" is based on "Sleep that knits up the ravell'd sleave of care" (Macbeth, II, ii, 36). Cf. "Shakespeare, stars," "Sleep and Insomnia," "Sleep, mythological figure."

Shakespeare, stars. Two quotations in the novel are from Shakespeare's Romeo and Juliet, and both are about stars. "Then I defy you, Stars" (32) is from one of Romeo's speeches (V, i, 24); "Take him and cut him out in little stars" is from one of Juliet's speeches (III, ii, 22). Murphy's memory of "an opportune apothecary" (86) is a clue to the source of the first of these passages: it refers to "I do remember an apothecary,— / And hereabouts he dwells . . ."; this line appears in the same scene as the first quotation (V, i, 37). Cf. "Game between . . . and his stars" (I), "Astronomy-astrology."

Shelley, Harriet and Mary. The novel contains a reference to the suicide of Harriet Shelley, "Shelley's first wife you know" (99), and an allusion to *Frankenstein,* a novel by Mary Shelley, the poet's second wife (124).

Sinners. Neary speaks as though "he were kneeling before a priest instead of sitting before two sinners" (215). Cf. "Belonged to the same great group" (I).

Sleep and Insomnia. Murphy is reminded of a comment of Neary's: "Sleep and Insomnia, the Phidias and Scopas of Fatigue" (238). Cf. "Sculptors," "Sleep, mythological figure," "Those that slept" (I), "M.M.M., Skinner's, groups."

Sleep, mythological figure. There are two references to Sleep as a figure in Greek mythology; in each instance there is also a reference to another mythological figure (or figures) related to sleep: "Sleep son of Erebus and Night, Sleep half-brother to the Furies" (175); "Greek urns, where Sleep was figured with crossed feet, and frequently also Sleep's young brother" (207; "Sleep's young brother" is Death). The second passage probably alludes to G. E. Lessing's *Wie die Alten den Tod gebildet.* Cf. "Sleep and Insomnia," "Shakespeare, sleep," "Furies."

Swift, allusions. There are two allusions to the works of Jonathan Swift in the novel. "Gilmigrim jokes, so called from the Lilliputian wine" (139) is a reference to the wine mentioned in the fifth chapter of *Gulliver's Travels.* "Wood's halfpenny" (170) refers to the copper coins minted in Ireland during the eighteenth century by William Wood; Swift, who was persuaded that the coinage was debased, advocated a boycott of Wood's coins in his *Drapier's Letters.* Swift also referred to the controversy in the third chapter of *Gulliver's Travels.*

Tantalus. There is a reference to Tantalus early in the novel (21); later a tempting pub is described as a "palatial tantalus" (121). Cf. "Moon by a striking coincidence" (I).

Telegrams. Cooper sends Neary two telegrams with similar texts; Neary writes two letters, with similar texts, to Wylie and Miss Counihan (57, 199). Cf. "Letters, Neary's," "He hurried back" (I), "When the boots" (I).

Telephone conversations. In two instances Celia calls Murphy on the telephone, and their conversations are described (7–9, 22); Murphy writes Celia two letters whose texts are described (22). All the letters and conversations have to do with whether Celia will return to Murphy. Cf. "Letters, Murphy's," "That is not possible" (I).

Thanks. On three occasions the irony in a character's expression of gratitude is emphasized by repetition: see "*I* thank you" (I), "Million Thanks" (I), "My. . . . Thank you" (I).

Ticklepenny, men. Ticklepenny is attracted to two of the men in the novel, Murphy and Bim (85, 258–59). Cf. "Homosexuals," "Fancy . . . not far short of love" (I).

Ticklepenny, reprimands. The narrator says, "Two sorts of reprimand were familiar to Ticklepenny . . ." (170). Cf. "Ticklepenny, things he wanted."

Ticklepenny, things he wanted. Bom mentions "one or two of the things that Ticklepenny most wanted" (169–70). Cf. "Ticklepenny, reprimands."

Time, personified. Time is personified twice in the novel (114, 278).

Tug and barge, coupled. Celia sees a "tug and barge, coupled abreast" (15). Later, when she sees the tandem kites, she is reminded of the tug and barge (152). Cf. "Kites, tandem," "Funnel vailed" (I).

Turf, Irish. There are three references to Irish turf: "gaelic prosodoturfy" (89); "The turf was truly Irish . . ." (130–31); "Turf is compulsory in the Saorstat [Ireland]" (197). There is also a reference to "the well-known English turf" (79).

Twins. Two characters in the novel, Bim and Bom Clinch, are identical twins, and their given names and nicknames are similar (156, 165). Cf. "Old Testament, twins," "Darling" (I), "Fancy . . . not far short of love" (I), "What is vulgarly called" (I).

Vibrations, flat. Murphy's vagitus "had not been the proper A of international concert pitch, with 435 double vibrations per second, but the double flat of this" (71). Cf. "Vagitus" (I).

Virgil, *Aeneid.* There are two allusions to the *Aeneid*: "*quantum mutatus* . . ." (87; *Aeneid*, Book II, l. 274), and a reference to Dido (195). Cf. "Miss Counihan, queens."

Vision. The narrator uses two similar terms, *voyeur* and *voyant*, to distinguish between two types of vision: "the vision that depends on light, object, viewpoint, etc., and the vision that all these things embarrass" (90). Cf. "Points of contrast."

Waitresses. Two waitresses appear in the novel, Cathleen and Vera (46, 81). Wylie orders "two large coffees" from Cathleen (46). Murphy's order to Vera also involves dual entities: see entries under "Murphy, lunch."

West Brompton. Two scenes involving Celia and Murphy are set in the West Brompton flat (6ff., 26ff.). Cf. "What . . . told me to get" (I).

Whiskers, large ruddy men with. Bim Clinch is described as a "huge red, bald, whiskered man" (156); Dr. Killiecrankie is described as a "large bony, stooping, ruddy man . . . with an antiquary's cowl whiskers" (257–58). Cf. "'Mr. Clinch,' said Dr. Killiecrankie" (I), "Mr. Clinch" (I).

Window, leaning out of. When Wylie leaves Miss Counihan, she leans out of an upper-story window to watch him depart; unexpectedly, however, he changes directions and returns (130–31). Later, Celia looks out an upper-story window to watch Murphy's departure, and when he unexpectedly changes directions, she thinks for a moment that he is about to return (142–43). In both scenes there are references to spikes on nearby railings (131, 142–43), and a cross-reference, "(Murphy's figure)" (131), links similar descriptions of the departing men: see "Heads in the pillories of their shoulders" (I). Cf. "Handfuls."

Wordsworth. There are two references to William Wordsworth (100, 106). Cf. "Wordsworth, allusions."

Wordsworth, allusions. The novel contains two allusions to Wordsworth's "Ode on Intimations of Immortality": "fields of sleep" (100) is from Stanza III; "Since Heaven lay about you as a bedwetter" (217) is based on "Heaven lies about us in our infancy!" in Stanza V. Cf. "Wordsworth."

Wylie as mimic. Wylie twice mimics the peculiarities of another character's speech patterns. Miss Counihan often says "—er—" when she is searching for a euphemism, and Miss Carridge sometimes repeats the last phrase of a sentence when she is being insincere. Wylie mimics both of them: he says "—er—" while speaking about Miss Counihan (60), and he says, "If you are quite sure you are quite sure" to Miss Carridge shortly after she repeats a phrase (227). Cf. "—Er—" (I), "Doubt" (I), "Principle of the thing" (I), "Miss Carridge, verbal repetition," "Miss Counihan, verbal repetition."

Wylie, communion. The narrator says that when Wylie comforts Neary, he feels "purer than at any time since his second communion" (51). Cf. "Sinners."

Wylie, women. Wylie is attracted to two of the women in the novel, Miss Counihan and Celia (61, 255). Neary and Murphy are also attracted to these women: see "Neary, former students of," "Friendships," "Murphy, women."

Index

Index

Beckett, Samuel (continued)
psychoanalysis, 69n6; style, 2, 3–4,
7, 176–80, 181–82; at Trinity
College (Dublin), 147n36, 164
Beckett, William, 49, 53n20, 62n9
Beethoven, Ludwig van, 22, 23, 26
Belacqua: character in *The Divine
Comedy*, 86, 204–5; character in
Dream of Fair to Middling Women,
21–22, 23, 24, 28, 29, 30, 31, 32,
178; character in *More Pricks than
Kicks*, 12, 36, 38–39, 40, 41–48,
49–50, 51, 60–61, 65, 67, 181, *see
also* "Echo's Bones"
Benedict XIV (pope), 168
Ben-Zvi, Linda, 144–45n16
Bergson, Henri, 160
Berkeley, George, 9, 14n12, 33–34n8,
87, 88, 89, 91,100n37, 102n48,
102–3n50, 201
Bilitis, 27, 34n9
Bim. *See* Clinch, Thomas
Black, Max, 144–45n16
Bom. *See* Clinch, Timothy
Borges, Jorge Luis, 33n7
Bouvier, Jean-Baptiste, 118–19n1
Bray, Mrs. (character in "A Case in a
Thousand"), 64, 65, 66
Brée, Germaine, 142n1, 145n20
Brueghel, Jan, 156
Bühler, Karl, 92
Burgess, Anthony, 63n18
Burnet, John, 99–100n33, 100–101n38,
122n28
Bury, R. G., 144–45n16
Byron, Lord, 180

Cain, 49, 50
Campanella, Tommaso, 118–19n1
Cangiamila, Francesco Emanuello,
168, 174n36
Cantor, Georg, 160
Carridge, Miss (character in *Murphy*),
9, 75, 78, 84, 91, 112–13, 115, 117,
208–9, 221
Cartesian philosophy. *See* Descartes,
René
*Cascando and other Short Dramatic
Pieces* (Beckett), 70n17
Case, Mr. (character in *Watt*), 135

"Case in a Thousand, A" (Beckett),
64–66, 68–69, 118, 179
Causality, 128, 129, 130, 164, 165
Celia (character in *Murphy*), 11, 12,
72–74, 77, 78, 79, 80, 81, 82, 83, 84,
86, 89, 91, 106, 112, 114–15, 116,
117, 177, 201–2, 207, 208, 213, 215,
216, 218, 219, 220, 221
Cemetery groundsman. *See* Doyle
Chaos, 116
Characterization, 10–11, 12, 13, 21,
23–24, 27
Chas (character in *Dream of Fair to
Middling Women*), 21, 24
Chaucer, Geoffrey, 20, 33n2
Chess, 92–93, 111, 202–3
Chesterfield, Lord, 117, 123n39
Chinnery, George, 156
Christ, 49, 50, 117, 122n37, 213,
214–15
Chronology, 176–78
Cicero, 100–101n38
Cicisbeo, 39
Clavius, Christopher, 161, 171n19
Clinch, Thomas "Bim" (character in
Murphy), 84, 105, 117, 207, 210,
213, 220
Clinch, Timothy "Bom" (character in
Murphy), 84, 213, 215, 220
Clockwork Orange, A (Burgess),
63n18
Clytemnestra, 31
Coe, Richard, 142n1, 174n38
Coetzee, J. M., 170n4, 171n12,
174n38
Cohn, Ruby, 4n11, 34n12, 53n16,
118–19n1, 142n1, 170n7, 183n4
Company (Beckett), 66
Con (character in *Watt*), 126
Conarium, 88
Content, 6, 7, 14, 17, 182. *See also*
Form; Symmetry
Cooper (character in *Murphy*), 74, 76,
80, 82, 83, 84, 92, 117, 118, 200,
203–4, 207, 208, 215, 219
Copeland, Hannah, 118–19n1
Counihan, Miss (character in
Murphy), 75, 77, 79, 80, 82, 83, 84,
86, 91, 111, 117, 180, 207, 208, 213,
214, 215, 219, 221

Index

226

Index

Index

Ronsard, Pierre de, 40, 52n9
Rosen, Steven, 142n1
Ross, G. R. T., 174n39
Ruby (character in *More Pricks than Kicks*), 38, 39, 40, 44, 49
Rules for the Direction of the Mind (Descartes), 125
Russell, Bertrand, 160, 171n18

Sacred Embriology (Cangiamila), 168
St. Jerome, 166
Saintsbury, George, 172–73n25
Sam (narrator in *Watt*), 10, 133, 136, 141, 142, 152, 157, 161, 177, 180, 181
"Sanies I" (Beckett), 175n42, 176
"Sanies II" (Beckett), 52–53n10
Sappho, 34n9
Sargeaunt, John, 170n9
Satire, 50, 51, 139, 159
Satires (Horace), 168
Schneider, Alan, 4nn8,12
Schoeck, Richard J., 61–62n2
Schopenhauer, Arthur, 9, 10, 14n12, 34nn12–19, 94, 95, 103nn51,55, 109, 121nn24,25, 124–25, 128, 129, 130, 132, 133, 134, 135–36, 137, 138, 139–40, 142–43nn2,3, 144–45nn16,18,19, 146nn25,31, 147–48nn38–40, 148–49nn43,44, 150n52, 165, 171n11, 173–74nn28,32
Scopas, 86, 218, 219
Scott, Nathan, 142n1
Scylla, 31
Seaver, Richard, 4n2, 35n21
Self, 10, 12, 27, 130, 138, 168
Semiramide, 31
Senneff, Susan, 174n35
"Serena I" (Beckett), 175n42
Severn, Mr. (character in *Watt*), 11–12
Shakespeare, William, 86, 99n29, 108, 121nn21,22, 218–19
Shelley, Harriet, 219
Shelley, Mary, 219
Shelley, Percy Bysshe, 145–46n23, 219
Silence, 16, 17, 18, 22–23, 79. *See also* Aesthetic of inaudibilities

Sinclair, John D., 34n11, 53n14
Sinclair, Peggy, 49, 53n20, 54n21
Skerl, Jennie, 144–45n16
Slattery, John Joseph, 156
Smeraldina (character in *More Pricks than Kicks*), 38, 40, 48, 49, 179
Smeraldina-Rima (character in *Dream of Fair to Middling Women*), 21, 24
Smith, J. A., 101n39
Smith, Frederik N., 53n11
Solomon, Philip Howard, 144–45n16
Sphinx, 31, 68, 69, 158, 159
Spinoza, Baruch, 94, 95, 103nn51,54
Spiro, Mr. (character in *Watt*), 168, 178
Steinberg, S. C., 123n41
Stories and Texts for Nothing (Beckett), 1. *See also* "End, The"
Strauss, the ostrich, 56
"Stultum Propter Christum," 55, 61–62n2
Suicide, 113–14, 118, 167
Suk (character in *Murphy*), 76, 85, 90, 106, 107
Surds, 153
Swift, Jonathan, 41, 50, 51, 118–19n1, 219
Symbolism, 162
Symmetry, 89–96, 110, 116
Synecdoche, 162, 180
Syra-Cusa (character in *Dream of Fair to Middling Women*), 24, 27, 31

Tancock, L. W., 170n3
Tantalus, 86
Tar-water, 89
Tennyson, Alfred, 20, 33n2
Terence, 68, 158–59, 166, 170n9, 173–74n32
Texts for Nothing. See Stories and Texts for Nothing
"That a Wise Man is Known by Much Laughing" (Donne), 48
Thelma (character in *More Pricks than Kicks*), 38, 39, 40
Things-in-themselves, 130, 131, 133, 137
Thomas, Dylan, 10, 15n22
Thomson, James, 165, 173n27

A Note on the Author

Rubin Rabinovitz was born in New York City. He received his B.A. (1959) from Rutgers College and his M.A. (1961) and Ph.D. (1966) from Columbia University. He is presently professor of English at the University of Colorado and has also taught at Columbia. He has written many articles and two other books: *The Reaction against Experiment in the English Novel, 1950–1960* (1967) and *Iris Murdoch* (1968).